The
Prince Rupert
Hotel for the
Homeless

ALSO BY CHRISTINA LAMB

Waiting for Allah: Benazir Bhutto and Pakistan

The Africa House: The True Story of an English Gentleman and His African Dream

The Sewing Circles of Herat: My Afghan Years

House of Stone: The True Story of a Family Divided in War-Torn Zimbabwe

Small Wars Permitting: Dispatches from Foreign Lands

I Am Malala: The Girl Who Stood Up for Education and was Shot by the Taliban (with Malala Yousafzai)

Farewell Kabul: From Afghanistan to a More Dangerous World

The Girl from Aleppo: Nujeen's Escape from War to Freedom (with Nujeen Mustafa)

Our Bodies, Their Battlefield: What War Does to Women

CHRISTINA LAMB

The Prince Rupert Hotel for the Homeless

A True Story of Love and
Compassion Amid a Pandemic

WILLIAM
COLLINS

Five per cent of the proceeds of this book will go to
The Ark, Shrewsbury's homeless charity

William Collins
An imprint of HarperCollins*Publishers*
1 London Bridge Street
London SE1 9GF

WilliamCollinsBooks.com

HarperCollins*Publishers*
1st Floor, Watermarque Building, Ringsend Road
Dublin 4, Ireland

First published in Great Britain in 2022 by William Collins

1

Set in Bell MT Std
Printed and bound in the UK using 100%
renewable electricity at CPI Group (UK) Ltd

MIX
Paper from
responsible sources
FSC™ C007454

This book is produced from independently certified FSC™ paper
to ensure responsible forest management.

For more information visit: www.harpercollins.co.uk/green

On that best portion of a good man's life
His little, nameless, unremembered, acts
Of kindness and of love.

William Wordsworth, 'Tintern Abbey'

They call us rough sleepers – I am not rough, I don't
sleep much and my favourite thing is cathedrals.

Simon 'Spoons' Boden, no fixed abode

We gave them hope but they gave us
something much more.

Mike Matthews, owner of the Prince Rupert

Shrewsbury

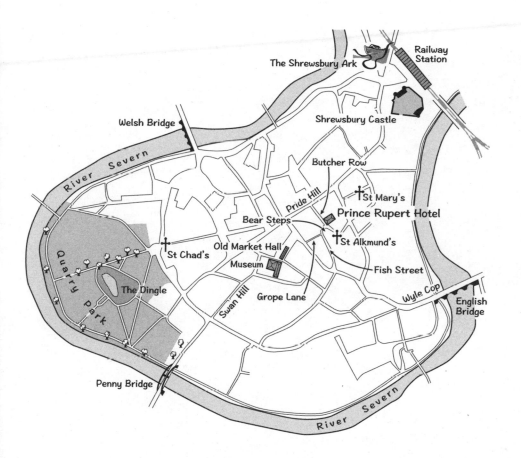

The Shrewsbury Ark

Railway Station

Welsh Bridge

Shrewsbury Castle

River Severn

Butcher Row

Pride Hill

St Mary's

Bear Steps

Prince Rupert Hotel

St Chad's

Old Market Hall

St Alkmund's

Quarry Park

Museum

Fish Street

The Dingle

Swan Hill

Grope Lane

Wyle Cop

English Bridge

Penny Bridge

River Severn

1.

Saturday, 14 March 2020

In an olde-worlde town of steeples, spires and higgledy-piggledy black-and-white houses on a hill, looped around by a river along which swans glide between an English bridge and a Welsh bridge, there stands a hotel like no other. High up in the town, reached along a cobbled alley called Butcher Row, it is a hotchpotch of timber-framed buildings dating back nine hundred years where a Bohemian prince once lived, and overlooks a square with a twisty tree and the church of St Alkmund's that was founded long before the Black Death.

'Let's meet at the Prince Rupert' has long been a common refrain in Shrewsbury, whether among ladies that lunch, business-people wanting to discuss deals, bridal parties planning a wedding or tourists wandering in wonder through the narrow streets of the medieval town centre.

Inside, on this Saturday, a welcoming fire crackled in the lobby and guests sallied back and forth past the portrait of a long-haired man with a romantic air. This was Prince Rupert, the Prague-born grandson of King James I, who stayed here in the seventeenth century trying to marshal Royalist forces during the English Civil War, and gave the hotel its name.

That day the Prince Rupert had sixty-one paying guests and the two restaurants and lounge bar had a steady stream of custom-

ers. The Camellias Tea Rooms were so busy that hotel manager Charlie was helping out alongside her daughter Gabriella, serving pots of Earl Grey and tiered cake-stands of scones, fruit slice and cucumber sandwiches while the tinkling digital piano played the theme from *Titanic*.

Upstairs, the hotel's sixty-one-year-old owner Mike Matthews was sitting in his wood-panelled office, the prince's old lounge, head in his hands. The computer screen in front of him revealed a summer full of bookings for the Prince Rupert's seventy rooms, thanks to the crowds that were going to descend on Shrewsbury for its food festival in June; for Let's Rock in July, featuring the eighties stars Adam Ant and Tony Hadley; and then in August for the folk festival and the Shrewsbury Flower Show, the world's oldest, dating back to 1836 when only carnations and gooseberries had been allowed.

Everything had been shaping up to be a good year. On television, however, as there had been for days, were terrifying images from northern Italy, where hospitals were so overwhelmed by a deadly virus that had come from China that they were running out of ventilators and doctors were having to play God and decide who to save. Some hospitals were so full they were treating people in car parks. Similar scenes were being repeated in Spain. Mike's cousin in Malaga was sending daily messages about the fear that was spreading across the country.

Mike called in the two fifty-something women he considered his 'right-hand men' – Charlie Green, the bubbly red-haired manager with a heart-shaped face, and Jacki Law, his watchful pale blond accountant, both as petite as he is tall. 'I think they will close us down,' he said. The women were surprised. The day before, almost seventy thousand people had gathered for the races at Cheltenham Festival. Boris Johnson, the mop-headed British prime minister, was playing the virus down, going to a rugby match at Twickenham with his young fiancée Carrie Symonds, shaking hands with all and sundry, and telling a press conference with his usual bluster, 'I'm absolutely confident that we can send coronavirus packing in this country.'

Mike shook his head. Italy, Spain, France, Germany and Greece were already in some form of lockdown, closing restaurants, shops and schools, and telling people to stay at home. 'It's economy versus life,' he said, 'and that's no contest.' He couldn't understand why the government wasn't shutting the borders, closing airports and seaports, taking advantage of being an island to keep the deadly virus out. It seemed to him as clear as daylight that weddings, banquets, business conferences and holidays would all have to come to a grinding halt.

His mind whirred. How on earth would he pay the staff? Some of them had worked there for decades. Part of the hotel was leased – how would he pay the landlord? Then there was the insurance, the mortgage, the utility bills and what about the suppliers – local farmers, grocers and butchers, as well as Tanners, the town's old wine merchants. He couldn't just say, 'Stop now, I won't pay.'

Centuries-old Grade II listed buildings like the Prince Rupert were not like a modern Holiday Inn you could just shut down. Behind the walls lay a myriad of pipes and wires that, if not used, could seize up. Water had to keep circulating or legionnaires' disease could take hold. If the boilers were shut down, they might not restart. The pipes were a mix of copper and iron – if hot water didn't flow, they would corrode. If the heating wasn't on and air wasn't flowing, mildew and mould would grow. And what about security: the hotel was a jumble of buildings with multiple entrances and exits, and it was right in the centre of town.

You couldn't just stop everything in its tracks. The Prince Rupert needed care and attention, like a living breathing thing.

Mike was particularly worried about paying Charlie and Jacki, who were so dedicated to the hotel and had no significant other in their lives – how would they survive without their jobs? He'd read about Nordic countries that were putting in place a furlough scheme whereby the government would pay 80 per cent of people's wages, which in his view was seriously generous. He couldn't imagine the UK doing that.

He called his bank manager to see if he had heard anything. 'I know as much as you do,' came the reply.

Back home that evening, a few miles away in the village of Cruckton, Mike paced the lounge. The news on TV was growing more and more alarming. There were now over a thousand cases in the UK, including the junior health minister Nadine Dorries, and twenty-one people had died. Anyone with a high temperature or 'new and persistent cough' was being urged to stay at home for fourteen days. The stock market was falling. People were starting to panic buy in supermarkets.

'I don't want to close,' he told his wife Diane. 'I need to find something to do with the hotel.'

The next day as he walked from the car park along Wyle Cop and up Pride Hill, the main shopping street, people were coming out of Tesco and Marks & Spencer laden with piles of toilet rolls.

In his office Mike began making calls and sending emails, offering the hotel to different organisations. He asked the NHS if it wanted to use the Prince Rupert to put up nurses and doctors from the Royal Shrewsbury Hospital who were worried about taking the infection home. He tried the police and fire service. Nobody responded. By that evening, as he left for home, he had given up hope. 'What am I going to do with you?' he said, shaking his head at the hotel's black-and-white timbered frontage in the pink early evening glow.

After supper he sat on his sofa with a cup of tea. Diane went upstairs to her room at 10 p.m., as she always did, but he stayed up, his mind racing.

It was twenty-five years since they had bought the Prince Rupert and the hotel was his life. Dotted around the living room were photos of their three children: the two eldest, James and Camilla, both now hoteliers themselves, and the youngest, Alexander, who was at university studying hospitality. It was because of them that Mike and Diane had moved back from the

Caribbean, where he'd spent ten years managing hotels such as the exclusive Sandy Lane resort in Barbados whose guests had included John Cleese and Michael Winner. He'd been having the time of his life there, but one evening, looking out over the turquoise water and twinkling lights, he thought about the need to find schools for their children and to be nearer his ageing parents back home, and decided he wanted a place of his own.

Mike amassed a bulging file of hotels that were for sale across the UK, but something about the Prince Rupert kept catching his eye. He had never been to Shrewsbury on the English–Welsh border – like many, when he thought of Shropshire, he thought of Ludlow, its ancient market town – so was intrigued to read the description of Shrewsbury in a Frommer's guide as 'the finest Tudor town in England'. When he went to see it on a trip back from the Caribbean, he had just two hours to walk around, and never did discover if you should pronounce it *Shrews*-bury, like the long-nosed rodent, or *Shrows*-bury, to rhyme with 'show' – no one seemed to know – but it looked to him to have everything you could want in a town.

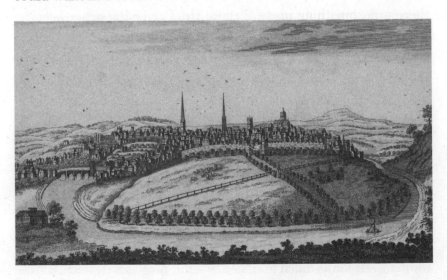

A view of Shrewsbury, engraved in 1771.

Set on two hills with a dip in the middle and the River Severn encircling it almost like a moat, Shrewsbury has an astonishing 660 listed buildings and had clearly once been very affluent, with all its highly decorated black-and-white Tudor mansions and handsome Georgian townhouses on cobbled streets. Many of these had been the homes of wool merchants and drapers, who were behind the town's commercial heyday from the fourteenth to seventeenth centuries. Its location across the border from Wales, on the highway to London and on the Severn to the port of Bristol had seen it dominate the trade in Welsh wool, and then in woven cloth, which went thence to Europe and later the Americas. Aside from its fine houses, the town had a Norman castle and abbey, a series of bridges and an ancient school to educate the scions of its wealthy, as well as the world's first iron-framed building, the flax-mill, known as the grandfather of skyscrapers. That wasn't Shrewsbury's only claim to fame (and draw for tourists) – one could also call it the birthplace of evolution, for Charles Darwin grew up there. It also had a couple of old coaching inns – the Lion and the Prince Rupert. Both had seen better days, but to Mike there was something magical about the Prince Rupert.

Buying it had not been easy. Even in its dilapidated state, he could not afford the £1.15 million price tag on his own, let alone the money for works, and his first partner in the enterprise proved unreliable. Eventually, in 2002, Mike managed to borrow almost £2.5 million to pay over the odds to buy his partner out.

Since then, he had renovated, added bits and created a court-yard terrace; there was always something to do with a hotel. In 2014 he had sold off some car parking spaces and borrowed money for a £2 million refurbishment that had taken the Prince Rupert from three stars to four stars. Guests had included Margaret Thatcher, the Liverpool football team and Monica Lewinsky, and rooms went for as much as £225 a night. Mike's wife and children had all worked there. He knew every nook and cranny, from the stone vaulted cellars with underground tunnels to the Jacobean staircase and the ancient rooms with their heavy wooden beams and ceilings that slanted so low you could easily touch them with your hand. He had even got to know the ghosts.

The first rays of dawn sun were lighting up the tiles when he finally drifted off into an uneasy slumber.

Around 4 p.m. that day, Monday 16 March, Pam, the reservations manager, asked if Mike had got the message from Paul on reception that someone from the council had called about housing. Paul was absent-minded and there was a frantic search to find the scrap of paper with a name, Tim Compton, and number.

Intrigued, Mike dialled. Compton came straight to the point. 'I guess this is a long shot and you'll probably say no, but the government is ordering us to bring in all rough sleepers off the streets because of this coronavirus, and I wondered if we might use your hotel.'

Mike was stunned. 'I bet we're the last hotel you tried,' he laughed.

Compton said nothing. 'I had included the Prince Rupert on the list of local hotels and B&Bs to try as a formality, never expecting them to agree,' he later admitted.

'How many are there?' asked Mike. He couldn't remember seeing many homeless people on the streets of Shrewsbury, maybe three or four in doorways. To be honest, he always quickened his step when he saw one, and if he thought about them at all it was to wonder why they didn't get off their backsides and get a job.

'Thirty to forty,' said Compton.

'Wow,' said Mike. He invited Tim for a cup of tea in the hotel lounge the next afternoon.

That evening Boris Johnson held the first of what would become daily briefings from 10 Downing Street, standing at the centre of three podiums, flanked by the scientists Professor Chris Whitty, the UK's chief medical adviser, and Sir Patrick Vallance, the chief scientific adviser. 'Now is the time to stop non-essential contact with others,' urged the prime minister, 'and all non-essential travel.' He added that people should stop going to pubs, clubs and restaurants to halt the spread of the 'new coronavirus'.

'I don't think there's been anything like it in peacetime,' said Johnson. 'Without drastic action, cases could double every five or six days ...'

Although there was some confusion – Johnson wasn't ordering places to close or banning public gatherings – businesses started taking matters into their own hands. Top London theatres announced they were bringing down the curtain on their shows, even *The Mousetrap*, the world's longest-running play. Airlines began cancelling flights and cruise companies said their cruises would be suspended until 11 April. One British ship, the *Diamond Princess*, had already been quarantined for weeks at a Japanese port after a major outbreak swept through, infecting seven hundred passengers and crew, of whom nine had died. If Mike had any doubt the Prince Rupert would have to close, it soon disappeared. Guests started calling to cancel. Before long only eight rooms remained booked.

After lunch the next day, he sat waiting in the lounge with Charlie and Jacki. Through the glass doors they watched a man with long hair and long beard, dressed all in black, saunter up to reception. 'Oh crikey, they've sent one already!' exclaimed Charlie. Then the man turned and they saw his Shropshire Council lanyard.

It was Tim Compton. He explained that the government had launched an initiative called Everyone In to get all the homeless across the land off the streets by the weekend, 'as their immune system was all shot', and they were considered particularly vulnerable to the disease and potential spreaders. Councils had been asked to round them up and house them in hotels and B&Bs.

'How long would it be for?' asked Mike.

'We've been told up to four months, but we think it will be just a few weeks,' said Compton. 'Until this is over.'

Jacki asked about funding. Compton said he didn't know the details, but they would obviously be compensated. He was very open. 'This won't be easy,' he said. 'They are very vulnerable – many are high-level drug addicts or alcoholics; some are convicts. Many have not slept inside for years.'

He did not expect Mike to agree. He'd spent most of his working life battling the stigma attached to rough sleepers, having spent ten years running the Shrewsbury Ark, the local homeless charity, before joining the council's housing department in 2019. When he'd told his colleagues that he was going to the Prince Rupert to see if it would house any homeless, they'd laughed.

'Maybe you could take one or two,' he suggested.

Mike looked at Charlie and Jacki. They were smiling. 'Let's do it,' they said. 'We can take them all.'

2.

Thursday, 19 March 2020

It was just after lunch when the first new guest walked in.

'Welcome to the Prince Rupert,' said Charlie, sticking out her hand with her usual friendliness, while exchanging nervous glances with Jacki. 'My name is Charlie and I'm the hotel manager.' The staff were all wearing plastic gloves and surgical masks sent by the council, which made her feel like an alien and hid her warm smile, but the killer virus was apparently in the air all around.

'Chris Bennett,' said the man, who was carrying a dirty rucksack and sleeping bag.

'Should they fill in forms?' asked the receptionist, trying not to look scared.

'Just the name and arrival date and time – it's two o'clock,' said Charlie. You could hardly ask homeless people for an address or credit card for extras. 'Maybe put Shropshire Council for address.'

'Can I take your luggage, sir?' asked Trevor, the porter.

The man stared at him. He looked okay, thought Charlie, mid-forties, quite clean, in smart jeans and trainers and zipped pullover. Not really how she imagined the homeless.

'What about the sherry?' whispered the receptionist, gesturing at the crystal decanter with which they used to greet guests on arrival. 'No, no,' said Charlie, 'let's remove that.'

'Let me show you to your room,' she said.

Apart from the welcome sherry, Charlie and Jacki had decided that they would treat their new arrivals exactly the same as regular guests. 'We have to,' insisted Charlie.

She led Chris Bennett upstairs to the first floor and opened the door to a room, showing him its en suite bathroom with Gilchrist & Soames toiletries and fluffy towels, the flatscreen TV, tea tray, ornate brass bed with Hypnos mattress, crisp white cotton sheets, plump Dorma pillows and fluffy duvet.

He looked astonished. 'I thought you were just going to give me a sleeping bag and send me out again,' he said. She wanted to hug him.

He sat on the bed, staring. 'It was all a bit surreal, going from being on the streets in the cold and the wind to being in a four-star hotel,' he said later.

'Would you like something to eat?' asked Charlie. 'Sandwich? Jacket potato?'

'Jacket potato with cheese and baked beans?' he said.

Charlie went back downstairs to tell the kitchen, then rejoined Jacki, who was running around with other staff getting rooms ready for their new guests. They were removing soft furnishings

like cushions, bed throws and extra pillows, as well as the leather folders with tourist information and the room service menu. This was not only to avoid damage but because the news was reporting that the virus could be transmitted via surfaces that had been touched by infected people. Door handles were said to be particularly deadly, so the cleaners were spraying them with disinfectant. They also took out the second bed from twin rooms to deter anyone from bringing back a friend. Lastly, they removed the tasselled ties from the curtains – somewhat alarmingly, the Shrewsbury Ark had told them to take out anything that could be used for suicide attempts.

That day it was just the pair of them running the place, because Mike had headed to Gatwick the night before to pick up his eldest, James, who was flying in from Barbados, where in a strange twist of fate he had his father's old job of managing Sandy Lane. James's wife Lindsay was due to give birth to their first child and had already flown back to the UK, staying with her mum in Christchurch. The couple were going to stay for a few months in Mike's flat in Bournemouth, which he had inherited from his parents, and he planned to settle them in then head back to Shrewsbury in a couple of days.

He kept calling the hotel to find out what was happening.

Wendy Faulkner, the manager of the Ark, and her assistant Rose Greenslade were busy rounding up homeless people from local streets, shop doorways and under bridges, and had told them that three rough sleepers would be arriving that day.

Late afternoon, the other two arrived together – Donny McIvens, who looked like a little old man, and Chez, who was tiny, with weathered skin, clad in skinny jeans and bomber jacket, and didn't seem to speak English. They'd been told he was Polish. Both had rucksacks. Chez also had a carrier bag, from which a teddy bear poked out, and a pile of blankets. Donny looked like a rabbit caught in the headlights and couldn't quite believe that they were allowed to stay. 'Is this okay?' he kept asking. 'Thank you, thank you.'

He seemed delighted by the television in his room, and was barely able to take his eyes off it, once Charlie had switched it on. She wondered how long he had been living on the streets. She offered them supper but both just wanted a sandwich.

'You know what, I don't think we can just leave them,' Charlie told Jacki. 'I'm going to stay.' She only lived a few minutes' drive away from the hotel and popped home to get a small case. Her two youngest children still lived at home – her daughter Gabriella, twenty-two, and son Fraser, twenty – and she felt awful leaving them. She thought of them as a trio, the Three Musketeers, but she could end up carrying the virus home if she went back and forth. Besides, she was sure they would cope. The pair bickered but never fell out – they had learned to cling together through all the problems with her ex-husband, their dad.

Fraser was so scared of the virus that he actually seemed relieved. 'Mum, if you're going to work there, you can't come home,' he said.

Charlie hugged them close, promised to call every day, kissed her two cats Henry and Tallulah goodbye, and drove off in her little grey Fiat 500.

Jacki had lived on her own for a number of years, since splitting up from her partner. Her cottage in Telford was too far away to go and come back that evening, but she said she would bring her things the next day to stay. Her main worry was her eighty-three-year-old mum, who lived alone in Wolverhampton, but Jacki figured she could drop off weekly shopping for her.

Neither imagined it would be for more than a few weeks.

That evening they continued getting the hotel ready. The Ark had warned them not to leave any temptation for their new guests, so Trevor padlocked the snooker room and they began removing all the bottles from the bar.

When they were finally done, they sat in the lounge with a glass of wine, wondering what their new guests were doing and what would happen. As hoteliers they were used to dealing with the unexpected and the demanding, from the opera diva whose agent kept calling from miles away to order her room service to the furry red handcuffs left in the four-poster bed and rolling comatose wedding guests in top hats into bed in the early hours. But this felt like dealing with the complete unknown – they'd seen these people on the streets but had no idea about their lives.

They called Mike. 'We've got three so far and they seem okay,' said Charlie.

He sounded more harassed than they did. Worried about all the reports of empty shelves in supermarkets, he had dragged James out of bed that morning, telling him, 'No time for jetlag, we need to shop!'

They had driven to every supermarket they could find – Sainsburys, M&S, Waitrose, Tesco, Aldi, Lidl, some as far as twenty miles away. 'Everywhere shelves were empty,' he said. 'No fresh food, no pasta, just cereal and tins of rice pudding. Not a toilet roll in sight – we had to buy Kleenex!' They had scooped up all they could on shop floors littered with empty boxes and plastic as if a stampede had been through. At one point in the chilled section in M&S, as Mike went to take something, a woman had shoved him out of the way with her trolley. 'It's a madhouse out there,' he sighed.

When Charlie came down to sort out breakfast next morning, the night porter told her that Chez had gone out in the night and not come back. Eventually they found him in the doorway of the Thai restaurant, just along Butcher Row, curled in a neat nest of blankets with two dollies next to him. He had not understood he could sleep in the hotel.

'We need Google Translate,' said Pam, when they brought him back. 'This is now your home, you are welcome to sleep here,' she tapped into her phone and converted into instant Polish. He looked at them in disbelief, then started to cry. Charlie patted him on the back and showed him back to his room.

A short time later the fire alarm went off. 'Oh God, they're smoking!' she exclaimed.

It was Chez. He had tried to go out through the fire door near his room. Pam got on the computer to translate 'no exit' into Polish and printed out a sign to post on the door.

That day six more arrived. 'Wow,' mouthed Charlie as the next one came in. His name was Derek Tyrer. He was the first to look really bad, with an untamed ginger beard, and he was absolutely filthy and smelly, talking non-stop to no one in particular. A message from the council instructed them to put him in a quiet room because he suffered from 'extreme paranoia'. Charlie took him to one on the first floor.

'Would you like some bubble bath?' she asked as she showed him in. She gave him a big bottle. Afterwards she discovered he poured in the entire contents to his bath.

Next to arrive was Mark Chapman, also filthy and smelly, with a dirty beanie over long straggly hair and beard, spotty face and dirty fingernails so long they were curling over. She guessed he was in his mid-fifties.

'Hello Charlie, how's your lovely daughter?' he asked.

She looked at him in shock. How did he know her name? He explained that he sold the *Big Issue* outside Tesco and used to see her and Gabriella come in together on Saturdays. He'd been on the streets for thirty-five years.

Shortly after that came Neil Hallam, a man with a voice so nasal he was hard to understand, who introduced himself as Stokesy, and Dave Pritchard. Both had long matted gingery beards and stank. Stokesy was in his fifties and originally from Stoke, hence his nickname, and had not slept in a bed for decades. Pritchard, who was thirty-nine, was covered in tattoos, including a duck on his forearm, and said he was known as Ducky. He had what looked like black teardrops tattooed under one eye, which one of the girls said meant he had murdered someone. He had been sleeping in the doorway of a restaurant near the river, where he said they wouldn't even give him a cracker, and he seemed overwhelmed.

'I'd never been in a place like this,' he said later. 'The effin' door handles are worth more than I am. I didn't know, could I touch things or will I get charged for it?'

The last to arrive that afternoon were a couple – Randolph, a tiny wiry man, and Tracy, a big girl with a pretty face framed by reddish hair and bellowing voice, who did not stop crying. They had been thrown out of another facility and had been sleeping in a tent, and couldn't believe they had a safe place to stay. They came with a mass of bags and belongings.

Tracy wept when Charlie took them to their twin room, touching the marble in the bathroom, and immediately asked if she could help with cleaning or anything. 'I grew up around pubs,' she said. 'That's where I met Randolph: he was cheffing.'

Rose from the Ark had come to the hotel to help with the first guests and had accompanied Charlie to their room. She was a woman of few words but it was the only way they got any information as the council weren't telling them much.

'I know you're on scrip, but do you need a sharps box?' Rose asked them.

Charlie's ears pricked up. Once upon a time she had been a midwife working at the Royal Shrewsbury and she knew that these small black plastic boxes were for needles. So they must be heroin addicts. A scrip, it turned out, was a methadone prescription.

A sharps box.

*   *   *

'Room 7 – champagne bottle in bar 6.15 p.m. as surprise for wife' read the hotel's logbook entry for that Friday. Already that seemed like another world. The last ordinary guests had checked out, apart from a retired couple who were regulars and two workmen in Shrewsbury for a job who were intrigued by the new guests and offered to help. Customers in the restaurants had dried up since the prime minister had warned people to stay at home at the start of the week, and at the end of Friday they closed the tea rooms. The Mother's Day lunch for Sunday was cancelled.

Mike had said that with most of the other guests gone the homeless could eat in the Royalist Restaurant, an imposing wood-panelled room with chandeliers, stained-glass windows and tapestries, and two knights in shining armour watching on from the fireplace. But the two women thought this was unwise. The tables were laid with crystal glasses and the walls were decorated with swords and lances. Nor did they want them to use the lounge bar, where regular residents might still go.

'What about the Darwin Suite?' suggested Jacki, referring to the beamed conference room on the first floor named after the town's most famous son.

'Good idea,' said Charlie. There clearly weren't going to be any conferences for some time.

It already had tables and chairs, so they converted it into a dining area cum communal room, bringing in a sofa, comfy chairs and the TV that would normally be in the hotel window showing promotional videos. At the back they set up a trestle table where breakfast and dinner could be served. They also laid out sandwiches and juice for lunch, but no one seemed to eat them.

The homeless had all disappeared during the day. They had no idea where they went. Charlie found it a bit scary not having a clue about their new guests.

The Royalist restaurant.

They all seemed to know each other. Some of them were rather alarming. Mark Chapman had a way of flourishing his hands like a magician. Dave Pritchard was very loud, as was Tracy, and loved to jump out from behind the partition in the Darwin to scare them. Derek Tyrer talked to himself, telling them he could hear voices or was talking to God.

Most of them reeked of smoke. Charlie and Jacki tried to keep them away from the oldest parts of the hotel, such as the twelfth-century mansion house with its Jacobean staircase, which the insurance company had told Mike was the most important thing to save in a fire, even if he had no idea how.

Charlie was overseeing closing those parts off when Jacki called her to come to the kitchen. 'The chef is throwing his dummies out of his pram!' she said. The head chef had resigned a few days earlier and one of his deputies had taken over. Used to creating sophisticated fare for their menu, such as confit of duck terrine with poached pear or seared king scallop with truffle puree, he was unimpressed by their new customers. 'I'm not cooking for the homeless,' he said.

That evening dinner was cottage pie. 'That was nice apart from the pickled onions,' said Donny when Charlie had picked up his plate. He had left a line of the offending onions on the side.

'What?' exclaimed Charlie. Back in the kitchen, she asked the chef, 'Is it normal to put pickled onions in cottage pie?'

'They'll have what they're effin' given!' he replied. 'They'll be asking for chips next!' He was also scared of the virus, as he had asthma. Food deliveries had to be left for hours in the cold room off the kitchen as a kind of quarantine in the hope that any virus attached to them would die off. A couple of days later they heard him shouting, 'I've gotta go, gotta go!'

By Monday, he would quit.

It wasn't just the kitchen staff that were a problem. The house-keepers were terrified of going into the rooms of their new guests.

It was agreed that they would work in groups of two. To start with, Charlie or Jacki also went round with them, and Gabriella, who had worked in the tea rooms, offered to switch to cleaning.

In one room they found bottles of vodka. Cider in another. They quickly guessed that some of their guests were alcoholics. Dealing with these very different new residents was exhausting. They were joined by Wendy Faulkner, the manager of the Ark, who had been thrown in at the deep end herself, starting the job in January and immediately having to deal with floods that had rendered people homeless, then a pandemic. She had come to see how things were going. 'You two look absolutely shattered,' she said.

But whenever Charlie spoke to Mike, who kept calling from Bournemouth, she assured him that everything was fine. He was dubious. He had told James, 'It looks like we're going to take in homeless. God knows how it will work.'

Mike soon had something new to worry about. That night on TV, he watched Rishi Sunak, the whippet-thin new young chancellor, announce a furlough scheme in which all employees would be paid 80 per cent of their salary by the government.

'Oh my God, the staff will all just go home and get the money!' said Mike.

One of his friends who ran a restaurant in Shrewsbury called. 'All my staff left, all sixty!' he told Mike.

Dame Louise Casey would also be taken aback. As soon as she realised the severity of the pandemic, the former homelessness tsar had come up with the Everyone In programme to get rough sleepers off the streets. She and her staff had been ringing round hotels to get them to take part, from budget inns in London to a caravan park in Cornwall. It would be a way of keeping their businesses going. 'Turned out no one had talked to the Treasury, and as soon as Rishi announced the relief package some of the hotels pulled out,' said Dame Louise. 'One in Brighton kicked everyone straight back onto the streets. I was like: "Speed dial Rishi, tell him don't f**king give furlough to hotels!" But it was too late.'

Some of the Prince Rupert staff couldn't carry on working during the pandemic, such as the barman, who had worked there twenty years: he was seventy and asthmatic so had to shield. But Mike began to get messages from others saying they would take furlough – receptionists, night porters, a chef, housekeepers, staff from the tea rooms. Charlie told him they had all gone home.

He was livid. He'd employed some of these people for years and with a flick of a switch they had gone, no loyalty. 'You quickly find out who is dedicated,' he told James. And how could they possibly look after all the homeless without staff? Later it would transpire that the employer had to agree to staff taking furlough, so some came back.

Thank God for Charlie and Jacki. They told him they had both moved in to the hotel.

Mike decided he would move in too, after his insurance broker called to ask how he was planning to secure the building, thinking they would be closing it and worried about the possibility of fire or theft. 'Well, actually we're going to house the homeless,' said Mike. There was silence.

'Don't worry, I will be sleeping on site,' he said rashly. In recent years he and Diane had grown apart anyway.

The Lion, Shrewsbury's other historic hotel, where previous guests had included Charles Dickens, Benjamin Disraeli and Niccolo Paganini, had changed its mind about taking in homeless and had closed down, ejecting its residents. Back at the Prince Rupert, more and more rough sleepers kept arriving.

One of the new arrivals was a young man called Tommo. After checking in, he went outside for a smoke. Not long after, Jacki happened to glance out a window. Tommo was bent double with his head in the flowerbed as if he were eating the flowers. She beckoned Charlie over. 'What's he doing?' she asked.

They went outside. 'I think he's on something,' said Charlie.

'Tommo! Tommo!' they shouted. Eventually he came to and stood up, zombie-like, his eyes red and hazy. They pushed him inside and up the stairs, swaying from side to side like a praying mantis, with one of the security guards behind them.

'What is it? What has he taken?' asked Jacki.

It was their first encounter with mamba, a synthetic cannabis substitute that was cheaper than weed and more potent. 'Will he be okay? Shall I Google what to do?' she wondered.

Tommo had passed out on the bed but he seemed okay, so they left him. When they came down, another Polish man, called Christian, had arrived and they put him in the room next to Chez so they could talk to each other. Also among the new arrivals was a couple, Julie and Andy, who like Randolph and Tracy had been living in a tent under one of the bridges. Andy was very tall and never seemed to stop moving, while Julie was rail-thin, white-faced and tearful.

Next came Shaggy, a gruff man with a ginger beard, in his thirties, nicknamed after the character from *Scooby-Doo*, and Martin Pippard, thirty-three, a wiry man who had been sleeping near the river in a concrete alcove under Telford Way until the floods had forced him out. 'I had a bit of carpet under me and a sleeping bag and pillow, that's it,' he said.

The problem was the Ark didn't seem to want to give out much information about the rough sleepers, seeing that as the responsibility of the council. But the council workers who came to process them usually worked in an office two miles away and had names but did not know the individuals.

Along with Mark Chapman and Dave Pritchard, Charlie and Jacki realised Martin Pippard and Tracy were alcoholics as well, from all the bottles in their rooms. Soon they would see them flat-out drunk.

Gradually the staff of the Prince Rupert gleaned a few details. Shaggy had set fire to his school at the age of nine. Tommo had just come out of prison. Dave Pritchard and Martin Pippard had been in jail for assault more times than they could remember. Tracy had started drinking at an early age from the drip trays under the beer taps in her grandad's pub.

'Oh God,' Charlie said to Jacki. 'Mr M is going to flip, his beautiful hotel will be trashed.'

That day Mike left Bournemouth to head back to the hotel. He called from the motorway.

'You're not going to like this …' began Charlie.

3.

Tuesday, 24 March 2020

Mike didn't recognise his own hotel. Two burly security guards had appeared on the door in unfamiliar uniform. The tea rooms were shuttered and the TV set showing promotional videos had disappeared from the lobby window. There was a large bottle of sanitiser at the entrance and one of the guards pointed a temperature gun at his forehead. Inside, everyone was wearing masks and gloves as if it were a hospital. At reception stood a couple of young women he didn't recognise – from the council, he later learned. In the lounge bar, instead of ladies who lunch, there were unfamiliar people sitting at laptops who looked at him like he was intruding – staff from the Ark. It felt horrible.

The usually bustling streets outside were deserted, and the town's many boutiques and cafés were closed. The night before, an unusually sober-looking Boris Johnson had made a speech to the nation, announcing, 'From this evening I must give the British people a very simple instruction – you must stay at home.' Only supermarkets and food shops could remain open. He called the virus 'the biggest threat this country has faced for decades'. And so had begun the country's first national lockdown.

The UK death toll had now reached 335. Mike's cousin in Spain, where they were about two weeks ahead, was sending ever more apocalyptic messages. There, more than two thousand people had died, so many that an ice rink in Madrid had been turned into a makeshift morgue. Soldiers had been drafted in and had found old people dead and abandoned in care homes. Mike shivered as he wondered if they were heading the same way.

There was another reason to shiver – the hotel was cold. The heating seemed to be off. He wandered into the kitchen. Every surface was crammed with stuff: loaves of bread, boxes of eggs, crates of fruit and veg, packets of sandwiches. 'Donations,' said Charlie, emerging from behind him. 'Something called the Food Hub is sending us all the things they normally send to the Ark. Don't touch them!' she exclaimed as he went to pick up a sandwich. 'We are supposed to quarantine everything for a day. And wash the eggs.'

She looked different, too, in jeans, jumper and leopard-print Doc Martens instead of her usual smart suit and heels, though he was relieved to see her.

'How's it going?' he asked.

'Okay …' she began.

'Why is it so chilly?'

'The guests complained about being too hot. I guess they are used to being outside. They've all got their windows open.'

'Which room are you in?' he asked.

'206.'

The Princess Charlotte Suite. Exactly the room he'd been thinking about on the drive up. It had a four-poster bed, a spacious bathroom with an oversized bath, a desk and a sofa to watch sport on TV, not to mention a lovely view of St Alkmund's and across Butcher Row to the old black-and-white timbered Abbot's House and the rooftops beyond.

'I'll go in room 209 then,' he said, trying not to sound put out.

'Oh, Jax is in there,' she said.

That was annoying. His favourite room was actually the Prince Maurice Suite in the twelfth-century mansion house at the back, a

lovely quiet room with wooden beams, a king-size bed, Victorian roll-top bath and antique chaise longue, where previous guests had included the astronomer Sir Patrick Moore and Colin Tennant, 3rd Baron Glenconner, the owner of Mustique. But he thought he needed to be at the front to keep an eye on things.

In the end he decided to take a room on the third floor, which was small but had a terrace with views over the church and square, and it was good for sunning and watching what was going on. 'So where are our new guests?' asked Mike.

'Having dinner in the Darwin. Come and see.'

He followed Charlie upstairs to peep in. There were about fourteen of them in the suite, mostly men, eating bowls of chilli con carne with garlic bread. Some of them had no shoes or socks on, he noticed. They seemed very quiet.

'I think they are scared of us,' she said. 'From stories they have told us, they have been treated awfully in the past. They are very wary of people.'

The next day Mike drove home to get his clothes and whatever he needed for the next few weeks. Inside the house, Diane backed away from him. As he went from room to room collecting things, she followed at a distance, spraying Dettol on door handles and everything he touched. Everyone was paranoid about catching the virus from surfaces and having recently recovered from pleurisy and, before that, breast cancer, she had even more reason to be concerned. Most of those dying were the elderly and she worried about passing it on to her ninety year old mother in a nursing home in Devon.

'I can only do this if I stay in the hotel,' he told her. 'I need to be there for the insurance and I can't come back and forth because of the virus.'

She nodded. Their old ginger-and-white cat Tango appeared, rubbing up against his legs. Could he stroke him? Could cats carry the virus?

His head a blur, Mike began stuffing belongings into cases – clothes, toiletries, his weights. He looked wistfully at his electric guitar but thought better of it. Alexander, his youngest son, emerged from his room. His university, like all of them, had been closed. 'I'm going to stay in the hotel for a bit,' said Mike.

As he got in the car and drove away, it felt eerie not knowing exactly what he was heading off to or for how long. The roads were empty.

Once again the hotel felt like a different building. He spotted some bearded characters lounging on the bench across the way on the church square. Some of them were smoking roll-ups and one seemed to be rolling the biggest spliff he had ever seen.

'I think I should make a speech,' he told Jacki and Charlie. 'You know, welcome them and let them know who I am.'

Neither of the women thought this a good idea but he was determined, so that evening they called everyone as usual for supper in the Darwin Suite. Mike drew himself up to his full six foot two and cleared his throat, his left eye twitching as it did when he was tense.

'I'm Mike Matthews, owner of the hotel,' he began. 'I want to welcome you, it's lovely you are here. This will be challenging for you all,' he went on. 'You're not used to living in a building or to us. And we're not used to you. But we want to make this home for you. As hoteliers we are used to providing a service. Whilst staying with us you will be treated as regular guests. Anything we can do, let us know.'

'For God's sake, no one's listening,' Charlie whispered to Jacki.

Mike went on to talk about Covid, which he called 'this terrible virus sweeping the world', reminding them not to touch each other and to wash their hands thoroughly and use sanitiser. 'I know you are all used to being free but we must all be careful and protect each other,' he ended.

Afterwards Randolph and Tracy came to thank him, to his horror sticking out their hands to shake his. He washed them thoroughly afterwards. Randolph told him that twenty years earlier he had worked in the hotel's kitchens. 'You were trouble then,' laughed Mike, though he didn't remember him.

Walking around the corridors the next day, Mike saw one or two of the new guests with their shirts off and was shocked at how skinny they were, with their ribs sticking out. When they were slumped in doorways in duffel coats he would never have realised.

'We must feed these guys up,' he urged Charlie. 'If nothing else we can make them healthy.'

She had told Mike about the chef quitting. Since then, the previous head chef had helped out for a few days to prepare some meals and go through everything in the fridges that could be used. He'd made some tomato sauces to keep, sorted out lamb shanks that could be used for a casserole and whipped up a sticky toffee pudding. But he had now left.

'We need to get a chef in who will cook hearty food, good nourishing fare from fresh ingredients,' said Mike.

'No, I will do it,' said Charlie.

'Is there no end to your talents?' he laughed.

'Look, I've brought up three ravenous boys. And I used to cook at Gary's social club for all those football players …'

'Seriously, do you have time?'

Charlie nodded. She relished it. She was a confident cook, who didn't need to measure ingredients. Though petite and mostly vegetarian, she loved feeding others.

From then on, every afternoon she would disappear into the kitchen, Jacki in tow, and begin chopping onions, carrots and potatoes. She started making vast toad in the holes, vats of chilli con carne, huge lasagnes, enormous bread and butter puddings, and apple and pear crumbles. She quickly worked out that they had to have dessert, and always with custard. Stokesy, who rolled the huge spliffs, turned out to adore banana flavour Angel Delight.

On Sundays there would be roast with all the trimmings.

Most of the new guests were hugely grateful, except Derek Tyrer who ran away whenever they tried to talk to him and wandered around muttering, 'This is just a money-making exercise.'

If the homeless were wary of the staff, they were even more scared of coronavirus. The new government restrictions allowed people out only once a day for exercise or essential shopping for food or medicine. Many of the addicts were on methadone, an opioid in the form of green linctus syrup, which blocked the high from heroin. It was mostly prescribed on a daily basis because it was just as addictive, so each day they would go out to collect it. Sometimes they stole from each other.

With nothing else for them to do but watch the endless, ever more alarming coverage on TV, they started hanging round the hotel more. 'We need things for them to do,' said Charlie. She nipped back home one day to bring in all her DVDs.

Wendy promised to bring in some games from the Ark. First she brought children's games – small plastic skittles and a bow and arrow, which were quickly broken. Later she sent over a Wii game console and Martin started playing the boxing game obsessively. Eventually they learned he had once been a semi-pro welterweight. 'I had a lot of anger management problems because of my stepdad and I banged him out when I was fourteen after he hit my mum,' he said. 'But then I watched *Rocky* and asked if I could start boxing. It was the best thing I ever did in my life. I used to train all week and travel round the country to fight, even to Scotland.'

Mike brought in a pool table and the hotel put out a message on a local Facebook group asking for anything. The local prison sent them a ping pong table. Charlie strung some fairy lights from the vast Tudor beams.

'It's brilliant what you're doing for us,' said Stokesy one day, bringing tears to her eyes. 'Outside, everyone treats us like dogs, but even dogs have kennels.'

'I'm going to stop wearing PPE,' Charlie told Jacki after the first week. 'It's creating a barrier between us and them.'

'What about the risk of getting coronavirus?' asked Jacki. 'People are dying.'

'We're all living here together in a bubble, just a big one. It just feels like if we wear this surgical stuff, it's as though we see them as unclean like everybody else does so they can't trust us. And it keeps misting up my glasses.'

She also wondered if they had already had the virus. Many of the hotel's guests had been Chinese, tourists or parents of students boarding at nearby Concord College, and one evening in January a Chinese man had been spluttering and sneezing all through dinner in the Royalist Restaurant. A few days afterwards all three had gone down with a lingering cough and flu-like fatigue that had taken a couple of weeks to go, symptoms that were remarkably like those now being described as Covid.

Most of all Charlie yearned to help their new guests. She'd always been the type of person who picked up stray birds. At school she befriended the kids who didn't have friends. 'I had one friend whose mum was a lady of the night and dad was nowhere to be seen, and my mum used to say she could see the nits crawling from her hair to mine,' she smiled. 'She used to tear her hair out.'

Charlie did not want to pry. But she did want to listen, something most of their new guests were not used to. The first to start opening up to her was Chris Bennett, who had offered to help with sweeping outside.

He was a roofer and joiner, he told her, and only recently homeless, having been on the streets since the day before New Year's Eve. Originally from Manchester, 'dad a copper, mum a seamstress who split up when I was five', Chris had always worked since leaving school just before GCSEs, apart from when he fell off a roof and broke both legs. He had come to Shrewsbury to live with his girlfriend and had been away a lot of the time, working on the building of the new HS2 high-speed railway, for which he'd been earning 'bloody good pay' – about £600 a week. 'Each time I came back the house was a mess, my money was all disappearing and she'd be smoking crack with her mates,' he said. 'In the end I told her to choose between them and me. She threw me out in the clothes I stood up in.' Having previously fallen out with his family, he had nowhere to go. 'I was scared,' he said. 'I'd never been on the

streets before. I had no phone, no cards – just £30 in my pocket, not even a toothbrush or hair clipper, and was walking round the streets feeling lost. I stood on the bridges and stared at the water, thinking about throwing myself in the river.' Eventually he had met Randolph and Tracy, who gave him a sleeping bag and advice on where to sleep.

When he heard about the pandemic, Chris was terrified he would just be left to die on the streets. Then someone from the Ark told him about the Prince Rupert. 'I'd never have come in a place like this,' he said. 'I wouldn't have expected you to be so down to earth.'

Most of the guests had been on and off the streets for years. At thirty-four, Shaggy was one of the younger ones and did not say much, disappearing off outside or staying in his room reading his collection of Lee Child thrillers, but one day he told them he was

a local boy. 'I've been in trouble since I was nine, when I was playing with a box of matches with a friend and we threw one in a bin
and the whole school burned down, so I was thrown out,' he said.
'Me and my dad are too similar and clash big time, so I moved out
when I was sixteen and been sofa-surfing or on Pride Hill pretty
much ever since.'

Shaggy had held various jobs, the last of which had been at a
local metal press, but had not worked since 2015 after breaking up
with the mother of his son. He said she had kicked him out and he
had been on the streets ever since. 'It's cold and miserable, and you
end up doing more drugs to try and forget,' he said.

'It was a bit intimidating at first,' he said of the Prince Rupert,
'but I know most people here. We've all been hanging round for
years.'

Others were struggling to adjust. One day Charlie came down
to shouting. Dave Pritchard was yelling at one of the people from
the Ark. 'You've done nothing for me, you fuckin' lazy bastards!'
he said. 'Now you're taking my letters.' His mum used to send him
letters care of the Ark, handwritten in tiny violet envelopes
containing money, and he'd become convinced that they were not
passing them on. Charlie and Jacki watched, alarmed at his sudden
rage.

'The Ark doesn't own these guys,' said Charlie. 'They're
free.'

'Get your mum to send them here,' they told Dave afterwards.

The next morning Mike got a WhatsApp message from a friend
who ran two pubs in Shrewsbury, asking if Michael Lambert or
another man were staying with them, as they had been filmed on
CCTV apparently trying to break into the Albion Vaults by the
station.

'No,' replied Mike. 'Never heard of them.'

An hour later, Wendy from the Ark called. 'I have someone I'd like you to take in,' she said. 'His name is Michael Lambert.'

Mike was horrified.

'Oh, he's a really nice guy,' she said. 'He just needs a helping hand.'

Shortly afterwards a couple of policemen dropped in. 'If Michael Lambert pitches up here, we would strongly advise you not to take him in,' they said. 'He was recently released from jail, has served multiple prison sentences and he is Shrewsbury's most prolific shoplifter. He will rob you blind. He is highly dangerous, a high-level drug taker and drug dealer. If he does appear, call us immediately.'

Mike didn't know what to do. Charlie was all in favour of him staying. 'Maybe we can turn him round,' she said.

Not long after that the security guards called. 'There's a new guy just arrived,' they said. Mike and Charlie went to reception, where Pam was talking to someone. The man standing there looked to be in his late thirties. He was wearing a baseball cap and had two earrings in his left ear. He was dirty, skinny and wary, and reeked of smoke.

'The Ark told me to come here,' he said.

'Your name please?' asked Pam.

'Michael Lambert.'

'Welcome,' said Charlie, trying not to look fazed. Whatever people may or may not have done in their past, she was not going to be deterred by the police. 'The most important thing to be when you grow up is kind,' she had always told her children, 'and true kindness is not conditional.'

She showed Lambert up to a room and gave him the key. They had switched to putting keys on plastic fobs, as they didn't want to lose the heavy old leather ones and feared they might pass on the virus. As she explained how the heating and television worked and told him about meal times, Lambert said he had got out of jail on

Christmas Eve and had been sofa-surfing at the home of someone called Bevan. He'd had to move out because of Covid. He had been on the streets since.

He was amazed at the warmth of Charlie, Jacki and Pam. 'I was surprised to be welcomed with open arms,' he said, 'but to tell the truth I didn't like the place at first. I'd never ever stayed in a hotel before. My family are travellers, rough and ready, and I thought it was too posh. Also, I don't like eating food in front of other people.

'Then I saw some people I knew from the streets, like Shaggy, Martin and Mark Chapman, and thought, Aha, it's not as posh as I thought.'

As soon as the police found out that Michael Lambert was there, they called all the local shops to warn them. In the hotel, Charlie, Jacki and Mike ran round screwing doors shut and stacking chairs in front of parts of the hotel that had been closed off to stop him getting to them. 'I hope we are not going to regret this,' said Mike.

At dinner, Mike was surprised to see this skinny figure with no shirt or shoes or socks standing waiting with his plate to be served. 'So you're the big Michael Lambert everyone is scared of!' he exclaimed. 'You look like Tarzan.'

It did not take long for Lambert to establish himself as a firm favourite. He loved Charlie's cooking, particularly the desserts, and quickly became known as the custard king. He might have served so many prison sentences that he couldn't remember the number, but he was, they all agreed, their politest resident.

4.

Saturday, 28 March 2020

He was a tiny figure, not even five feet tall, swamped by a bright-red puffer jacket and rucksack twice his size. His name was Richard Marshall, but everyone called him Titch.

He came in looking very scared and very young, huge bug eyes on stalks as he approached the reception desk. With him was a pugnacious-looking man who was holding a bulldog. The man had tattoos across his forehead and chin, and said he was Richard's uncle John.

'We don't take dogs,' said Charlie apologetically.

'We were told the Prince Rupert was taking people in,' said John in a strong Glaswegian accent.

Mike heard the raised voices and went to the lobby. He could see John was spoiling for a fight, which was the last thing they needed. 'No dogs here I'm afraid,' he said firmly. 'I'm a dog lover myself but our insurance company doesn't allow it.' Still complaining, Scottish John, as they called him, left with his dog Sky, but Richard stayed. They had, he said, been sleeping in the doorway of the Town Fryer, a local fish and chip shop.

Soon he was irritating the others. He might have been small but he was hard to ignore, talking loudly and nasally, his head cocked to one side like a bird, almost every sentence interspersed with 'd'ya know what I mean?'

Mike was instantly drawn to him, thanks to his broad Mancunian accent, having grown up there himself before his parents moved to the south coast when he was nine. Serving dinner in the Darwin, after piling everyone else's plates high, he gave Richard just one potato. 'You're only small so here's a small plate,' he said.

Richard looked shocked, then burst out laughing.

'You're from Manchester, I hear,' said Mike. 'So am I.'

'You don't fuckin' sound it,' replied Richard.

They quickly discovered a shared love of Manchester United. Mike could see that behind his swagger and loud voice, Richard was trying to overcompensate for his lack of height and physicality. As for Richard, he saw 'Mr M', as he called him, as the father figure he'd never had. Jacki became 'mum'. He began to open up.

Titch and Mike.

Though he looked much younger, Titch was thirty-one and had, he told them, been sofa-surfing since the age of twelve, when his father died. 'My mum was in the bath and my dad started having a fit, coughing blood, so I called an ambulance, but it was too late,' he said. 'He was an alcoholic but I didn't know. They both were. My mum would come home from work and get cans of beer to drink while watching TV and I just thought that's what parents do. They deserved to drink because they worked every day.

'My dad was a very strict man – if he pointed at the ceiling, we would have to run upstairs. I was the youngest. Later I found out he wasn't even my real father.'

After his father died, Titch soon dropped out of school. 'My mum couldn't cope, so they put me into care but I ran away from the children's home and got in with gangs,' he said. 'I started stealing because I didn't have any money to live from: they would put me through house windows to get car keys or wallets, as I was small.'

As his legs were so short, he was also the one who would get caught if the police came, while the others ran off with the loot into nearby streets or to the canal. Eventually Titch ended up in prison, where he spent seven or eight years for burglary and car theft. 'In prison they used me as a guinea pig for drugs,' he said. 'Because I was small it would affect me more quickly, so they could see if something was good or bad. Like them canaries in mines. People are always taking advantage of me.'

Titch was also epileptic.

Once he got out, he went to live with an uncle. Unfortunately, the uncle was also a drug user. 'He used to inject heroin in his groin and got an infection and died, so I ended up on the streets again. Then I was with the guy who threw a hand grenade into a pub in Manchester to kill some rival. Now every morning I wake up and hear explosions and screaming, so need to smoke dope to block everything.

'I've been an addict – I smoke weed and mamba,' he added. 'Every day I say I want to give it up because it's going to kill me, but on the streets, you're walking around and someone offers you drugs, so it's hard to say no. It kills the time when you have nothing good to think about.

'I've tried self-harming, tried hanging myself. I've even thrown myself in front of a bus, but always someone helped and I never managed it. Never managed anything really …'

For a while Titch went to the Isle of Man to stay with another uncle who had a farm with horses, but that didn't work out. Somehow he ended up in Birmingham, sleeping in doorways. That's where he met Scottish John, the man he called uncle. 'He bought me a train ticket and I thought we were going to Scotland. Instead we came here. Never been to Shrewsbury, but it's a nice place. As soon as I arrived, I thought this could be a fresh start, but then the pandemic came.'

The pair had been put up in the Lion but were evicted when it closed, so they slept in the Town Fryer doorway, which was where they had heard about the Prince Rupert. 'This feels like an opportunity,' Titch told them. 'It's like a home. I feel like I've got my life back, like I'm not homeless. You see something in us. On the streets people look at you like you are dirt: you're just a junkie.'

Mike remembered going Christmas shopping in London a few months earlier and passing a man who had been slumped forward on the pavement in Piccadilly, his head on the stone slab, clearly intoxicated. 'My reaction was the same as hundreds of other shoppers,' he later recalled. 'We all just walked by.'

He was horrified by Titch's story. What would he have done if he had had a childhood like that, abandoned at the age of twelve? He remembered how angry he had been when his parents moved to Plymouth, and getting into fights in his new school, where the headmaster had said, 'None of your Manchester ways here, boy!' Would he have had the resilience to survive?

How could someone just drop out of the system like that? Sadly, Titch was not unique but was one of many described by Anne Longfield, the Children's Commissioner, in a report entitled 'Pass the Parcel', as 'children no one knows what to do with'.* With more than eighty thousand children in care in England, she would go on to call the system 'infuriatingly inadequate', warning 'a children's social care system that is supposed to protect vulnerable teenagers is frequently putting them in even greater danger. Often, we may as well be handing over children directly to ruthless gangs and criminals.'✝

This was precisely what had happened to Titch, and Mike determined to help him. 'What would you like to do if you could do anything?' he asked.

Titch told Mike he would like to have a job refurbishing furniture. 'Once I worked at Sir Alex Ferguson's house, as a cousin of mine had a contract doing some work and I helped tiling. I got to meet him. It was the best thing ever. Can you imagine Sir Alex, legend, speaking to me Richard Marshall, no fixed abode?

'And I want a place of me own to live. I don't understand why I walk around and see these empty council flats. I think I could look after myself. I might struggle a bit but with some help I could do it.'

Helping Titch wouldn't be so easy, however. To Charlie, he was like a Peter Pan figure who had never grown up. 'He has no idea how to do basic things,' she fretted.

Sometimes he would disappear and she and Jacki would keep having to go and find him. By now they recognised the red-eyed zombie look of someone who smoked mamba and knew from Chris Bennett that the best remedy was to get them to drink orange

---

* 'Pass the Parcel', Children's Commissioner report, December 2019.

✝ 'Out of Harm's Way', Commission on Young Lives report, December 2021.

juice, as the sweetness revived them. 'Mamba is poison,' Bennett said. 'At the end of the day it's wheel cleaner. It's an addiction. It gets into your blood and when you don't get it, you get such sweats you wake up with your bed sodden and all phlegmy like spiders' webs coming out of you.'

'I feel bad every time I do this,' said Titch. 'But you can't get off drugs if you don't tackle the problem, which is my life is shit and I am depressed.'

Tommo, who had been doing the mamba handstands in the flowerbeds, was taken away by police, having breached the terms of his probation. Before being sent back to prison, he came to the hotel begging to go to his room. 'I've left some family photos,' he told a mystified Jacki.

'I've checked the room, there's nothing there,' she said, refusing to let him go up.

'It's my mamba, I need it,' he whispered eventually. A small packet was hidden behind the headboard.

Outside, the streets of Shrewsbury were silent and deserted. In the evenings pools of yellow light from the old streetlamps fell on empty pavements. For the first time Mike found himself waking to birdsong. Sitting on his balcony with a coffee brought by Charlie, watching doves and seagulls circling over the ancient spires and rooftops, it felt like they and the homeless had the beautiful old town to themselves. 'Is it odd to say I am enjoying myself?' he wondered.

Inside the hotel, the atmosphere grew more relaxed, sometimes boisterous. To Charlie, it felt almost like a carnival, at least until the fights broke out. Without discussing it, the three of them developed a routine – a triple act, whereby Charlie loved everyone, Jacki didn't trust anyone and Mike was the voice of reason, saying 'Hold on a minute, let's think about this over coffee.'

Some of the guests joined in to help clean, Chris Bennett sweeping, Tracy hoovering and Titch clearing plates after meals. Stokesy liked messing around with the plants – he told them he loved flowers and that many years ago, before his mum went into hospital for an operation and never came out, he had worked with his father in his landscaping business. Shaggy told them he was a chef and had once worked in the pub next door, the Bull Inn. 'I love cooking,' he said. 'I used to cook with my mum but cheffing is unsociable hours and too high pressure.' One night he cooked them all sweet and sour chicken. 'It's better than Charlie's food,' said Tracy to Charlie's annoyance.

Some came down hair washed and shiny, clean-shaven, like different people. 'It's lovely to see the transformation,' said Mike, after Charlie or Jacki had exclaimed in wonder, 'Have you seen Dave or Martin?'

Some did it sooner than others – it would take Mark Chapman a month. After the first wash, he'd take pride in his appearance, changing clothes, and wearing an impressive-looking medal that turned out to have been purloined from someone he knew who had done a half marathon.

By then many clothes had been donated from local people and shops who had heard what the hotel was doing, and they had laid these on tables for the residents to go and choose from. Chris Bennett lit on some leather trousers and put on an impromptu fashion show. 'I had thousands of pounds of designer clothes,' he told them. 'Armani, the lot. But my girlfriend threw me out in the clothes I stood up in.' Mike was amazed how picky they could be for people who had been wearing the same tracksuit for five months. 'I'm not wearing that!' they would exclaim, rejecting his late father's Church's shoes (taking only the laces) or Austin Reed jacket, or his wife's Jaeger jumper.

Maybe it was the fear of the pandemic and all being stuck together like a family of misfits, but gradually the homeless guests began to talk more freely. They learned from Martin that his step-dad had abused him from an early age and had gone to jail, and that Shaggy had been abused by one of his teachers for two years before setting fire to the school. 'Back in those days no one listened,' he said. 'I got called a liar.'

One evening Chris Bennett brought a photo album into the Darwin Suite to show them. It was of a holiday in a luxury hotel in the Turkish beach resort of Marmaris in 2017 with his ex-girl-friend, her son and his two beautiful teenage daughters. There were a number of gaps – he had removed all the pictures of his ex. In one photo of Chris on a beach staring soulfully out towards a sunset over the sea, he was almost unrecognisable from the worn-down man who was living in their hotel.

It was late in the evenings that their true characters came out and some of them would sit with Mike, Charlie and Jacki in the

Chris on holiday in Turkey.

lounge bar and start telling stories. Mike particularly enjoyed talking to Mark Chapman, who was known as the grandfather of the street for his decades in the open air. He was quiet compared to some of the residents, and Mike found him 'a wise head, a real gentleman and an intellectual, who loved to talk about cooking, travel, politics, often replying with cryptic Eric Cantona-style one-liners in between shots of vodka'.

Charlie and Jacki would crack up at some of his remarks. 'Enjoy your dinner, Mark,' they would say.

'Don't make a meal of it,' he'd fire back.

Sometimes in the lounge bar, he would put on his glasses, saying, 'Now I don't want to make a spectacle of myself ...'

He told them he'd left home at fifteen because of a clash with his father, joined the army, then worked as a chef and been jailed in

Amsterdam for punching someone who had tried to take the money he was withdrawing from a cashpoint. Occasionally he would launch into polemics on the state of the nation and failures of government, how it only served the privileged. 'They'll find a way to make money from this pandemic, mark my words,' he said. 'We are all just ants under their Old Etonian boots.'

'Wouldn't you like to live in a house?' asked Mike one evening.

'You know what they say – wealth comes from within,' replied Mark. 'I don't have a problem with people wanting success and material things – I am just not interested in getting on that merry-go-round.'

And with that he would down another shot of what he called his 'medicine'.

One day Mike was catching up with James on the phone, checking in on how he and his pregnant wife were doing, and he noticed Michael Lambert looking interested.

'My son,' Mike said. 'His wife is expecting my first grandchild. Do you have any children?'

'Six,' nodded Lambert. 'From three different women – or maybe four!' Aged between two and eighteen, four of them were in care – the three youngest adopted and one fostered. He still saw only his two eldest daughters, though not often. 'But I want to see them more,' he said. 'It's why I came back here when I got out of jail.'

Mike nodded. Until Chris Bennett had showed them his photo album, he hadn't imagined that the people he saw sleeping on the streets might be parents. 'Not much of a dad, right, that's what you're thinking?' said Lambert. 'I guess that's what they think. But I didn't have much of a role model.'

Lambert explained that he had been born in Germany, where his dad was stationed with the army. His parents split up when he was two and his mum took him and his five elder sisters to the market town of Whitchurch, about twenty miles north of Shrewsbury. From there they had moved to another nearby Shropshire town, Market Drayton, when he was twelve. Bullied at school, he was expelled at thirteen. He was just fifteen when his mum left with his elder sister and went back to Germany, and he was put into care.

'She never explained why she left me but took my big sister,' he said. 'I cried and cried. I felt no one loved me. After that it was downhill, a life of crime and drugs, in and out of jail ...'

It started with getting in with the wrong crowd, and by sixteen Lambert was on heroin. 'Before I knew it I was taking it every day,' he said. 'And shoplifting to pay for it. I never really thought about whether it was right or wrong,' he added. 'I just needed the fix – it was like a devil inside me.'

Soon he was in prison. Out at twenty-one, he got into a relationship and his first daughter was born. That ended after two years when he landed back in jail. After that he was with someone else for five years and had another daughter, but left in a fury after coming home one night in the early hours to find her in bed with another man.

'Basically, each time I would get in a relationship, have a kid, then it broke down and I ended up back in jail,' said Lambert. 'Then I'd get out, into another relationship, have another kid, then go to jail again.'

The problem was his addiction. He had, he said, tried to sort it out by taking methadone, but 'the wrong people were always there tempting me. I am too easily led. I had a period of seven years when I was clean with my last but one partner, but then got in with my neighbour and went down. That's always been my downfall. I come out of a relationship and into a life of crime ...

'Afterwards I'd always think, Why? It's not got me anywhere,' he said. 'I'd take drugs to get rid of the problem but however much

I took, the problem was still there. I'm not proud of what I've done but at the time I didn't think I was hurting someone, as long as I got money for drugs I didn't care. It was mad, now I sit here and think about it.'

Lambert had lost count of how many times he had gone to jail. 'It's got to be fifteen or sixteen … Petty mostly, shoplifting, also witness intimidation. I could have made better choices,' he added.

Mike didn't know what to say.

Lambert claimed to be clean since his last stint in jail and back on methadone, and was glad to have been brought in. 'Life on the streets is no picnic,' he said. 'I've had people throw things at me, kick me in the face and shout abuse. I think a lot of people think, They want to be like that. For a lot of us, it's not we want to be on the streets like that, we have no choice.'

Chris Bennett was sceptical. 'Anyone serious about getting clean takes Subutex not methadone,' he said. 'Subutex is a blocker. Methadone is just a substitute, stopping you feel ill, until you can score. It's worse than heroin. It's even harder to get off and makes your mouth so dry it destroys your teeth. It was developed by the Nazis to keep their soldiers fighting. That's why they say High Hitler.'

5.

Tuesday, 31 March 2020

By now the hotel had thirty-three residents and they'd had to start using rooms on the second floor, putting up there those who were less troublesome.

Charlie, Jacki and a few other staff were on a training course. The last course Jacki had taken was on floristry, she said, and, before that of course, accountancy. She'd always liked flowers and gardens, and dreamed of one day having a little flower shop. Now she was on a Zoom class about how to deal with a heroin overdose. They all sat in a semi-circle in the hotel lounge, staring at the laptop screen. It was the first time any of them had used Zoom, so it took a while for everyone to work out how to start it, where to look and how to unmute.

The call had been organised by the Shropshire Recovery Partnership, a local organisation that worked with the council on addiction, and was to instruct them on what to do if one of their new guests passed out. There was a lot of nervous giggling as a man on the screen held up a long yellow plastic container that looked like a toothbrush box. Inside were two needles and a syringe containing naloxone, an anti-overdose medication, which had to be injected into a muscle, they learned.

If someone stopped breathing and their lips started turning blue, they were to approach from a distance saying, 'Wake up, open your eyes', all the time being careful to avoid discarded needles. If the drug user did not come round, they were to put the person in the recovery position, open their airways and make sure they weren't swallowing their tongue. The instructor demonstrated how to do this using a dummy. Then they were to take out the syringe, unscrew the top, insert a needle, hold it like a pen and stick it in the person's thigh or bottom, through their clothing if necessary.

'I don't think I'd want to do that!' exclaimed Jacki.

Even more complicated, they were supposed to inject just half of the naloxone while keeping the needle in to see how the person reacted, as although the medication quickly brought people out of withdrawal, it wore off just as quickly and they could go straight back into overdose. They were then to give the second half and 'leg it', as it was likely an addict would be aggressive when coming round.

For Charlie, who had been a midwife and dental nurse, accustomed to needles and administering injections, it was nothing extraordinary. But for Jacki and the others, it was unimaginable and scary. As an accountant, Jacki was used to being in the back office, doing the bills and VAT returns, chasing debts, paying invoices and wages, and the end-of-day accounts. When she first started at the hotel, she'd kept in her office upstairs, very quiet, working long hours on spreadsheets as the work was new.

She had grown up in Wolverhampton with an elder brother, their father an HGV driver and mother a lithographer for a local distribution company, on one of those streets of terraced houses where everyone was in and out of one another's house. Her nan and two of her aunties lived on the same street. Always a tomboy, playing football and making dens in the park with other kids, she left school at sixteen wanting to be a car mechanic and enrolled on a YTS scheme. 'One day I'd want to be a truck driver, the next a hairdresser, but I never wanted to be an accountant!' she said.

However, seeing most of her friends earning more money in the local washing machine factory, Jacki left the YTS and joined them. The work was boring, so she and a friend went and worked at a campsite in the Welsh resort of Black Rock Sands, doing bar duty. When she came back, someone told her of a job going as a filing clerk in Walsall for a parts company. She took evening classes in accountancy.

For a while she lived with a partner in the countryside with two spaniels and a stream where ducks swam, running a business together from the barn. But that had not worked out and she had found herself on her own, nearing forty.

The Prince Rupert had given her a new lease of life. Mike had been looking for an accountant and Jacki was recommended to him by his auditors. 'It was a change and I wanted to move on,' she said.

When he showed her the kind of spreadsheets he used, she pretended to be familiar with them. Her only experience of hotels had been staying in them when travelling with previous boyfriends, lovely holidays leaving winter behind and chasing the sun to faraway places like Thailand, Vietnam and Mexico, despite her fear of flying. She'd also done a Caribbean cruise and gone to New York and dined at Windows on the World on top of the World Trade Center, even though her fear of heights meant she sat with her back to the view.

She had only really had one brief relationship since, and was, she said, quite happy alone in her cottage overlooking the River Severn. She spent her free time walking, running (if not as much as Charlie) and meeting up with friends. One of her favourite things to do was going to live music – 'anything from AC/DC to Michael Jackson'. She also regularly checked in on her ageing mum, particularly since her dad had died.

Jacki's colleagues in the hotel found her a woman of mystery. While Charlie wore her heart on her sleeve, often colourfully dressed, Jacki preferred neutrals, sensible trousers, jumpers and boots, and her expression could be inscrutable under her long straight blond hair that was tending to grey. She wore two watches, one of which had been her dad's and neither of which showed the right time.

She had a series of admirers. One year bouquets arrived for her twice a week for a month. One Valentine's Day, she got a message from reception to come down, as there was a man waiting with some flowers. He handed her a white envelope. Inside was a key. She looked at him blankly. 'If you come outside, it will become apparent,' he said. She followed him. He was, he said, from the local garage.

Parked in front of Camellias Tea Rooms was a silver SLK Mercedes convertible tied with a ribbon. 'I saw a lovely one in black,' she grumbled. 'And the engine is underpowered …'

When she went to collect it from a service later that year, her key wouldn't work. 'That's not your car any more,' said the garage owner. 'It has been swapped for the black one next to it – a three-litre V6.'

It was on lease and eventually Jackie returned it, going back to her Golf. Her colleagues in the hotel were intrigued and envious, some saying she had sent it to herself. Mike was fascinated. After sixteen years the pair had learned to rub along with each other. External auditors always praised her accuracy, but Mike found her 'much more than a figure cruncher', telling people, 'Jacki truly is dynamite.'

For her part she got used to his practical jokes, such as phoning her pretending to be an Italian waiter. Over time Jacki got more involved in the public life of the hotel, filling in on reception, working Christmas Day and New Year's Eve, valet parking cars in the pouring rain. A hotel could take over your life, she discovered.

But never like now. Everything had happened so quickly. Like all of them, she'd had no idea what to expect and was still rubbing her eyes at the whole thing. 'It makes you realise what you've got and how you can suddenly lose it,' she said to Charlie.

She felt sympathy for the alcoholics among the guests because she had experience of that in her own family, but she found the drug addicts harder to understand. For their part, the homeless were fascinated by her – Titch would call her mum, others the 'Ice Queen'.

Mike was not happy with the Zoom class, and was concerned about the insurance implications of staff trying to treat people who might potentially die. Afterwards the hotel received a supply of naloxone kits to keep behind reception. Most addicts had their own, but they often used the needles for other purposes. 'I hope we never have to use them,' said Jacki.

6.

Wednesday, 1 April 2020

The earliest written mention of Shrewsbury is from 901 in the charter of Wenlock Abbey, where it is referred to as *Scrobbesbyrig*, a Saxon name meaning 'Scrobb's fort' or 'the town in the shrubland'. By then it already had four churches, including St Alkmund's (next to the Prince Rupert) and St Mary's (behind it), and fortifications had been built to keep out the marauding Welsh. By the Middle Ages it was flourishing as the centre of the wool trade,

Butcher Row.

even having its own mint, and most of the street names in the centre date back to that time. Some have obvious meanings, like Milk Street and Fish Street, where dairy and fish were sold, and Butcher Row, along which you can still see some of the hooks from which carcasses were hung and the gully that ran red with blood. Then there is Wyle Cop, which means 'hill' in old Welsh. Off the top of that runs Dogpole, where horses used to be traded and which apparently used to be called Duckpole because to enter it you had to duck under a pole. Murivance, leading up to the old town walls, was derived from the French words *mur* and *avant*; and Pride Hill, the main shopping street, was named after a prominent wool merchant. At the top is High Cross, where executions used to be carried out.

Just in front of the Prince Rupert are the Bear Steps, the oldest part of the town, site of the bear pit, and you can still see the metal ring the animal would have been tied to before fighting. Local guides stop there to tell tourists how in July 1403, Henry IV had set out from that point for the bloody Battle of Shrewsbury to

defeat the rebel forces of Harry 'Hotspur' Percy, a battle immortalised by Shakespeare in *Henry IV Part 1*, and after which the nearby town of Battlefield was named. Hotspur's mutilated corpse was later displayed on the High Cross at the top of Pride Hill as a warning.

Between Bear Steps and the old Abbot's House is a narrow passage called Grope Lane, the old red light district. On either side of it are intricately decorated black-and-white Tudor buildings that lean into each other so much you can shake hands across their upper storeys.

It was down this alleyway that Mike and Charlie would run each evening, crossing the square in front of the old Market Hall, then along Coffee House Passage and down Swan Hill to the river. There they would cross the Penny Bridge (though the toll was now twenty pence) and head along the towpath, below the lush playing fields and imposing brick buildings of Shrewsbury School, where Mike's sons had studied in the same classrooms as had Darwin and where Richard Ingrams, Paul Foot and Willie Rushton had started a satirical magazine that became *Private Eye*.

'So beautiful,' sighed Charlie, looking at the banks of waving daffodils and the setting sun turning the river aflame under the weeping willows. After all the rains and floods in February that had left the Severn still swollen, it had turned into the perfect spring. If nothing else, the weather Gods were smiling on them. It would end up being the sunniest spring since 1929.

The news was relentlessly bad. More than six hundred people were dying a day and intensive care wards across the country were filling up, with some hospitals reportedly running out of oxygen.

Their evening run was the one time of day when they could have a break. Charlie had loved running since her school days, particularly hill running through the woodland paths up onto Grinshill ridge with its rocky platforms from which you could see far across the valley towards the Shropshire Hills. Behind it was the Grinshill quarry – the sandstone mined here had been used to build the English and Welsh bridges in Shrewsbury, as well as the library, castle and many of the town's imposing buildings.

It was thanks to her running that Charlie had discovered her first pregnancy, at the age of nineteen, shortly after marrying Gary. Her breasts started hurting when she ran and when she told her mother this she suggested why that might be. Later on, as their marriage soured, running had become Charlie's one release from difficulties in her life. Now fifty-three, after four children, she was still fit, wiry and fizzing with energy.

Almost ten years older, Mike, whose rugby-playing days were long over, sometimes struggled to keep up. They looked an odd couple, Mike a foot taller than her. Apart from exercise and fresh air, the run also gave them time to think and to talk without inter-ruptions about what was going on in the hotel.

Sometimes they talked about other staff and whether they were really committed. That morning a receptionist had quit with no

notice, saying she was not comfortable with their new guests. Mike was furious. 'I think we can manage without her,' said Charlie. 'I don't think we can have anyone who is not fully on board.'

Mike nodded. He kept thinking about his conversations with Titch and his stolen childhood; Michael Lambert being abandoned by his mum; Chris Bennett and his holiday snaps; Shaggy being abused at school; Dave Pritchard being beaten by his dad so much he couldn't go to school and telling Mike with tears in his eyes that he couldn't see his children or wife or mum.

Yes, some of them were hardened criminals, loud and scary to look at like Pritchard, and you might cross the road if you saw them while out shopping, but this camouflaged what they really were. Michael Lambert, who was supposed to be so dangerous, kept thanking them for everything and seemed to him a big softie. It just felt like they'd had no real chance in life, no one to turn to when things went wrong. Others, like Chris Bennett, had ended up on the streets because of an unfortunate relationship.

That wasn't Bennett's only misfortune. When his girlfriend kicked him out, the first people he'd met were Tracy and Randolph. Although they told him about the Ark, when he asked them where they were going, it was to a drug dealer. He spent his only £30 on heroin. 'They taught me how to do it, I put the needle in my arm and I woke up twenty-four hours later sick and addicted,' he said. 'The first time it makes you throw up, but it also gives you the best feeling you ever felt in your life. If you don't have it, you feel like dying and you'll do anything to get needles. People who never committed a crime in their life will go into a shop and steal.'

Occasionally Charlie and Mike would be joined on their daily run by Martin, the former boxer. The first time they invited him, he'd just had dinner and had been drinking all day and ended up vomiting in the castle car park. But after four weeks of circuit training via Zoom with someone from the council, Martin would leave them all for dead. When they caught up, he'd often tell them about his past life travelling around to tournaments.

'You know, I thought before if you swept all the homeless up in a net they would be all the same, but I'm realising they are all very different,' Mike said to Charlie.

He remembered going to meetings of the town business council at which shopkeepers would complain about rough sleepers and having to wash down and disinfect their doorways before they could open in the morning, yet nobody said we need to solve homelessness – it was accepted as a fact of life. Their local MP Daniel Kawczynski had reportedly once told a one-legged drug addict in a wheelchair begging outside Parliament to 'get a job,' though he later insisted he was simply offering useful advice.

Mike considered spending a night in a doorway himself to see what it was like, but realised one night knowing you would be back home the next morning was really not the same. It was also becoming clear to him that solving homelessness was about more than giving them a roof and a key, even if they did keep losing them. You needed to understand what pressed that button in the first place to end up on the streets and how to bring them back.

One of the people who seemed to know more than most was Lenny Worthing, housing coordinator for Shropshire Council, who had been coming to the hotel most days and had twice been homeless himself. 'Homelessness is about 101 things,' he'd told them. 'Housing is a small part of a bigger picture. Put someone in a house who is an alcoholic, they are still an alcoholic.'

'I don't understand why we are not getting help from any services,' Mike complained to Charlie. 'For the first time ever you have all the homeless of Shrewsbury in one building. Surely that's a great opportunity to work on them.' For two weeks he'd been waiting, naively thinking some service would come in to help, to provide counselling for mental health and addiction or at least to check on them, even take their blood pressure, but he had begun to realise that wasn't going to happen.

Everyone was working from home. Schools had closed and Wendy from the Ark was, like working parents across the country, having to home-school her children, so spent much of her time on her smallholding with her family and chickens. When he'd asked the council officials, Mike was told no one would come in because of coronavirus, but that they could set up virtual sessions with counsellors from the Shropshire Recovery Partnership. This seemed mad – none of the homeless had diaries or laptops, few had smartphones and the laptop they had set up in the Darwin was very public. The Ark would eventually give them all tablets, but they quickly sold them to buy drink or drugs.

Even when they did have Zoom sessions, Chris Bennett complained they were a waste of time. 'You get this twenty-one-year-old girl who has never taken a drug in her life telling you blah-de-blah and reading stuff off a computer. How can she dictate to people who have been doing it thirty years? They make you jump through hoops, telling you you have to wait a couple of weeks. I need this help now – in two weeks' time I could be locked up because the need for drugs has made me commit a crime. And if they do do anything they just throw methadone at everyone.'

Mike had begun to wonder whether they could do something themselves. Their guests were clearly comfortable with them – so much so that they had started to moan about the food. Tracy put vinegar on everything, including Sunday roast, and mayonnaise on the lasagne. To Mike's amusement, Michael Lambert had moaned about the gravy that Charlie made from boiling bones overnight as stock. 'An armed robber complaining your gravy is too thin!' he'd teased.

'You know we could do more than give them accommodation and food and clothes,' said Mike. 'We're all here together in this hotel. Do you think we could actually rehabilitate some of these people, as no one seems bothered about that? If we could just help twelve or thirteen ...'

When Mike had mentioned this to Lenny from the council, he laughed. 'If you can help just one, that would be amazing. It's not just about getting them on their own two feet. I'm already seeing a change in the way they look – their skin, their weight – from how you're feeding them up.'

Mike and Charlie discussed whether they should have rules, but decided the hotel would have none apart from no smoking inside, which the guests kept ignoring, and not being allowed out after midnight. The main focus, after all, had to be on keeping the residents safe from the virus. They took the view that what happened in the hotel stayed in the hotel unless it was really dangerous to others, although the guards noted down anything untoward in the logbook and reported it to the council.

'We treat them like guests – except we put our arms around them,' Charlie always insisted.

No one had given them any instructions, so they were just 'winging it'. It was only afterwards they would find out that other hoteliers taking in the homeless had been very strict and if guests didn't obey, simply shut the door on them. Instead, on one of their runs, Mike and Charlie had come up with a concept they called CCR – care, consideration and respect. 'Maybe the biggest thing we can do is give them time to heal,' suggested Charlie.

Mike looked at this woman with new eyes. Though they had developed an extremely close relationship in the six years she had worked at the Prince Rupert – once he had even fed her cats while she was on holiday – he realised you didn't really know someone when they were just coming to work and going home. Now they were all living together, an island of troubled souls with a plague all around, he felt he'd never met someone with so much love to give and who so wore their heart on their sleeve.

He often thought back to the day in 2014 when Charlie came in with her CV, gave it to his daughter Camilla who was on reception, then disappeared. Catching sight of this petite redhead from his office behind, he had overheard and asked, 'Who was that, zooming in and out so quickly?'

At the time Mike was looking for someone more mature and worldly-wise to come into what was mostly a very young team, and he was also desperate to find a head housekeeper with a proper grasp of cleanliness. 'Wow,' he said, looking at Charlie's CV. 'Well, she must be clean: she's got children and is a midwife and ran her own care agency. God knows why she is applying here.'

In fact Charlie had been told by her husband to 'go out and get an effin' job', because his own business was going bankrupt. She had had to give up her care agency because she was spending so much time looking after their daughter Gabriella, who was unwell. She wandered round Shrewsbury trailed by her youngest Fraser,

leaving her CV in shops and offices, and had walked into the hotel 'knees knocking'.

When Mike rang, Charlie was in the Aldi car park with Gabriella and wondered, Who is this posh man calling? He invited her for an interview and said there were three vacancies – his PA, restaurant manager or head of housekeeping. She asked which was available soonest and he said the last, so she went for that.

Mike soon realised she had a rare gift for people. 'I couldn't work out how all our customers knew Charlie: they used to put on TripAdvisor "lovely meeting Charlie!",' he said. 'I started to realise she was connecting with guests on corridors and I was losing potential PR by keeping her upstairs. She needed to be front of house.'

Within a year he had promoted Charlie to assistant manager and within five, hotel manager. He soon wondered how he had coped without her. For her part, sometimes Mike drove her mad with his mood swings, but she always came back. He never actually believed she had been a midwife. 'People put all sorts of things on their CVs,' he said.

Then one day they had a wedding party staying and the bride's limousine broke down in front of the hotel. Mike's wife Diane offered to drive the bride to the wedding and he invited the lady chauffeur in for a cup of tea while she waited for the tow truck. 'I know her,' said Charlie, asking 'Hi, how are the children?'

'Oh my God, hi!' replied the woman, her eyes wide.

'I delivered her two children,' explained Charlie.

Back at the hotel after the day's jog, they could hear shouting in the corridors. 'Oh no, what now?' groaned Mike.

Invariably, such fracas seemed to involve Tracy, who it turned out had been lending other guests money for drink or drugs when they were desperate. When they got their benefits from the post office, she was demanding repayment at exorbitant rates – £40 or even £45 for a £20 loan – stashing it all away in the capacious leopard-print bag she carried everywhere. She seemed to know exactly when people got their Universal Credit payments and the lucky ones who got the more generous PIP, which Mike had never heard of but stood for Personal Independence Payment and was an allowance for those who struggled to do everyday tasks.

'You fuckin' bitch!' people would shout. 'You're making me pay double what you lent me.'

Randolph, her partner, was selling them the drugs, so the pair of them had a good business going.

It was, thought Charlie, inevitable that someone would see the Prince Rupert as an opportunity. Shady characters had started appearing around the front of the hotel and disappearing off with guests behind the church. Drug addicts couldn't believe they had a safe place to shoot up.

'If you put a load of druggies together in a hotel, what do you expect?' asked Michael Lambert. 'A lot of things were going on over money. I quickly got into arguments I didn't need to and ended up punching another resident.'

Shaggy agreed. 'The whole thing gave me headaches,' he said.

Randolph had appeared with a bike and sometimes they would see Michael pedaling off on it furiously.

'Where's he going?' Mike would ask Charlie.

'Well, I don't think it's just exercise ...'

'I used to fetch drugs for everyone on Randolph's stolen bike,' Michael later explained. 'I'd collect the money and bring them back, then I got a cut.'

The hotel logbook began noting more and more disturbances. 'John Patrick came in shouting and swearing,' it read one day. 'Asked to calm down and leave the premises.' That was referring to Scottish John, who often came back, kicking the bin and shouting late at night, exasperating Mike who was trying to sleep.

Charlie would take out food in Tupperware and beg, 'You're pissing off the boss. Please go away or he will call the police.'

Whenever there were fights, the security guards refused to get involved and it was Charlie and Jacki, barely five foot tall and size-four feet, who usually broke them up, prompting Mike to call them 'my two little Rottweilers'. They preferred Mark Chapman's description – 'the angels'.

Factions had begun emerging among the guests. It soon became clear that the alcoholics and drug addicts, particularly those who were injecting, did not get on. And that some of those who had said they were clean or 'just did mamba' were shooting up in their rooms.

Richard annoyed the others by informing on them, and he quickly became known as Titch the Snitch. When a table went missing from the Darwin, it was Richard who told Mike that it was in Randolph's room. The security guard sent to recover it returned saying he had refused to give it back, so Mike had to go himself. 'You can't just take tables,' he said. 'It's a communal room.'

Inside Randolph's room, Mike was alarmed to see not just the table but a metal bar, about seven foot long, that looked as if it had been purloined from scaffolding. 'What on earth?' he exclaimed.

'I want to do exercises to get fit,' said Randolph. 'Weight training.' He made as if to lift it up, almost whacking the window.

'No way,' said Mike. 'The kind of exercise you want to do with that is called hitting someone or breaking in somewhere. That thing is leaving the hotel.'

Randolph ignored him.

Mike was exasperated. 'Aren't the security guards supposed to stop things like that coming in?' he asked Charlie.

'Don't worry, Mr M,' she said. The next time Randolph went out, she opened his room and removed the pole, putting it in a skip.

* * *

Mike decided he needed to identify leaders he could rely on and focused on Dave Pritchard and Chris Bennett, both of whom were strong characters, if very different, and seemed to command some respect among the others. Chris was quiet and watchful, and seemed sensible – he had always worked and never done a day in jail, and was desperate to have a normal life again. Dave was the polar opposite – boisterous, extrovert, complex. Chris was a drug addict and Dave a high-level alcoholic.

Dave described himself as 'not HRH but HLH' – hard to love homeless. 'I am bloody hard work,' he admitted. He loved to hide behind the partition in the Darwin Suite and jump out to scare Jacki or Charlie when they were serving dinner. But if they told him off about anything, he would shout, 'Don't treat me like a child!'

Dave was local, born in Hope, a small village on the outskirts of Shrewsbury. His dad was a metalworker and biker, and had, he said, 'kicked the shit out of me since I was a kid just as his dad probably did to him'. Dave's mum worked as a playgroup carer and tried to protect him. Yet when he told his story, he always defended his father. 'He was just trying to make me as hard as he could,' he said. 'He was my best mate and worst enemy.'

His foster brother would also join in – 'Sometimes I was so black and blue I couldn't go to school,' said Dave. He insisted he didn't care. 'Why would I go to school? My dad had engines. Besides, I was extremely dyslexic. Most of the teachers thought I was thick. Only the metalwork teacher Mr Jones loved me because that I knew.'

Dave's brother was, he told them, killed in a cage fight. By the age of fifteen, Dave was in a young offenders' institution. Like Michael Lambert, he said he had lost count of the number of times he'd been to prison. The worst came when, in his late twenties, he finally turned on his dad. 'He'd beaten me from a young age and one day I just lost it. When you have a hammer smashed on your head, I proved a point, don't fuck with me.'

He too was a dad – of seven children, six from his ex. 'The lights went out, the snow came down and I met her ...' was his cinematic description of their meeting. They had two girls and four boys, the eldest now twenty-one. He also had another twenty-one-year-old from a different relationship.

He was happiest, he said, when they were together and he ran a garage selling motorbike parts called Ducks Bitz, after his nickname Ducky. But she had left him for another man and an exclusion order meant Dave was not allowed near any of the family, even his beloved mum.

Jacki was the first to spot their latest arrival. 'Come and look at this gorgeous guy, he looks like Mick Jagger,' she told Charlie.

He had long hair, snake hips, cowboy boots and a gravelly voice. When he opened his mouth, however, his teeth were all missing and the words he uttered were 'Go fuck a horse!'

'It must be Lionel!' said Charlie. They had heard that someone with Tourette syndrome was arriving and they were intrigued. He also suffered from schizophrenia and dementia, they were told.

Even Mike was impressed with Lionel. 'He had a real style and swagger about him,' he said. Lionel seemed to change outfits six times a day. He also kept asking to move room. He would come to Jacki, saying, 'Can I change my room, miss?'

'What's wrong with it?' she replied.

'Nothing,' he said. 'I just want to change.'

'Okay, give me the key and we will move your stuff,' she would say.

He'd hand it over and half an hour later she would give him the same key and he would be perfectly happy.

7.

Thursday, 2 April 2020

Underneath the words 'Do Not Disturb' on the sign hanging on the door, someone had scribbled 'Drunk'. Gabriella couldn't help laughing. That was typical Dave Pritchard.

She had waitressed in the tea rooms for four years, since she was eighteen, but now these were closed she had opted to stay on as a cleaner rather than ask for furlough and be at home alone. Every day she arrived with a big smile, her auburn hair tied to one side in a long plait, white fluffy jumper accentuating her olive skin and deep-brown eyes.

At the beginning she felt scared, not knowing what to expect. She had only seen homeless people on the streets and had never heard of the Ark. To start with she was going into their rooms in twos or threes with her mum and other staff who had stayed on, like Kim or Leonie, but she quickly realised the guests were 'not monsters', even if some of them were rather alarming.

One day Randolph and Tracy would be screaming at each other and demanding separate rooms, the next they'd be smooching and saying, 'I can't live without you, babe.' To Gabriella, it felt like living in an episode of *The Jeremy Kyle Show*. 'Sometimes they were so off their faces they couldn't remember who I was,' she laughed.

Derek Tyrer hated people going into his room and would stack chairs, cushions and blankets in front of the door as a barricade. They could hear him muttering away to himself inside.

Some rooms, such as Michael Lambert's, they would get high just walking in. Others were sweet. They would find Titch lying on his bed, his face smeared with hot chocolate from the sachets he'd licked, watching *Mrs Brown's Boys* on TV and laughing out loud. He had stuck a Union Jack on his wall and a photo of him and Charlie, and kept his room tidy, proud to have a place of his own.

Stokesy had decorated his room with plants, though his bath would be black with dirt. Most immaculate was the room of Chez the Pole – he had even arranged a little patchwork quilt on his bed with a red teddy bear on top and a small mat by the side for his slippers.

The room they most dreaded cleaning was Shaggy's, which was littered with needles, blood and balls of hair. Yet he had a pile of

books by his bed and had stuck up photos of his son, an adorable little boy. Mark Chapman's room stank of food, as he had a slow cooker into which he would put his dinner from the Darwin and leave for days.

Many did not flush their toilet. Every room took an hour to clean, there was so much mess. Gabriella was patient with the new guests, who she knew were not used to living inside, but told her mum that she was getting fed up with all the clothes piled on the floor – or even in the shower – instead of in the wardrobes.

Some guests were very appreciative of their work, while others got angry. Some tried to hide things. Gabriella knew all about hiding things. When she was fifteen, she had stopped eating. It started in secret, throwing her breakfast out of her bedroom window, not using her lunch money at school. Charlie didn't real- ise to begin with, accepting her explanation that Gabriella was dieting. With all four children still at home, she would serve dinner in huge tureens, not noticing how little Gabriella was taking.

To Charlie, her children were everything and she had strived to recreate the idyllic country childhood that she and her elder sister had enjoyed. Swimming in rivers, building dens, dancing around at home to her parents' records like Fleetwood Mac or the Mamas and Papas, writing poems and stories. But whereas Charlie's parents adored each other, she and her husband always seemed to be shouting at each other. This got worse when his family scrap-metal business, which had funded their comfortable lifestyle, large house in Grinshill and speedboat, began to leach money and eventually went bankrupt.

'We lived in a posh farming area with invites to hunt balls and barbecues, and my dad didn't like it,' said Gabriella. Not wanting to join in with the smoking and drinking, Gabriella found herself ostracised and bullied at school, telling Charlie, 'No one likes me, they think I'm weird.'

She also overheard her dad telling her mum to 'stop Gabriella eating so much, she is getting fat'.

When Mez and Callum, the two elder brothers she idolised, went to Australia in January 2012 for a year abroad, Gabriella gave up. Lying to Charlie that she had eaten at school, she also started taking laxatives and exercising obsessively. 'Every time I got on the scales and weighed less felt like a victory,' she said.

When they moved to a smaller house, where they were on top of each other, Gabriella felt her dad blaming her for being poorly and for the collapse of her parents' marriage. Her weight dropped so much that her periods stopped. Charlie took her to hospital for tests for conditions such as thyroid disorder. But she knew – by then Gabriella was just six stone, so skinny they could see every bone protruding.

When their family GP told them she was anorexic, Gabriella shouted, 'No, I'm not!' He told her she must either admit it and be given help or go home and get thinner and more ill. 'I suppose I might be just a little bit,' she agreed. 'I just wanted to fit in at school.'

She was given an eating programme with nutritious Fortisip drinks, told to stop burning calories by exercising and was visited regularly by nurses who weighed her. But she still went running and secretly did hundreds of sit-ups, even though she had so little fat that they left her backbone raw.

Eventually she lost so much weight that her skin turned scaly like a lizard's and she became so weak that she was put in a wheelchair. Her muscle had so withered that she couldn't even push the wheel and her mum or younger brother Fraser would push her, occasionally bringing a weak smile to her face by doing wheelies. When they took Gabriella shopping in town, sometimes Charlie felt people tutting at her, as if it were her fault.

It was like 'a living hell', watching her beloved daughter doing this to herself and feeling powerless to stop her – anything she said to her making it worse.

Gabriella continued to deteriorate. Her skin got so dehydrated that the patches wouldn't stick for tests to monitor her heart and her arms were so thin that it was impossible to find a vein to take blood. In the end, doctors told them her heart and internal organs were so compromised that she could die at any time and she was so dehydrated her kidneys could fail. Charlie had to sleep next to her, making up a bed on the floor, and holding her hand because she had taken to scratching her forehead until it bled.

'I knew what I was doing to myself but I just didn't want to be there any more,' said Gabriella. 'People think anorexia is about anxiety or about an obsession to be thin, but it wasn't that – I felt I had no control over my life. I couldn't control the girls bullying me or my brothers leaving or my parents' marriage falling apart, and this was the only thing I could control. I got a thrill out of this, of nearly fainting,' she added.

By September 2013, there seemed no option but to admit Gabriella to a special hospital. The first place they went to in Stafford had no doors on the rooms and to Charlie, the kids looked like zombies. There was no way she was leaving her there. They found what seemed a more caring place in Stoke. Even there, said Gabriella, was 'full of other kids screaming out for help and self-harming'.

'All they wanted was feed me up to get the numbers up on the scale and get me out, not really deal with the problem. There was just one doctor who told me it as it was – he said, "You look like you have been in a concentration camp."'

In mid-November doctors told Charlie there was no hope and to get her sons to come home to say goodbye. For Gabriella, it was her beloved brothers coming back that turned things round. Somehow she rallied and on New Year's Eve 2014, she was released from hospital.

Charlie had spent so much time looking after her daughter that she'd had to give up her care agency – which is why that summer she'd ended up leaving her CV at the Prince Rupert. Gabriella had missed so much school that she left with just three GCSEs.

After she recovered she started working in the hotel's tea rooms, which had given her confidence. She knew she talked too much sometimes to cover up her insecurity and she still got panic attacks, particularly if she ran into one of the girls from school, and sometimes had to call her mum to help her.

The Prince Rupert's very different new clientele under the pandemic had changed everything. The hotel logbook had gone from noting taxi reservations, champagne orders and early check-ins to listing fights and police and ambulance call-outs.

'Tracy and Randolph shouting over money,' read a typical entry. 'Argument between Chris Bennett and Richard. Kicked Richard twice. Mark Chapman been drinking all day. Weed himself.' Some of the remaining staff found it difficult. 'We didn't have proper PPE,' complained Kim, who partnered Gabriella in cleaning.

Yet for Gabriella, her new job, while often deeply unpleasant, was more rewarding. 'Seeing the homeless made me realise I wasn't the only crazy one,' she said. 'I wanted to give someone the help I didn't get.'

It was nice to walk along Pride Hill and see them smile and wave at her.

The new guests could, however, be exasperating. Such as recent arrival Deena, a tiny woman in her thirties with short spiky hair who could have passed for a young boy but told Gabriella she had children. She had decorated her room beautifully with throws on the chairs. Titch was particularly taken with her. The pair were spotted canoodling in the churchyard, much to the amusement of the other guests.

Charlie proffered bath foam to everyone who checked in, encouraging them to take baths, but was surprised by how many they were taking. Later she learned that steam intensified the high when doing drugs. One day they saw water cascading through the reception ceiling. Charlie ran upstairs. It was Deena's room. Inside, the bath was overflowing with bubbles almost up to the ceiling. Stokesy was out cold on a chair, a heroin syringe by his side.

'Don't worry, it's okay,' said Deena.

'No, it's not okay,' replied Charlie. 'Don't do it again.'

8.

Friday, 3 April 2020

It was about half past midnight and Charlie was fast asleep when her phone rang. One of the security guards was on the line. 'There's a situation on the first floor,' he said. They always spoke as if they were in a TV police drama.

She pulled on some clothes and ran out. She could hear the shouting even before she got down the stairs. It was Deena. 'I'm fuckin' rattling!' she was shouting in her deep voice. 'I've got to get out, you've got to help me!'

No one was allowed out of the hotel after midnight, except for a smoke just outside. Inside her room, Deena was pounding around, throwing chairs and other stuff and banging her head against the walls frantically. She looked like a wild animal, her pupils dilated, and she was making a huge amount of noise for such a tiny figure.

'Stop it, Deena!' pleaded Charlie. 'Please calm down.'

'You don't understand,' screeched Deena. 'I'm rattling!'

'What do you mean, you're rattling?'

Charlie and Jacki had acquired a whole new vocabulary since their new guests moved in – 'scrips' meant methadone prescriptions, 'gear' was heroin, 'white' was cocaine – but this was new and she reached for her phone to Google.

'She means she needs her gear,' explained Tracy, who had come out of her room along the corridor to see what all the fuss was about. 'Don't worry,' she added, 'I'll calm her down.'

Charlie was dubious. Tracy and Randolph were often the source of problems in the hotel. As she feared, whatever Tracy did made things worse, sending Deena even more berserk, causing sweat to pour off her. They learned afterwards that Tracy had given her more pills.

'Don't you understand, I need drugs!' yelled Deena. 'I need someone to go and get them for me.'

What to do? No one from the Ark or council stayed in the hotel at night and they'd had no training apart from the Zoom session on overdosing. The guards had disappeared round the corner muttering, as usual claiming it was not part of their job.

Jacki had also come down. 'Is it an overdose?' she asked, worried they would have to use one of the yellow kits.

'No, it's the opposite, I think,' replied Charlie. 'She is needing drugs.'

'Isn't that the point of the methadone they take?'

'I don't know – maybe she isn't taking it.'

Neither of them had ever seen anything like it. 'Rattling is the worst feeling in the world,' Shaggy explained afterwards. 'It's like flu times a million. I wouldn't put my worst enemy through it.'

'We need to wake up Mike,' said Jacki. When he came downstairs, he too was horrified.

'Calm down, Deena,' he said firmly. 'Stop it now.'

The screaming got louder than ever. 'This is unbearable,' he said. 'How can someone so small make so much noise? I think we have to call 999.'

Mike instructed one of the security guards to stay outside the bedroom door, not to move or let her out, and went downstairs to check on the police. When he came back up, the guard had gone. Mike wandered the corridors and found him round the corner.

'Why are you here?' asked Mike.

'I'm not staying anywhere near that room,' he replied. 'That woman is too aggressive, she's dangerous.'

'But you're the security guard!'

'Nah, I'm not doing it.'

Mike shook his head and returned to Deena's room. Two police-men were just arriving. To Charlie, they looked like Darth Vaders in their black gas masks with grilles either side. Inside, Deena was kicking and screaming, snarling at anyone who came near. 'Get out of my bedroom, I hate police!'

'Deena, calm down or they will arrest you,' urged Charlie.

'I won't calm down!' she shouted. 'They can't fucking arrest me!'

Finally they managed to get her into the Darwin Suite and sat on a seat. She calmed down for a bit. 'I'm sorry, Mr M,' she said. 'Sorry Charlie, sorry Jacki, I'll be as good as gold now, I promise.'

'Phew,' said Mike.

Then she started up again, rocking back and forth, raging, eyeballs rolling back in their sockets.

'This is going to go on all night,' Mike told the police. 'You'll have to take her in.'

'I'm afraid we can't,' said the lead officer.

'What do you mean?'

'She hasn't committed an offence.'

'But look at her, she's going to hurt herself.'

At that point Tracy reappeared. 'Oh yes they can,' she said. 'You have to say she's damaged your property, criminal damage, then they will have to arrest her by law.'

'Is that true?' asked Mike.

'Yeah,' nodded the policeman.

'All I have to do is say she caused criminal damage?'

'Uh-huh.'

'See, I told you!' crowed Tracy. 'They don't tell you that, you need me to tell you.'

'Okay, thank you, Tracy,' said Mike. He thought for a moment. 'But I don't think she has caused criminal damage ...'

'What about the carpet and lobby ceiling from flooding her room the other day?' asked Charlie.

'Yes, that's true, I have to call in a decorator. Okay, officer, well, I want to report criminal damage to my property by this woman.'

The policeman radioed through to the station for help and a riot van arrived with reinforcements. Deena was read her rights and handcuffed, then dragged down the staircase, clawing at the banister and spitting as she went. In the end it took seven of them to get her downstairs and into the police van. Once inside, she was moving around so much the van was rocking back and forth.

The other guests all seemed to be out of their rooms or watching from their windows. Some were cheering her on. Even from above you could hear the shouts of 'I'm fucking rattling, you've got to help me!'

Finally the van drove away. Mike stood outside watching it go, shocked. Charlie could see he was worried about the reputation of the hotel. Those four stars were not easily gained. Only a few days earlier he had heard a fracas outside his office window and seen police pinning down this filthy bearded character. 'Is this one of yours?' they had called up to him.

He'd laughed at the time, telling Charlie, 'Oh God, is that what they think of the Prince Rupert?' But now he thought again. In the hotel business he was used to dealing with drunks at weddings, often carrying passed-out people to bed. But the world of drugs and dependence was very different. No amount of Yorkshire puddings and Sunday roasts was going to solve that.

It was about 3 a.m. when Mike finally got to bed. He lay down, head in his hands. 'What have I done?' he groaned.

There was only one person he could talk to. He picked up his phone and started FaceTiming a number in California.

9.

Wednesday, 8 April 2020

Everyone was shaken after Deena was taken away. Mike insisted they needed to go on as if nothing had happened. With so many residents, they had gone from doing cooked breakfasts of bacon butties and eggs to putting out a selection of cereals, pastries and juices. Jacki laid them out around 8 a.m. as normal – their guests were used to getting up early to clear their rubbish from shop door-ways before they opened. Earliest of all was Mark Chapman, who would be down at reception for his morning vodka shot and knock at Martin's door at 6 a.m. for breakfast to shouts of 'Go away!'

Despite the disturbed night, Mike had been awake at dawn, Googling heroin addiction and how to deal with it. 'We need to know more about our guests,' he told Charlie and Jacki. 'We must get alongside them more, find out who they are and what they are and take some kind of control – we know now the police won't, security won't, the Ark won't …'

Charlie nodded. She wondered aloud to Jacki later, 'What does he think we have been doing?'

It wasn't just what happened with Deena that was gnawing at him. A few days earlier he had overheard Shaggy saying to Michael Lambert, 'These guys are making a fortune from us.' Furious, he took them both into the churchyard and told them that he got £85 a night for room and board from the council.

'Maybe it seems a lot but you have to understand even with this money our revenue has fallen by a third,' explained Mike. 'It gives us money to pay wages and bills but doesn't let us renovate or pay the mortgage. Just the mortgage is £12,000 a month and leasing the townhouse is another £7,000 a month. And though you could argue that the homeless have been a resource in a brutal commercial way, by doing this we missed out on government grants we would have got had we closed.'

They seemed satisfied. But a gloom settled over the hotel. The news from outside was unwaveringly grim. Deaths were regularly hitting more than eight hundred a day and hospital admissions had reached record levels. The first of the so-called Nightingale hospitals, emergency field hospitals that could take up to four thousand patients, opened in London's ExCel centre, built in just ten days by army troops working round the clock. The prime minister, his key adviser Dominic Cummings, Health Secretary Matt Hancock, Chief Medical Adviser Chris Whitty and Cabinet Secretary Mark Sedwill had all gone down with the disease. Even Prince Charles had had it – no one, it seemed, was safe.

Shrewsbury had been less affected than many places, but every so often an ambulance siren punctuated the silence.

Security at the hotel had been doubled by the council to four guards, not because of what happened with Deena but thanks to two other residents who had arrived that week: Leonard and his girlfriend Marianne, who looked terrified. The staff soon found out why. 'Look at this,' said Mike one day. It was an email from the council telling him that Leonard owed a lot of money to some Liverpool-based drug dealers and there were three choices: either they pay the debt for him which they couldn't, move him somewhere no one knew or keep him in the hotel with more security.

'Surely keeping him here safe is best,' said Mike. 'How serious is it?'

The council gave him the recent example of an eighteen-year-old girl in nearby Oswestry who owed £80 and had her face slashed with a knife eighty times to teach her a lesson. These were apparently the same drug dealers.

'Okay, that's serious,' he replied.

'Let's do a cream tea,' suggested Charlie.

'What?' exclaimed Jacki.

'Come on, it will cheer everyone up.' It was Dave Pritchard's birthday in a few days and Charlie had been planning to make a cake, but it was a glorious spring day and suddenly a cream tea seemed the perfect idea.

She sent Gabriella to fetch the tiered cake stands from the tea rooms, then the three of them set about mixing and baking. They did the whole works. Scones with strawberry jam and cream. Mini melt-in-the-mouth chocolate brownies. Light as air Victoria sandwich. Slices of moist fruit cake. Tiny crustless sandwiches of egg and cress or thinly sliced cucumber. All beautifully laid out on the stands, and Jacki cut some flowers and arranged them.

'Those are gorgeous, Jacki,' said Charlie in surprise.

'I always wanted to be a florist,' she replied. 'I even did the flowers for my dad's funeral.' She scrolled through her phone to show them a photo of a stunning display of red roses on the coffin.

Once everything was done, they went knocking on all the doors and told the residents they had a surprise for them in the Darwin. From inside the rooms came moans of 'Leave us alone!' Some of the guests were passed out on their beds. But they cajoled and dragged, and gradually most of the residents drifted into the Darwin. Once inside, seeing the spread, their faces lit up.

'Tea for two and two for tea!' shouted Dave Pritchard. 'It's like being at one of them bloomin' posh hotels in London.'

*   *   *

'Look at this!' said Mark Chapman. There was a newsflash on TV: 'Boris Johnson moved to intensive care'.

A group gathered round the television to watch. Reporters were standing outside St Thomas's Hospital with serious expressions, but there wasn't much detail. None of the residents lingered. Most had long felt alienated from a government that they felt did nothing for them, though Mike was surprised how closely some of them followed politics, when he got into discussions with them.

Some of them piled plates with cakes and sandwiches and gathered outside in the sun with pots of tea. They sat on the stone wall around the twisty locust tree and lounged on the benches by the church and the Bear Steps, which would normally have been

crammed with tourists looking at them disapprovingly, if they looked at them at all. It was lovely to have the town centre to themselves.

Across the way was the old Abbot's House and the doorway to Philpotts sandwich bar, which in normal times would have had a queue outside. Someone said they had slept there one night and this prompted a conversation about which doorway or park bench they had each been sleeping on and which was best.

'I went to the Indian by the Vaults because it was a restaurant,' said Dave Pritchard, 'but did they give me food, did they fuck? Not even a bloody cracker! A smile would have been nice ...'

Some doorways, they said, gave better protection from the elements, while others were better located for begging. 'We chose

Town Fryer as the doorway was deep and wide so more comfortable,' said Titch.

'I'd never thought about that,' said Jacki.

It turned out that there was a real hierarchy on the streets. As a local born and bred, Shaggy stayed on Pride Hill and was king of the street – he would take money from any others who were in his spot. 'You can clear a hundred quid on a Saturday,' he said.

Those who were on their own chose doorways that had CCTV cameras so they wouldn't be kicked or robbed. Most had been urinated on at some point. Friday nights after the pubs closed was worst, said Michael Lambert. 'You get yobs come into town to kick a homeless. I've been kicked in the face,' he said. 'But you're a human being the same as everyone else.'

For that reason some of them preferred to sleep outside of town – Mark Chapman in the woods and Martin under the Telford Way bridge.

Mike was shocked. He was as guilty as anyone in the past of never stopping to talk to them, maybe even crossing the road or hurrying on, but the idea of kicking or urinating on someone clearly down on their luck, what did that say about society?

'One thing I always wondered is why do so many homeless have dogs?' he asked. 'Surely it makes it harder to get housing and also what about the cost of feeding them? Dog food is not cheap.'

Natalie, another recent arrival, laughed. 'People give you more money if you have a dog. They don't care about us, but they do care about the animals.'

They're right, thought Mike uncomfortably. Nine out of ten Brits would stop if they saw a dog sick or in trouble, but not if it was a dishevelled person.

'It's also security,' said Mark Chapman. 'And companionship,' said Stokesy. 'If you have a dog, you have a sense of purpose, something to care for, to talk to.' He told them he used to have a baby squirrel, which lived in his pocket. 'I fed it nuts,' he said. 'It used to run away and come back again. Then someone reported me to the Environmental Agency and they forced me to let it go. I was heartbroken.'

The image of this hardened heroin addict with his pet squirrel melted Charlie's heart.

The drug addicts were the hardest of their guests to get through to. They were far more secretive than the alcoholics, who often just conked out with silly smiles on their faces and had to be picked up and carried back to their rooms, Mike taking the arms and Charlie and Jacki the legs. 'Mark Chapman been drinking all day. Weed himself,' recorded the logbook for the previous day.

By now they were familiar with mamba, which was smoked in roll-ups like weed but was actually synthetic. It had been legal until 2016 and sold in newsagents and off licences in shiny packets with names like Voodoo or Holy Smoke, even though on the back were printed the words 'Not fit for human consumption'. Now it had been criminalised and was sold in clear bags mixed with plant matter to look like weed. It was cheaper than weed (usually just £5) and more dangerous, often containing ingredients like paint-stripper.

Why did they take it? 'To kill time,' said Titch. 'If you're out of it for a couple of hours, that's a couple of hours not to think about things, about having no family, no home, no help …'

It seemed hopeless, thought Mike. Yet some of these people had been thirty-five years on the streets – that was almost thirteen thousand nights. He doubted he would last one in the freezing cold with no bathroom. They were clearly survivors.

Despite arguing a lot in the hotel, they undoubtedly had a strange kind of bond. 'It's like jungle drums,' said Charlie. 'Though they fight each other, sometimes rob each other, at the end of day they are a community and know if one is being preyed on.'

They used the public toilets as their bathroom, though Charlie had at times stepped over deposits in the town's narrow alleyways that she would rather not have seen on her way from home to the hotel. Before Covid, the only help they got was from the Ark, which they could go into during the day to do their washing, take showers and get something to eat. Few of them seemed to have a good word to say about it. 'You know sometimes we'd have been outside all night freezing and arrive at its offices in the pouring rain at five to nine, and could see them all inside with the lights blazing and heating on, but they would refuse to open till 9 a.m.,' moaned Dave Pritchard. 'And the coffee is dreadful,' complained Andy.

As for actually trying to solve homelessness, no one had ever talked to them about it. 'Homeless don't vote,' pointed out Mike's friend Robin Hooper, who used to be chief executive of Shrewsbury Council.

Charlie headed back inside to start on dinner. 'Can we have English breakfast for dinner?' some of them pleaded.

'After afternoon tea?' she asked. 'I guess they're craving carbs,' she said to Jacki.

Some of the guests went back to their rooms but others drifted off into groups. A few disappeared behind the churchyard – by now Mike knew what that meant. Michael Lambert set off on the bike. As he went back inside, Mike caught sight of Jacki chatting away to Dave Pritchard. Their most difficult resident had taken a real shine to her. 'Ooh, here's the missus!' he would call out whenever she walked into a room. Watching her now, Mike smiled. Jacki was animated in a way that he had never seen in sixteen years of her working there. Like a different person.

'You know what, I love you guys!' Pritchard called out.

Charlie and Jacki were preparing dinner when they heard a shout like a wounded animal. 'What now?'

The post had arrived and there was a birthday card for Dave Pritchard from his ex, who now lived with another man and who he was not allowed contact with. He ripped the card in pieces and stormed back to his room. When they knocked, he wouldn't answer.

Late that night Charlie called Mike. 'I can hear someone on the roof,' she said. He peered out from his terrace and looked out the windows of the third floor. 'I can't see anyone. Go to sleep.'

He lay in bed, thinking. It felt as if an ocean of pain and trauma rose and swelled inside that one hotel, but also an ocean of kindness. Outside, over the rooftops of Shrewsbury, hung a huge pink moon, a supermoon, the closest and largest moon of the year.

10.

Easter Sunday, 12 April 2020

The whoop of excitement could be heard from downstairs. It was Titch. 'I've never had a chocolate egg before!' he told Charlie, running down, clutching a big boxed foil-covered egg with the happiest of smiles on his face.

'That's so tragic,' she said to Jacki. 'Imagine never getting an Easter egg as a child.'

When her children were little and they lived in the big house, Charlie used to organise elaborate Easter egg hunts in the garden every year. Trying to recreate her own picture-perfect childhood of love, music and laughter had not been easy with a controlling husband who could turn puce and explode into rage at the slight-est thing, but her enthusiasm was infectious. The children made each other cards and Easter egg trees out of twigs, which they decorated with paint, ribbons and glitter and planted in pots with eggs hanging from them.

She still bought them Easter eggs in their twenties.

She was thrilled when a few days earlier, two big deliveries of Easter eggs had arrived at the hotel from the local branches of Marks & Spencer and Holland & Barrett, who had heard about their guests. She and Jacki had piled the table in the Darwin Suite high with eggs and made a sign telling everyone to take one.

Even the most hardened addicts seemed delighted, tearing open the boxes to get to the brightly foiled chocolate, unable to believe they were all for them. There were so many that Charlie made an Easter egg pavlova, as well as bread and butter pudding from hot cross buns and chocolate. 'Sugar explosion!' laughed Jacki. 'Are you sure that's a good idea – aren't they high enough already?'

That afternoon they had the usual Sunday roast, this time with turkey. As always Derek Tyrer infuriated Jacki by trying to snatch the serving spoon.

Helping dish out crunchy roast potatoes, parsnips, carrots, slices of meat and thick gravy cooked from stock to the line of homeless, then watching Tracy pour vinegar over it and others drown it in mayonnaise, Mike wondered why they bothered.

Several of the guests insisted they only ate gluten-free food, something he found baffling – how could they know on the streets? Richard Boffey claimed to be allergic to garlic. Others refused to eat sausages or tomatoes. Charlie spent days boiling bones and making stock for the gravy, while the potatoes were roasted in duck fat or goose fat, and for what? Only Mark Chapman seemed to appreciate it – the former chef would sniff the gravy and exclaim, 'Mmm … lovely seasoning.'

Watching them all, Mike realised almost a month had passed and wondered how long they would be there. It was clearly not going to be the few weeks that had initially been envisaged.

That day had seen a new arrival, Jamie, a local man in his forties, who told them he had been in trouble since he was little as he had ADHD (attention deficit hyperactivity disorder) and his parents couldn't cope so he'd been taken into care. He had been in and out of prison since the age of sixteen, when he ended up in a young offenders' institution after kidnapping a boy who had been bully-ing his younger brother. 'I only wanted to scare him,' he said. 'I'm homeless because of life.'

The government was due to review lockdown measures that week but few expected anything to change. The UK death toll had passed ten thousand – and worldwide there had been more than a hundred thousand deaths. Boris Johnson had been discharged from hospital that day to go and convalesce at Chequers, and he issued an Easter message, thanking the NHS for saving his life. He insisted progress was being made in 'a fight we never picked against an enemy we still don't entirely understand'.

With warm weather forecast, the government and its scientists were urging everyone to stay at home. Full-page adverts in the newspapers warned, 'Stay Home this Bank Holiday Weekend – Don't Put Your Friends and Family in Danger'.

On their evening jog along the avenues of lime trees by the river and through Quarry Park, past the bandstand, Mike and Charlie noticed park benches had been taped off to stop people sitting on them. Also closed off was the Dingle, the beautiful sunken garden created by Percy Thrower, who had been Shrewsbury's park superintendent for decades but was better known as Britain's first TV gardener.

Spring was Charlie's favourite time of year, with an explosion of daffodils along the riverbank and cherry blossoms casting a frothy veil of pink.

'A good day, I think,' said Mike as they stopped to catch their breath and watched the swans gliding past.

The following morning a message came from the owner of the Bull Inn next door. Someone had tried to break into the pub in the night. They had called the police and CCTV had shown a man climbing out of a first-floor window of the Prince Rupert and across the roof towards the pub.

'I know who that is,' groaned Mike.

The room he had come out of was Chris Bennett's, and it wasn't hard to work out who the figure exiting the window was.

Police were called. Michael Lambert insisted he had gone out not to rob the pub but to collect cigarette butts to get the tobacco out and make a roll-up. 'It was raining and I wanted a smoke,' he said. 'I knew the pub garden had a covered smoking area where there were lots of butts. It's a dirty thing, I don't like doing it, but didn't have any option.'

Mike persuaded the police to take it no further as nothing had been stolen, but he was furious. Shortly after, he saw Lambert on the staircase and blocked his way. 'Michael, can we talk man to man?' he asked. 'You cannot stay here, jump out of windows and try to burgle pubs. If you do that, you're going to have to leave and I don't want you to. Can we have an agreement?'

Michael drew himself up as if about to challenge the bigger man, then thought better of it. 'All right, fair dos, I'm really sorry Mr Matthews,' he said. 'I won't let you down, don't worry,' he added, patting Mike on the back.

'I think that was an important moment,' Mike told the two women afterwards.

They were not so sure. Later they went and piled more chairs against the doors blocking off the old parts of the hotel, and toilet rolls too so they would see if anyone had tried to get through.

That afternoon Mike found a delegation waiting outside his office. He let them in, wondering what they wanted. 'The thing is, Mr M, we're getting a bit tired of all this fresh veg and healthy food,' they said. 'Couldn't we have pizza and chips some time?'

11.

Thursday, 16 April 2020

'Sir and Lady Clementi arriving today,' read the reminder note for the day in the logbook. 'Welcome note, chocs, prosecco to go in room compliments of hotel.'

By now such entries from a pre-Covid world seemed surreal. Underneath, the security guards had written: '04.20 We call paramedics for Mark C. He was not very well. Spent night outside drinking. Returned this morning VERY DRUNK.'

'8.15 a.m. Police arrived to check if everything in order.'

'Andy and Julie had argument. Andy walked out.'

The latter had become a frequent entry, leaving Charlie to comfort a tearful Julie. 'I always make bad choices,' she sobbed. 'I went off the rails because of violent partners. Violent partners, violent friends …'

On each of Julie's tiny wrists was tattooed a girl's name and date of birth – her two daughters, aged ten and eight. Neither of them was she allowed to see. She was permitted one letter of communication a year and even that she struggled to write, not having finished school. There was also supposed to be a DVD of the girls that she could watch at Christmas, though this was shown on a laptop under supervision in the library so that she could not post anything on social media. 'As if I would,' said Julie.

She had filled her hotel room with girly toys, rainbow-coloured unicorns, sparkly hair-clips and pink bobbles.

Charlie gave her a hug. 'I know about bad choices,' she said, thinking about her own marriage and how she had stayed all those years under her husband's thumb.

A skinny doll-like woman of thirty-six, with a pale elfin face, wispy brown hair and lots of silver rings on hands that fluttered like birds' wings when she spoke, Julie had arrived with her boyfriend Andy right at the beginning of lockdown. She had seemed terrified and had taken a while to start to open up.

At six foot five, Andy towered over her and was always moving fast. To Mike, he seemed like someone who lived in the shadows. They had all noticed how any time Julie spoke to anyone else, Andy would get annoyed. They would see her running after him down Butcher Row, going down on her hands and knees, begging him to take her back.

'I didn't like being single,' she told Charlie and Jacki when they urged her she could do better. 'I want to have someone to be there, to watch telly with ...'

Julie had grown up in Shrewsbury, she told them, and her problems had started at school. She had a condition called irritable hips, which caused her hips to pop out of their joints, and was in and out of hospital, missing school. 'I had really crooked teeth and was very thin so I was bullied a lot,' she said, 'to the point I would go down the road after I left for school and call home from the phonebox pretending to be reception, saying, "Julie is not well and needs to come home." Then I'd spend the day lying on the sofa watching TV.'

While it seemed to Julie that her younger sister couldn't do anything wrong in their mum's eyes, she always felt like the black sheep. She ended up leaving school at fourteen, having failed every exam, and began working, cleaning shops and pubs, and as a carer for the elderly. She also started getting involved with the wrong kind of men. 'My mam said, "I wish you would stop attracting idiots."'

Julie moved in with a boyfriend and gave birth to her first child, but he left and she met another man and quickly got pregnant again. 'He didn't believe he was the father, even though he never allowed me out, so he jumped on my stomach and I gave birth at eight and a half months and the baby, a boy, was stillborn,' she said.

'One day I came home and found my daughter in the bath in a strange way. She told me, "Daddy did something to me." I walked in the front room and slapped him and screamed, "Why did you do it?" He said, "Well, you weren't here." I told him, "She's two! Aren't you disgusted with yourself?"'

By then Julie was pregnant again. After her second daughter was born, the father saw the baby every day and one day brought her back, saying she'd had her bottle. 'I later discovered that because she was crying to excess, he'd put heroin in the milk,' said Julie. 'Then we had a fire door at the flat which slammed shut and he whacked her head with the doorframe without telling me and fractured her skull. I took her to hospital because she didn't stop crying and I got blamed, and they took the children off me. My little girl had three heart attacks because of the drugs.'

Desperate for distraction after losing her children, Julie connected with Andy on Facebook and they met for a drink. 'He's a charmer, nice, good-looking. I thought, He's Mr Right.

'Eighteen months down the line, he started to change,' she said. 'One day he pushed me off a chair flat on my back and kept stamp-ing on my face and I thought, I am going to die at the hands of this man. Eventually police came and I went to hospital and the doctor said, "Do you want the good news? There isn't any, both your eye sockets are shattered." The police said, "Andy's done that" – he'd been cautioned and fined for beating a previous girlfriend – and I said, "No, I had a fight with some girls."

'But when I told Andy, rather than being apologetic or grateful, he said, "Oh, so now they are looking for some fucking innocent girl," and he started punching my stomach and shattered my ribs. I went to my mam's and she asked why I was wearing sunglasses. When I took them off, she cried.'

In 2016 Andy was sentenced to jail for four years. Julie visited him every day and drowned her sorrows in drink – 'cider, vodka, anything I could get hold of' – until one day she found herself in hospital with no memory of how she got there. A doctor told her she'd had fifteen fits and if she drank again it would probably kill her. Her dad collected her from the hospital and she told him, 'That's it, I'm not going to drink more.' Since that day, she said, she hadn't touched alcohol.

But she was doing drugs, encouraged by Andy, who was a regular user. Heroin was her thing. She had started in 2018 when he got out. 'Within a week and a half I was really addicted and would do anything to get more,' she later admitted. 'I would sit outside begging to get £10, then buy a bag, but that was not enough so it would be, what can I do now? If you had a pipe, you'd want another one and another one, lie down, feel spaced out for a bit, then want another. At my worst I could easily do eight or ten bags of gear and £120 worth of white between three of us.'

Drugs had also almost done for her. 'I'd started dreaming I was being murdered, that people were strangling me or tying me to a railway line,' she said. 'Eventually, a couple of years ago, Andy took me to A&E and the doctor told me my organs were shutting down and that's why I was hallucinating. He said you can either have an operation or die – it's your choice. I said, "Well, you don't mince your words." So I had surgery, five operations. They cut open my arms and removed all the bad tissue.'

She still didn't stop. Eventually they both got evicted from their homes and ended up sleeping in a tent under Tubbs Way for about a month. After that coronavirus hit. They went to the Ark to be verified as homeless and two days later, on the Sunday, went to the pizza shop to charge their phones and found a message telling them to go to the Prince Rupert.

'I was scared,' said Julie. 'When we were about three doors away, I stopped and said to Andy, "I can't do it. I can't go in there."'

Charlie and Jacki recalled how, when the couple came in, Julie hadn't stopped crying. What Julie didn't know was that Andy had applied for housing from the council without her, telling them that she was the problem. 'You don't understand, she's a nutter,' he told Mike. He was so charming that initially they believed him.

'You ever been to jail, Andy?' Mike asked one day.

'No, no,' he replied.

The power of drugs was something that none of the hotel staff had ever really thought about before, let alone understood. 'I could put out a line of plates of the most delicious food, roast chicken and all the trimmings for our guests, and right at the end a plate of drugs and they would ignore the food and just go for that,' mused Mike.

That temptation would be tested more than ever when, on 20 April, Samantha arrived. A tall slim woman in her mid-thirties, with long brown hair, strange tattoos on her hands and arms that she'd done herself, and the tell-tale missing teeth of a drug addict, she was, unexpectedly, brought in with her mother, who seemed lovely and was clearly distraught.

Samantha might have been from a good family but she had fallen in with the wrong crowd and become a hardened heroin addict. She had been in prison for theft and had recently miscarried after being badly beaten by her ex. She was in a bad state. She carried a dummy, which she often sucked on. Initially Charlie linked it to her losing a baby, but soon realised that the dummy was to stop her clenching her jaws and grinding her teeth. So

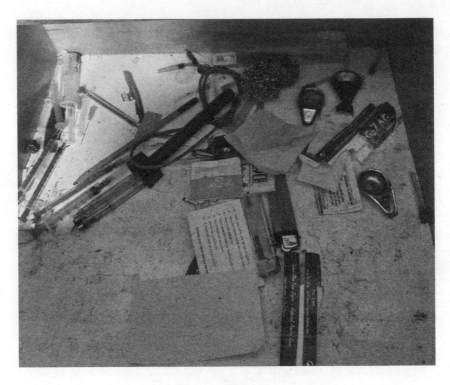

A hotel drawer full of drugs paraphernalia.

many addicts suffered from the same gurning and it was why so many of the guests had bad teeth.

They had never seen anyone pump their body with so many drugs. Samantha had an abscess the size of a golf ball in her groin and she would inject heroin directly into it to get a faster high. She was supposed to be on methadone, but nobody seemed to be checking whether she was taking it.

In her room's chest of drawers, where guests would normally put lingerie, socks and T-shirts, she had all the paraphernalia of addiction – syringes, needles, little plastic sachets, a bag of sugar, lighters, cigarette papers. Stokesy's room was just along the corridor and she was soon in and out of his too.

It quickly became clear that to fund her habit, Samantha would steal from anyone. Guests started complaining about things disappearing from their rooms. She hadn't been at the hotel long when one day her sister came to take her out. After a while her mum called Charlie in tears to tell her that Samantha had stolen her sister's purse then used the bank cards to empty the account. 'I'm exhausted,' she said. 'I just don't know what to do with her.'

Once Charlie went into her room to get her off her bed to come and have dinner and a needle fell off her. 'How to solve a problem like Samantha?' she wondered.

12.

Wednesday, 29 April 2020

It was the big day. The hotel was going to be on national television.

It had all started with an email a few weeks earlier, forwarded by the council, from Dame Louise Casey. Mike had no idea who she was and had had to Google her. He quickly discovered that the whole idea of Everyone In had been her initiative and he was impressed to read that she reported directly to Boris Johnson.

A woman with little tolerance for nonsense and long experience of working with the homeless, Dame Louise had worked for five prime ministers, including running the Rough Sleepers Unit for Tony Blair's government and the Troubled Families Programme for David Cameron. Most recently, she had been an adviser on homelessness for the Australian government and had flown back to London from Sydney in March, just before lockdown, to start a new job for Boris Johnson, carrying out a review of the government's homeless strategy.

She'd emerged from Heathrow to find the streets already deserted, apart from manic shoppers. 'My taxi driver told me I was his only fare,' she said. 'I realised the pandemic had changed everything.'

The following morning she had gone straight to Whitehall and the office of Robert Jenrick, the housing secretary. 'Can we talk –

I'm downstairs,' she texted him from the lobby. 'A message like that from me usually means nightmare,' she later laughed. She told Jenrick it was 'mission critical' to get everyone off the streets. 'I had lived through the TB outbreak in London in the late 1980s when I was working for Shelter and that only affected the homeless,' Dame Louise said. 'I thought this would be the same, that those of us in houses would be safe.'

This would be no easy task. There were an estimated 280,000 homeless people in England and Wales, of whom 37,000 were rough sleepers. Remembering how deserted her hotel in Sydney had been before she flew back, Dame Louise suggested requisitioning hotels. In London, where there were around five thousand rough sleepers, Mayor Sadiq Khan's team had already had the same idea but had so far only got one hotel.

Dame Louise was particularly concerned about the two to three thousand people who were staying in communal shelters. 'I wanted to close them down because it seemed to me they were not safe in a pandemic,' she said. 'I managed to get JVT [Jonathan Van-Tam – the deputy chief medical officer] on the phone and asked him, am I right that people can't be in communal settings, and he said yes.'

So that Friday she sent out the email that became known as Everyone In, to councils and homeless charities across the land, saying, 'We need to have all rough sleepers in by the weekend.' Soon she and her team and local councils were requisitioning hotels and lodgings everywhere. When she heard about the Prince Rupert, Dame Louise was intrigued. 'It's a wonderful thing your hotel and you are doing,' she wrote to Mike. 'To know that such vulnerable people are being looked after is just life-reaffirming.'

She went on to ask if he would mind if she put him in touch with Victoria Derbyshire for her morning show on the BBC. 'I really rate her … she and her team are brilliant and honourable BBC people … I am proud of what you and everyone in Shrewsbury has done here and would love you to get some good news out of it.'

Mike showed the email to Charlie and Jacki. 'Why would the media be interested in us?' he mused. 'We're just a hotel. Though I guess we do have a very different kind of guest.'

They thought it was a good idea that might be a fun distraction for their residents, who were starting to get bored, and would also enable them to speak out for homeless people. When she heard about it, Pam was less sure, worried it would draw unwanted attention to the hotel.

The main challenge had been who to put forward. Who could they trust to speak? Eventually Mike decided on Chris Bennett and Dave Pritchard, as they were so different. Charlie wasn't so sure. Pritchard was so volatile he could 'go off with a pop', particularly since getting the birthday card from his ex a few weeks before. Afterwards he had sent her a message on Facebook asking if the kids were okay. He'd then borrowed Chris Bennett's phone to call her. 'He told me he was calling his solicitor,' said Bennett. 'I wouldn't have lent him it if I'd known, as I knew he had a restraining order and I could have had my phone taken off me.' The next thing they knew, the police turned up at the hotel. Because Dave had ripped up the birthday card, he couldn't prove his claim that his ex had initiated contact. 'No matter what I do I am screwed,' he said.

He was excited when Mike told him about the interview, and called his mum. 'You won't believe it, I'm gonna be on TV!' he said, telling her to watch.

None of them had any idea how the media worked, although Mike had met plenty of celebrities in his days at Sandy Lane, as well as some who had stayed at the Prince Rupert, including Alan Shearer and Ian Wright doing *Match of the Day* when Shrewsbury Town FC were on an FA Cup run and hosted Liverpool.

The day before the interview, a BBC research team called them for a preparatory chat and tested the Zoom. Not long after, the BBC called back and said they only wanted Chris. 'We've researched the black teardrops tattooed under Dave Pritchard's eyes and seen it symbolises two murders in prison,' they explained. In fact, one was in memory of his dad and the other a badly drawn ace of spades.

Mike didn't have the heart to tell Dave the truth. 'They really liked you but time is short so they can only have one homeless interviewee and flipped a coin,' he said.

'That's me all over,' replied Dave. 'Always the flip-side. That's my life. Don't worry, I'll go and drown my sorrows.'

Mike was nervous when they went on air but also excited to speak about a subject he had become so consumed with. He explained how the project came about and the initial wariness between staff and guests, as well as his own lack of understanding about homelessness. 'When you're living together, you can't help getting to know these individuals and start to understand their predicament,' he said. 'Now we're like an extended family.'

Chris Bennett told a bit of his story, starting off being scared and suicidal 'in a world of lost' on the streets just before New Year. 'It's been brilliant to be fair, from six weeks ago not knowing what I was going to do to be let in this hotel,' he said. 'I thought I was just going to get a sleeping bag. Instead I was brought to the hotel and asked if I wanted a room. It's shocking.'

Victoria Derbyshire seemed fascinated by the project, asking Chris Bennett about his plans. 'Now I have a future to look forward to,' he said.

Mike interrupted to hold up Chris's right hand. 'Look, one of his issues was he'd just come out of hospital after an operation where he had a spider bite and got a serious infection. His hand was double the size.'

'I will have to change trade,' said Chris. 'I can't be a joiner or roofer any more because of my hand, I can't clench it. I'm not getting any physio …'

'Would you say you have become friends?' they were asked at the end.

'A hundred per cent,' said Mike.

Chris nodded. 'I think the world of Michael and all the staff, they go out of their way.'

Within an hour of the interview the other residents were teasing Chris about his spider bite. Mike didn't understand. Chris had told them that he woke up with the bite while sleeping rough and had gone to hospital, where it became infected. Eventually someone explained that the infection had in all likelihood been caused by Chris injecting heroin. 'I guess they have lived a life of lies since young children,' said Mike.

With people all locked down at home, watching far more television than usual and keen to find some good news amid all the bad, the interview struck a chord. Soon they were getting emails and the hotel phone was ringing off the hook with people wanting to help. Envelopes started arriving in the post with donations, ten- or twenty-pound notes accompanied by little handwritten letters, clearly from old ladies or men.

Charlie was so overwhelmed she cried. 'I didn't realise there was so much kindness out there,' she said.

So many clothes poured in that they turned one room into a walk-in wardrobe, where the guests could help themselves to new outfits. Many of the items were brand-new, from Primark or Marks & Spencer, still with labels.

Offers of free physiotherapy for Chris also came in, which he did not take up.

However, Dave Pritchard was devastated to have been left out. 'I was absolutely gutted,' he said afterwards. All the work Mike,

Charlie and Jacki had done building him up threatened to be lost. Just as he had with his father, once again Dave felt he was not good enough. They would have to spend hours with him reassuring him. Soon other media contacted them and Dave refused to have anything to do with it. A few days afterwards Mike was on Radio 5 Live speaking to Nihal Arthanayake with Shaggy, who talked of how he had dreamed of being a pastry chef.

'These are real fighters,' said Mike. 'I challenge anyone to sleep on a bench in the middle of winter with no food, hot water, bathroom, no hot drinks, it's really tough. I can't comprehend what it's like for one night, let alone years, and we have individuals staying with us who have been doing it three or four decades.'

Asked about his hopes, Shaggy told the audience, 'I'd like to be working, see my little boy, now I see a future.'

'Proud of you, mate,' said Mike after the recording.

The next star was Titch, who found himself in *Newsweek* under the headline 'Coronavirus Gave Me a Second Chance, Otherwise I'd Still Live on the Street'. To Mike's amusement his photo appeared on the same page online as that of Donald Trump.

Not all the attention was welcome. Some of their neighbours in nice houses near the church were less than happy about the new residents. One across the road kept videoing them, so much so that they christened him the Peeping Tom. Every so often he would phone, demanding, 'Can't you keep them quiet', and complaining about their foul language.

Mike was furious. 'If we had a wedding with fifteen or twenty drunken people outside in top hats making noise, you wouldn't care,' he said.

One day the Peeping Tom called the police, protesting that too many people were sitting outside. Officers came with cones, police tape and plastic barricades, and blocked off the stone steps by the

map of the city where people liked to sit. 'Really, was that necessary?' asked Mike.

On 3 May, Andy moved out of the Prince Rupert to a flat behind
the church and a job in a pizza parlour, begging them not to tell
Julie where he was.

Only afterwards would they discover that he had not only been
jailed but he was a sex offender and was not allowed near schools.
Mike was horrified. When he found out on a Zoom call with the
council, he asked, 'How could you let us have someone like that in
here?'

They apologised profusely, insisting they had been unaware and
that in the rush to house everyone he had slipped through the net.
But the case had been reported in the local papers.

Julie would later tell them that Andy had even taken control of
her bank account so she had no access to her own benefits. He
used it to buy drugs and had been caught selling them. Julie said
she wanted to stop taking drugs. 'I am only thirty-six,' she said. 'I
don't want to be living my life all the time thinking about where
the next bag is coming from.'

13.

Wednesday, 6 May 2020

He would have been thirty-two that day. Her guardian angel. Lockdown meant that they could not hold the annual ritual of family and friends releasing age balloons from the rocky ledge on top of Grinshill, where as a teenager he had carved three letters, 'MEZ', the name by which everyone knew him. His real name was Merrick and no matter how much love and how many fairy lights she spread around everywhere she went, Charlie would never get over losing him. His roguish bearded face smiled out from her phone and her living room at home was like a shrine to him, with large photos on the walls next to the pair of sculpted angel wings she bought after his death.

Nearly five years had passed since that Monday in June when she had gone home to change, in preparation for a big group coming in that evening for dinner in the hotel restaurant.

The day had been warm and she sat in the sun with Gabriella in the garden of the little rented cottage where she lived with her second son Callum. She and Gary had separated the previous year and they'd been living in the cottage six months, her two younger children having stayed with their dad in the big house down the road. Gabriella had popped in on her bike. She had turned eighteen ten days before, an age that at one time none of them had thought she would make.

It was hard to believe that two years earlier she had been so thin that you could count her bones and so weak that she was in a wheelchair. They'd been told she could die of a heart attack at any time and Charlie had slept on the floor next to her.

Things finally seemed to be turning. After twenty-seven years, Charlie was at last free from the husband she had married too young and, she felt, had turned her into a mouse. Now she was flourishing in a job that she was enjoying. She knew some of the other women at the hotel made comments, resentful of how quickly she had been promoted and how frequently Mike consulted her, but she could live with that. After what she had been through with Gabriella, she thought she could live through anything. She smiled as she watched her daughter cycle off. Olive-skinned and dark-haired like all her children, Gabriella was turning into a beautiful young woman.

Charlie went into her bedroom to change, when she heard frantic yelling outside her window. 'Charlotte, Charlotte! Come out!'

That voice still sent shivers down her spine. The voice of her ex-husband. Reminding her of the things he used to shout at her: 'You are nothing, you are last!' she'd heard often, his eyes red, the veins in his neck bulging, so different to the charmer of their first few years together during which she had been flattered by this older man interested in her, and the nice life he gave her.

'What do you want?' she called down.

'It's Mez, he's been in an accident,' yelled Gary. He was on his hands and knees, hitting the road.

Her heart stopped. She ran downstairs. Gary told her that police had come to the house to tell him Mez had been knocked off his motorbike just down the road and had been airlifted to Stoke Hospital. Gary was in no state to drive, so Charlie jumped into the driving seat of his BMW. On the way they passed Gabriella and told her to throw her bike in the hedge and get in.

Shortly after, they saw Callum and Fraser coming the other way in Callum's car and stopped them. The boys had seen the air ambulance but had no idea it was for their elder brother. They got in and Callum took over driving, so Charlie could call the hospital. She also phoned Mike to tell him there had been an accident and she would be late.

The accident had happened about three-quarters of a mile away at the junction of the turn-off to Grinshill from the A49. Mez had been at his girlfriend's and was heading along the main road when a large Toyota 4x4 pulled out in front of him, knocking him off. As the bike skidded and rolled across the tarmac, he was hit by a car coming the other way.

When they got to Stoke Hospital, they were taken to a side room. 'He's alive but we're working on him,' they were told. He had suffered severe trauma to the head and left lung, a doctor explained.

They sat in silence. It seemed just minutes before a doctor and nurse came in. This isn't good, thought Charlie. 'I'm afraid he's gone,' said the doctor.

Charlie felt like her entire world had fallen from under her. Numbly, she followed the doctor into the ward with Gary and their children. It was like *Casualty*, the curtains round the bed. Inside, Mez was lying covered up, connected to a respirator, the only visible damage scuffs to his knuckles, just as if he had been playing his beloved rugby. It couldn't be true. What they couldn't see was the back of his head caved in like an egg.

They all stood round the bed crying. Gary started wailing like a banshee. 'I'm sorry, you can't do that here,' said the doctor, ushering him out.

Fraser was only fifteen so Callum took him outside, but Charlie and Gabriella stayed at the bedside. They held Mez's hands as the respirator was turned off and slowly, slowly, like a little butterfly, his heart fluttered to a stop.

Charlie called Mike. 'He's gone,' she said. Mike didn't know what to say.

Back home that night, Charlie huddled in her bedroom with Fraser and Gabriella, and her elder sister sat with them until eventually they fell asleep. When dawn broke the next morning, Charlie ran across the fields to the crash site and searched frantically for bits of Mez's motorbike that hadn't been cleared away. As cars whizzed by, she sat sobbing by the side of the road, clutching the pieces to her chest as if they were part of him, her heart utterly broken.

She still had to make the hardest call of all – to her parents, who adored Mez. They were on holiday in Greece, probably having a wonderful time, and she was about to destroy everything. Her mum would never recover and would die two years later.

Mike had told Charlie to take as much time as she needed but she refused to stay off long, saying she needed to work. She worked like a mad thing. He would find her in the back bedrooms in the old part of the hotel, scrubbing and cleaning, sobbing her heart out, and comfort her.

'I wouldn't have survived if it hadn't been for the love of my family or the support of Mike,' she said.

He comforted her too, when the case came to trial the following year. The driver of the car that caused the accident was found guilty of causing death by careless driving yet fined just £2,500 and disqualified for fifteen months. The boys were so upset they wanted to burn his house down.

Her beautiful Mez had been her protector. One of the last times she saw him he had come into the living room and said, 'I told Dad to stop bullying you.'

It seemed so cruel for this to happen just as she was emerging from the fog of all she had gone through with Gabriella and her ex-husband. For a long time Charlie thought she would never recover. 'It was like hell with my eyes glued open,' she said. 'They took my daylight away.'

She blamed herself for Mez's death. Her ex-husband blamed her, as he did for everything. Gabriella blamed herself, saying Mez had come back from Australia because of her illness, despite Charlie telling her repeatedly that he always would have come back, he was a homebird.

A plaque engraved in his memory was installed on a bench by the church at the foot of Grinshill. He'd loved to climb and camp in its caves with Callum when they were boys, or ride its tracks on dirt-bikes. Once he had biked up and rescued his little sister and her friends when they had gone up there for a party and not come back.

Losing Mez made Charlie see how one wrong turn could destroy a life and how easy it would be just to give up and not to have to feel the pain any more. Or to try to forget the pain with alcohol or drugs, as so many of their homeless guests did. Sitting by the road that morning after his death, she too had thought of ending it all.

Instead she made herself leap out of bed with a smile as she always had, poured her grief into writing poems and hugged her surviving children even closer. She told herself over and over that there was blue sky behind the clouds, even if she did not believe it. The pain never went, constantly catching her unawares, but as the years passed she had forced herself to learn to live with it, helped by family and friends.

Working with the homeless the last couple of months had given her a new sense of purpose and dozens more people to mother-hen. 'They thought we were helping them, but they were helping me,' she said. She often felt as if Mez were watching from above, giving her strength, chuckling at some of the craziness.

She told some of them about him and showed them his photo. 'I recognise him!' exclaimed Dave Pritchard. 'He bought parts for

his bike from my Ducks Bitz.' She had no idea if that was true but she liked the connection.

Mez's birthday was always a particularly hard day, but at least this year she had other things to focus on. Later that day, Callum sent a photo of two giant silver balloons, a '3' and a '2', he had released from Grinshill ledge, where Mez's initials were engraved, floating up into the sky.

14.

Friday, 8 May 2020

It was VE Day, seventy-five years since the guns fell silent at the end of the war in Europe. The government had declared a national holiday, though it didn't feel very different as most people were working from home and many were on furlough. There was a two-minute silence at 11 a.m. Across Britain, people were dressing up in wartime clothing and holding socially distanced street parties.

In normal years the Prince Rupert would have been the first to be decked in bunting and Union flags. This time, however, life with the homeless guests was proving so hectic that they had not organised anything.

For many around the country VE Day was a welcome distraction. The UK death toll had reached more than 33,000, the highest in Europe, having overtaken Italy a few days before. Surprisingly no one in the hotel had caught coronavirus. Shropshire had lower rates than most of the country and Charlie and Jacki had of course endlessly warned their guests to wash their hands and spray them with sanitiser from the bottles that were dotted around. But they wandered about the town touching who knew what.

Shortly after the two-minute silence, Mike was showing off photos of his first grandchild Lara on his phone, just two days old, and the girls were cooing at her cuteness, when they heard a commotion in the lobby.

Two taxis had arrived from the White House in Telford, a budget hotel that was also being used for the homeless. From the first had come a well-dressed couple in their forties who could have passed for regular guests, except for their piles of belongings, and gave their names as Hannah and Neil, and from the other cab had come a man with a thick neck, shaved head and tanned face called Mick.

The security guards had asked them to put their bags down at the side of the lobby while someone at reception took their names and processed their information. The man on his own was trying to hold on to a large rucksack but the guards were insisting he place it with the others. No sooner had he left it than the rucksack started shuffling.

'Mick, that bag is moving,' hissed Hannah, who appeared to know him.

'It's okay,' he replied.

But one of the guards had also spotted it. 'There's something in that bag, man,' he yelled. 'It's moving. It's a rat!'

They made Mick open the rucksack. Inside, in a toilet bag, was a young magpie, which shot out and began flapping round the lobby.

'That's a wild bird, man,' said the guard in astonishment. 'You can't keep it in a hotel. You better catch it and let it go.'

'It has a broken wing,' said Mick. 'I'm looking after it.' The guards insisted he take it outside and release it. It hopped around for a while on the cobbles in front of the hotel.

'If it can't fly it's going to get eaten by a cat or a fox,' said Neil helpfully.

Mick picked it up and placed it on a branch of the twisty tree. The magpie stopped for a while, one wing askew, then suddenly flew into the sky, past the church and over the roofs and steeples in a lopsided way. Mick was really upset.

'That was my bird,' he muttered. 'I wish we'd stayed at the White House.'

Hannah did not agree. 'I knew this was a really historic hotel and was excited to see it,' she said.

A few days later, out of the corner of her eye, Charlie spotted something through the lounge window. 'What's that?' she exclaimed. 'Oh my God, there's a snake in reception!'

She ran through the door. Mick had a huge snake coiled round his neck. 'They call me Mick the Snake,' he said. 'Reason obvious.'

'We don't take pets,' said Charlie, standing well back.

'He's very gentle,' said Mick, stroking its mottled skin. The snake was a six-foot-long boa constrictor that he said he fed on dead mice and rats he purchased in the exotic pet shop. 'His name is Titch.'

'We've already got one of those and that's trouble enough,' said Charlie. 'You'll have to take it outside while I call the council.' She heard shrieks as Mick went and sat on the bench by the tree.

Samantha came running in. 'I'm telling you there's a huge fucking snake outside!' she shouted. 'And it's not the drugs!'

It turned out that a friend of Mick's daughter had been looking after the snake but had panicked and threatened to let it loose. Eventually Tim Compton from the council came to the rescue, offering to give the creature a temporary home. 'I already have a parrot, a snake and a greyhound,' he told them. Afterwards he organised for Mick to move to a former night shelter near the station that was run by the council, where he could keep the snake in a cage.

They were sorry to lose Mick – he was 'a bit of a geezer', who had been in and out of jail for burglary and had never lived on the streets but lost his home after the landlord got behind on the mortgage and the house was repossessed. In jail he had learned to draw and paint, and he showed some of his work to Charlie. 'His pictures are beautiful,' she told Jacki.

Hannah and the snake.

After he left, Mick would often come back to visit with the snake, terrifying Julie and some of the other women. Hannah's younger brother was a reptile expert who had kept snakes when they were children so she was used to them and would wind it round her body like a fur wrap. Charlie was also keen to try.

'You're not catching me with that thing,' said Jacki.

Things always happened just as Charlie and Jacki were preparing dinner. One evening they were about to serve when someone came running, shouting, 'Something's happened to Mark Chapman!'

Mark was a constant worry, often falling downstairs, sometimes swallowing his tongue. They would find him, carry him to his room and ten minutes later he would be gone again.

They rushed outside and saw a small crowd gathered outside the Japanese restaurant in Fish Street. Mark was lying at the bottom of the steps apparently out cold and there was lots of blood.

'I'll call an ambulance,' said Charlie.

'What happened?' asked Mike.

'Someone thumped him and he fell down the steps,' said one of those gathered. 'Look, there's the guy who did it ...'

Mike ran down the road after the man – he was with Stokesy. Mike reached for his phone. 'Be very careful,' said Stokesy. 'You call the police and you're a marked man in this town. We stick together.'

'Tough,' said Mike, trying to keep his hand from shaking as he dialled. 'I'm on the phone to them right now.'

By the time he got back to Mark, the ambulance had arrived. 'Was it you who called the police?' asked one of the paramedics.

'Yes,' replied Mike.

'They already radioed to say they won't come.'

'What? Why?'

'It's VE night and they are going round breaking up street parties and house parties. Apparently there are hundreds of them.'

'You've got to be kidding,' sighed Mike. By then Mark had come round but was refusing to get into the ambulance. 'I'll only go if Charlie comes,' he said. She wasn't allowed to travel with him because of Covid restrictions but she got in and he followed, gripping her hands tightly he was so scared.

*   *   *

That night in the hotel lounge, Mike, Jacki and Charlie watched on TV as the Queen spoke to the nation. 'Never give up, never despair,' she urged. 'Our streets are not empty, they are filled with the love and care that we have for each other.'

'She needs to come to Shrewsbury,' observed Charlie.

After the address, people were invited to go out to their door-steps and sing 'We'll Meet Again', Dame Vera Lynn's wartime classic. Some of the Prince Rupert's guests were gathering around the entrance but not for singing.

'Not again,' sighed Mike. Almost every evening, it seemed, clusters of people would gather in the lobby around eleven, clearly waiting in anticipation. He went upstairs to his balcony and sure enough there came Michael Lambert riding up on the bike. Once he got to the door, he'd be opening his pockets, saying look what I have, then vroom, one by one they'd go racing up to their bedrooms to avail of whatever assortment of heroin, crack cocaine or mamba they had ordered. It was like the Deliveroo of drugs.

Back downstairs, Mike bumped into Titch. 'If Michael Lambert was not here, how would they get their drugs?' he asked.

'Get rid of Lambert and the drugs will stop overnight,' said Titch.

'That's it,' Mike told Charlie later. 'Lambert has to go. We've got to get drugs out of the hotel. It's killing the place.' He organised a Zoom meeting with the council, at which it was agreed that Lambert would be moved. But afterwards Lenny Worthing came to meet Mike in the hotel lounge and urged Lambert be given one last chance. 'Just give him a warning,' he said. 'We can fix him.'

Charlie joined in. 'He's making so much progress,' she pleaded. 'And he loves my custard!'

Only later would Mike realise that Titch had been eyeing the business for himself.

*　*　*

Around 3 a.m. Mark Chapman discharged himself from hospital. He had a broken wrist, shattered elbow and lacerations all over his head. Unable to get a taxi at that time and with no money, he phoned Dave Pritchard and told him. Dave got out of bed, walked the three miles to the hospital and walked him back again.

Charlie was exasperated that Mark had not stayed to be properly treated, as the homeless were always at the bottom of the list for treatment and it would be much harder as an outpatient.

'Wow, you guys really stick together, don't you?' said Mike. 'When you're at a corner with nowhere to turn, you're there for each other.'

15.

Saturday, 16 May 2020

'Let's take Titch with us shopping,' said Mike.

Every morning Mike, Charlie and Jacki headed up Pride Hill like the Three Amigos to the big Marks & Spencer to collect expiring sandwiches, salads and fruit packs — sometimes as much as three pallets full — which they would put out in the Darwin

Charlie and Jackie collecting sandwiches.

Suite as snacks. They would also buy whatever Charlie needed to cook dinner.

That morning Titch had asked Jacki if she would look after his bank card so he couldn't just spend all his benefits on drugs. 'You know me, Mum, if I have a pound I spend a pound,' he told her. Several of them had started using Jacki as a bank, trusting her with £20 notes to keep for later in the month.

She shook her head at Titch with her wry half-smile. More than any of them, he tugged at her heartstrings – it felt to her as if he had never had a chance in life.

Titch had been having a rough time recently, bullied by some of the others, they subsequently discovered, because his uncle Scottish John had been arrested for raping a young girl in his tent on the other side of the Welsh bridge. Rape and paedophilia were offences that their guests took against very strongly.

Wanting to cheer him up, they suggested he accompany them shopping. 'Okay, Dad,' he said to Mike.

A few days earlier Boris Johnson had made a statement, changing the government advice from Stay at Home to Stay Alert, so there were more people on the street. No one quite knew what the advice meant but people could now go outside as much as they wanted, meet friends in the open air and they were being encouraged to go back to work if they could not work from home.

It was all part of a three-stage route out of lockdown that, if Covid cases continued to fall, would see some schools and businesses open in June. Shops, hairdressers, beauty salons and part of the hospitality sector would potentially reopen in July, depending on the all-important R number (which measured the spread of the virus) remaining below one.

For the first time the government recommended the wearing of masks in crowded places, having previously said there was no evidence that they were necessary. Occasionally Mike and Charlie would see people wearing one – they once saw a man in Tesco in what looked like an old gas mask from the war.

As had become usual, if they did see other passers-by, they did the corona-swerve to avoid them. That morning, however, they noticed people waving. 'We've become celebrities,' said Mike. Then he realised it wasn't him they were waving at.

'All right, Rich?' people were calling. Titch just waved.

Once they were in the Marks & Spencer food hall, Mike grabbed a trolley, Jacki pulled out the list and they started scouring the shelves. 'Tinned tomatoes, kidney beans, salmon fillets …'

'Wotcha doing?' demanded Titch in his loud Mancunian voice.

'Shopping,' laughed Mike.

'Whaddya mean?'

'Well, we have this list of things to buy,' said Jacki.

'Fucking hell!' exclaimed Titch. 'You've got a hotel full of shop-lifters – why don't you just give us the list every day and we'll organise it for you?'

Mike tried to shush him, worried someone would hear.

'Look, their CCTV doesn't cover liquor or wine,' laughed Titch. 'And if you line your bag with silver foil, it won't set off the alarm. And if it does, well, we just leg it down the hill – catch us if you can!'

They got back to find a commotion outside the hotel. A group of the guests were sitting by the flowerbeds enjoying the sunshine and Tracy had spat in Julie's face.

The pair had been at loggerheads for days because Tracy had apparently slept with Andy, but that day the argument was over money and drugs. Tracy had been difficult from the start. Not only had her money lending and exorbitant interest rates caused tension, but she herself was a huge drinker and drug taker. She'd wheedled her way into getting a room at the front so that drugs could be thrown up to her window.

Anytime anyone saw her photograph on the hotel's Facebook page, they got messages like 'OMG, she's the biggest thief in Shrewsbury, what is she doing there?'

Like Julie, when Tracy went to get clothes from the donations, she only wanted those with labels. Charlie was convinced they were selling them. 'They had entire racks in their rooms,' said Hannah.

Most of the fights in the hotel involved Tracy and Randolph, who knew when people got paid and once stole Mark Chapman's vodka. 'Tracy was always winding people up,' said Jacki. One evening while serving dinner in the Darwin, with Charlie down in the kitchen making pudding, Jacki could tell something was going to happen. 'There was real tension in the air between Dave Pritchard, Randolph and Tracy – something over money,' she said. Michael Lambert was lurking around. Suddenly Randolph picked up a chair to hit Dave. Everyone started shouting. Jacki grabbed the chair and tried to pull it out of his hands, and they fell on the floor. Dave then grabbed the chair to hit Randolph and as Jacki tried to get it back, they all fell on top of each other again. Lambert unhelpfully punched Pritchard in the face.

The noise could be heard in the kitchen. 'Fight!' exclaimed Charlie to Pam. They ran upstairs to find mayhem and security nowhere to be seen. The three women managed to break it up eventually and Pam was furious with Tracy. 'I've eaten bigger things for supper than you,' she told her.

Tracy was left seething but gradually everyone settled down and ate their pudding. However, Jacki was hobbling – in the scuffle her ankle had got whacked and it had swelled up like a balloon.

Shortly after that Randolph was moved out, after the council belatedly realised that the couple were subject to a restraining order and were not allowed to be together. But he still kept coming round the hotel, trying to cause trouble – on one day the logbook recorded him trying to enter the building nine times and a few days after that Michael Lambert claimed that Randolph had jumped out of the bushes and tried to attack him with a hammer.

Tracy continued to cause problems. She would pretend to be helpful, offering to clean the rooms of guests who had come for only a couple of days, as did Titch, but the staff later figured out they were scoping the rooms to see if guests had left any drugs. One day, when Samantha had passed out in the Darwin and an ambulance had been called, the staff realised she didn't have any pyjamas.

'I'll go to her room and get them,' said Mike. 'I'll come!' said Tracy. In the room, she started opening all the wardrobes and rummaging through drawers.

'I've found them,' said Mike.

'I'm just seeing if she needs anything else,' said Tracy, opening more drawers until Mike managed to marshal her out.

When Samantha returned to her room afterwards, she told them someone had been through her handbag and taken her methadone and money.

Shortly after the spitting incident, a woman walked past the hotel with a shopping bag and Tracy tried to snatch it. 'Give it, it's mine!' she demanded. Shocked, the woman protested and Tracy thumped her. The security guards dragged Tracy off and made sure the woman was all right, though because of Covid she didn't want anyone to come near.

'I knew we had problems but this is way beyond,' said a horrified Mike.

After security lodged a report with the council, Mike asked them what they recommended.

'We need to move her,' said Lenny.

'Is that your final recommendation?'

'Well, it's up to you if you really want to keep her but we wouldn't recommend it.'

Afterwards Mike, Charlie and Jacki talked in the kitchen for ages. Mike wanted time to reflect. From what the council had told them, they knew Tracy had been an alcoholic since she was about twelve. 'Surely our job is to understand this is the level we are dealing with and try to turn them around?' he said. 'But maybe this is her true personality she is showing.'

'She's a tough cookie but she can be sweet,' said Charlie.

'Sweet?' exclaimed Mike. 'I think we have to tell her to go.' He felt physically sick. The blood drained from his face. He knew Tracy was highly complex but it still felt as if they had let this person down big time.

'I'm going back on the streets,' she announced when he told her. She came downstairs with a huge swag bag, having taken off the duvet cover and filled it to the brim with toiletries, food and anything else she could find. They gave her some cans of cider from behind reception.

The council transferred Tracy to the White House in Telford, where Hannah, Neil and Mick the Snake had been staying. Not only was it much less luxurious but, according to Hannah, the rooms were not regularly cleaned and the guests were treated like children, made to stand in white circles chalked on the ground to keep them socially distanced.

They later heard that Tracy lasted less than forty-eight hours there, as she got into a fight. Every so often she would reappear and ask them to take her back in. 'I wasn't that bad,' she'd say.

'No way,' they'd reply.

Shortly after Tracy's departure, the police called and said, 'We've got one of yours by Tesco.' Charlie rushed up there with a security guard. It was Lionel, the rock-star lookalike with Tourette's. He was bare-chested and barefoot, and spitting and swearing at two policemen. Charlie crouched by him. 'Lionel, come home,' she urged.

He refused, swearing and spitting.

'If you keep doing that, we'll arrest you,' said one of the police.

'That's just how he is,' Charlie tried to explain. 'Please, Lionel,' she said, trying to take his hand.

He shook his head. 'Go fuck a horse!' he shouted.

'Lionel, come, it's cottage pie for supper,' urged Charlie.

He looked at her. 'Oh, okay,' he said. He followed them back. Ten minutes later he was at reception with his key. 'Miss, can I change my room?' he asked.

'After supper,' said Jacki. As usual she would give him back the same key.

16.

Friday, 22 May 2020

'So where are these famous ghosts, Mr Matthews?' asked Hannah in her husky voice, flicking back her long chestnut hair with shiny bronze nails.

Since arriving a few weeks earlier with Neil, who she had introduced as her carer, though they seemed rather close, they had quickly become the hotel's most glamorous residents. He was tall and laconic with floppy dark hair and a broad West Country burr, while she was ethereal, usually dressed in hippy chic, and described herself as an 'empath and an artist'.

As soon as Hannah heard about the ghosts, she wanted to know more. Several years before, the hotel had featured in a television series called *Great British Ghosts*, which some of the homeless guests had found on YouTube. It described Shrewsbury as the most haunted town in Britain and the Prince Rupert as one of the country's most haunted hotels. Among the tales of apparitions recounted was one of a young man in room 7 who was said to have shot himself after the girl he loved left him for his best friend and whose ghostly form would materialise at one of the windows.

Sometimes, late at night in the Darwin, the homeless would wind each other up, as well as the security guards, who they had discovered were terrified of the ghosts. One member of security, a lovelorn Sikh who had developed a crush on Jacki and kept asking

Mike for advice on how to woo her, claimed that doors often banged in the night when he was sitting in the lobby and that once a pen flew from the reception desk to the wall.

Hannah was fascinated. 'I do tarot readings,' she said. 'I used to do them for friends by the Buddha round the firepit in my garden. I'm really a pagan hedge-witch.'

Neil chortled. 'He thinks it means I dragged myself out of a hedge with sticks in my hair,' said Hannah. 'He doesn't understand about herbal magic and connecting with your inner spirit. Ignore him.'

'If you think about it, this hotel is nine hundred years old — that's a lot of memories embedded in its walls,' said Mike, who had no idea what she was talking about. 'It must have seen many deaths and tragedies. I think there is a passionate sadness in this building, where a person has been trapped in this loveless relationship.'

'That's so romantic,' sighed Hannah. 'I knew there was something here – I've seen images behind me in the big mirror on the landing and sometimes the doorknob rattles.'

Most of the ghost sightings had been in the oldest parts of the hotel. In the sixteenth-century Tudor building, the temperature often dropped in the corridors and the ghost of a hotel maid called Martha could be seen wandering next to the Prince Rupert Suite or inside it, fluffing the pillows of its four-poster bed. Guests had reported finding a depression in the bed, always in the same place. The guards claimed a Portuguese cleaner had fled in terror because she had felt a presence so strong it had pushed her over.

Eeriest of all was the Prince Philip Suite, said to be haunted by the spirit of a jilted bride. Abandoned by her lover on the eve of their wedding, she is said to have hung herself from the rafters. Single men staying there alone regularly woke in the early hours to a spectre of a hanging woman who then vanished. 'It's the only room I wouldn't stay in,' said Mike.

He showed them a photograph taken on his phone in one of the haunted rooms in which orbs appeared to be floating all around him. Hannah's eyes widened. Dave Pritchard started making ghostly noises. 'Stop it!' said Julie. 'Can't we talk about something else? I don't like this.'

'Well, I've definitely heard creaking floorboards and door handles rattling,' said Michael Lambert.

'That's the mamba!' laughed Pritchard.

'I sometimes hear a child's voice,' said Martin.

Jamie was scared because he'd once kidnapped someone and feared revenge. Mark Chapman was as philosophical as ever. 'What's a bump in the night?' he asked. 'It's the living we need to be most wary of, not the dead.'

'There's a girl on my corridor who keeps walking up to my door,' said Chris Bennett. 'I can hear the steps, but when I open it there is never anyone there. I don't know, is it me, did I imagine that? All I know is it's pretty annoying when I'm watching TV. I'm like fuck off!'

Hannah was intrigued. Charlie and Jacki were just as intrigued by her and Neil. The couple, in their early forties, were more sophisticated than other guests and had never lived on the streets. Indeed they were clearly still in shock at losing their homes.

Neil's father had been principal of Ludlow College and his mother a legal secretary. Hannah told them her father was a blues singer who'd toured all round the world and when she was a teenager he'd taken her and her two brothers to Chicago, where one night they slept through a tornado, waking up to destruction. After her parents divorced, her mum married another blues singer, a man called Jim Bruce, who used to perform with her dad. Her mother worked in the archives at Somerset House and wrote short stories, including one about a beekeeper who dies and a swarm of bees appear at her funeral.

Both, however, had the tell-tale rotten teeth of the addict and Hannah walked with a crutch because of osteoporosis, which she said had been caused by years of ballet.

They had come from Ludlow, perhaps Shropshire's most beautiful market town, after being evicted from the house Hannah had lived in for twenty-three years and where she had brought up her two sons. 'I was a brilliant mum,' she said. 'I looked after all the kids on the estate. They came to me if they were hurt and I did lots of art with them.'

How she lost the house was a convoluted story that started with her ex-partner forcing her to take drugs then going to jail for repeatedly acquiring cars and not paying the tax or doing the MOT and driving without a licence. 'He was an idiot,' she said. 'I was always told, never ever put a man before your house. I was told that by my friend Mary, Sadie Frost's mum, who also lived in Ludlow and hung out with the Beatles – her husband painted their psychedelic Rolls-Royce.'

Hannah had become a mother very young, having left home at fifteen. 'My mum came from a rough background in Woolwich – her dad was a motorbike repairman and her mum a factory worker – and no one cared what time any of the kids came in or where they were. My nan worked in the Woolwich Arsenal, making munitions in the war and told me stories about going dancing in the docks with the sailors during the Blitz. She and I used to get on really well – people say I am like her.

'My mum was the opposite – over-the-top protective,' Hannah went on. 'She wished her parents had been doctors and teachers, and was all about being the perfect mum, making jam and marmalade and sending me to ballet. But I just wanted to party and meet boys, so I rebelled, spending most of the nineties going off to raves, dancing, with long dreadlocks, putting on parties in barns and forests around Shropshire and the Welsh border, and then in a converted bus with a man called Spike to Somerset Tor for the summer solstice and on to Glastonbury. Blasting reggae tunes into a crowd of half-naked men and women dancing as if they were possessed was one of the most moving moments of my life. Neil was always there somewhere. At fifteen I ran away completely and by sixteen was pregnant.' A couple of years after that Hannah's biological father died of a brain tumour.

In Neil's case, he grew up endlessly in trouble. 'I struggled to read and write, and they said I was lazy and stupid,' he said. In fact he was dyslexic but didn't discover until later. 'Every time I entered a class, my main thing was to get thrown out before the embarrassment of being asked to read something out loud and them realising I couldn't. My dad was a headmaster but when I left school, I'd never read a book.'

He got a job waiting tables in a restaurant that was popular with day-trippers to Ludlow. One day in peak tourist season, the chef didn't turn up and a coach party of pensioners arrived with lunch reservations, prompting panic. 'I'll do it,' said Neil. He ended up doing sixty plates of plaice, chips and peas. He'd been taught to cook by his mum, often helping her do teas for his dad's rugby club, and his aunt and uncle had a restaurant, so cooking was in the family.

By the age of nineteen he was running a restaurant and then the kitchen of a hotel in the Welsh resort of Knighton. He had also started smoking grass and within a couple of years he was on probation after his house was raided and he got caught with some.

The long hours and stress of running a kitchen was getting to Neil, giving him really bad dermatitis on his hands, and he realised he could earn more doing fewer hours working in a factory. He went for a job in what he thought was a plastic mouldings factory and froze when the interviewer asked him to do a test. 'I'm not good at reading and writing,' he said. They assured him it was more a series of puzzles. He found it easy and was given the job, which turned out to be paint-spraying bumpers and spoilers for high-end Bentleys, Rolls-Royces, Aston Martin DB7s and Rover MGF sports cars.

'I had a nice car and was earning good money – £10.80 an hour back in 1996 – and living with my girlfriend and we had a son,' he said. 'I had some money put by and was going to buy a house for £69k in Ludlow, but I bottled it – the biggest mistake I ever made. Instead I bought a Mark 2 Ford Transit van, like bank robbers use, and a caravan and a one-way ticket from Plymouth to Santander, and we spent a year travelling round Spain and Portugal.'

They were in a lay-by in the south of France, wondering what to do next when they got talking to a Dutch man and his young family, who told them he was a carpenter and had just bought a farmhouse in Holland that he needed help doing up. They ended up going along, staying in the garden in their caravan and Neil working with him. When the house was finished and rented to some new people, they said they could stay in the garden. 'We thought that was weird and they were too,' said Neil. 'She was about six foot four and turned out to be a prostitute, working in brothels on the motorways, and he said he was a top landscape gardener.' Neil got a job delivering cakes, then baking bread and eventually painting furniture for a contemporary design company. 'One day someone at work showed me the front page of *De Telegraaf* and said, "Isn't that your street?" It was a photo of my neighbour, who had been arrested – it turned out he was a conman and she was on the run, hiding from the father of her two kids, who was an Israeli diamond dealer. I was smoking a lot of weed at the time and felt like I was in some kind of soap opera. It was all so surreal.'

Eventually they moved back to Ludlow, where Neil split up with his girlfriend and picked up a serious heroin habit. 'I was always up for getting wrecked, whether it was dope, Es or heroin, and I had spare money so started doing it at weekends then more,' he said.

He began bringing heroin in from Holland, where it was just £12 a gram and far cheaper than the UK. 'I was getting in loads of trouble, as every time I came back to Ludlow, police were waiting for me.'

Somehow Neil avoided jail, something he said the local police never forgave him for, but he could not stop. 'Heroin makes you feel nice and calm and forget,' he said. 'I thought it made everything much easier.'

Instead he decided he needed to leave. 'If you bought the *Sun* or *Mirror* on a Thursday, there were loads of ads for jobs in Holland.' This time he worked for Mitsubishi and Caterpillar, spraying fork-lift chassis. After some time he returned to Ludlow, got back with his partner and son, and they moved to Hereford and had a daughter. There he got funding from the Prince's Trust to set up a carpentry workshop, making furniture and shelves. 'I taught myself, watching YouTube videos,' said Neil. Nearby was the MOD Barracks at Brecon and he started getting contracts there, including one to replace all their sash windows. At one point he had fifteen people working for him.

'All the time, I was doing heroin every day,' he said, 'but I never went to jail and never stopped working. I even worked Saturdays. I was addicted to earning money to buy it.'

Eventually he split up with his girlfriend again and moved to Bristol. That's where he was when he reconnected with Hannah, who he had known when they were teenagers and then their sons had been good friends since primary school. She was not in a good state. Having fallen foul of the authorities for not declaring the bedroom tax – after her sons moved out, leaving her with a spare room – she had descended into a spiral of drinking and anti-depressants. Neil took her to stay with him in Bristol, then moved into her house in Ludlow to look after her.

Back in Ludlow, he soon crossed swords with a local policeman. After some of Neil's friends visiting from Bristol were stopped and searched for drugs – he believes because they were black – they reported the policeman. 'After that he was out to get us,' said Neil. Before long, police carried out a drugs bust on their house and broke the door down.

'I'd made an apple crumble and when I make crumble, I always make double the topping to keep for another one and they thought it was white powder,' said Neil. 'They claimed we were running county lines drugs.'

In the end the police found nothing, though refused to give Neil back his crumble topping. The housing association billed them £1,500 damage for the broken door and issued an eviction order, listing ninety-two complaints over five years, none of which they had heard before, according to Hannah. A court hearing was set but they failed to attend, they said, because the letter was sent second class and arrived after the date. They were evicted.

They moved out as ordered on 19 March 2020. A day later all evictions were put on hold because of Covid. 'If we'd stayed till the twentieth, they wouldn't have been able to move us,' said Hannah.

It was the beginning of a nightmare. 'I'd lived in my place ten years until I moved in with Hannah and she'd been there twenty-three,' said Neil. 'Not having anywhere was a bit of a shock.'

Hannah shook her head. 'They say everyone is two wage packets away from being homeless,' she said.

Homeless in the midst of a pandemic, they were sent to the Travelodge in Ludlow, then on to the White House in Telford. 'It was bedlam,' said Hannah. 'One girl was all dressed up in Julia Roberts over-the-knee boots and told me, "I'm off on the beat, do you want to come?" I said I didn't know what she was talking about, so she said, "Looking for punters." I told her that's not my bag. Then a group of Pakistanis beat Neil up in a case of mistaken identity.'

That's where they met Mick the Snake, who bonded with Hannah over their interest in art, clearly taking a fancy to her and giving her some art books, which he wrote messages in. One day he opened a drawer in his room to show her the magpie he'd found with a broken wing and been keeping. 'No one cleaned the rooms, so you could do what you like,' said Hannah.

After two months there, moving to the Prince Rupert had been a huge relief. Hannah was so thin when she arrived that Charlie thought she looked like a stick insect, telling her, 'We need to feed you up.'

'I'm really grateful. It's something that will stay with me for ever,' said Hannah. 'Don't get me wrong – we have our good days and bad days, but what Mr Matthews has done is really put his bollocks on the line.'

Once they knew about her art, they'd arranged for her to have some art materials and she designed a house number for Charlie, made graffiti tags for other residents and had even started working on an acrylic of Prince Rupert.

Mostly they kept to themselves, Hannah becoming an almost Greta Garbo-like figure. They clearly saw themselves as above the other residents. 'We are totally different to these street sleepers,' said Neil. 'I had a drug habit for years and years but I always worked – never even had a day sick – and brought up my children. My son is twenty-six and now works for a famous chef, and my daughter seventeen, and I speak to them every day.'

Both were on scrips and insisted they were not doing drugs. 'Look, we're not angels,' said Hannah. 'I've been stuck on methadone for eighteen years.' She took seventy millilitres of the green

liquid a day. 'It tastes horrible, like menthol, but if I don't have it, I can't function. I can't sleep, eat, sit still, I feel like I'm dying – in fact if someone gave me a gun I'd shoot myself. You know it was developed by the Nazis in the Second World War as a painkiller for people who lost limbs, not long-term use.'

Jacki was cynical. She couldn't help noticing how, when there was a drug deal to be done, Hannah left her crutch and sprinted up the road. Her own ankle was still swollen and painful from the fight in the Darwin – she could only wear flat Converse.

Just as Mike's view on the homeless had been turned upside down by living among them, a quarter-century of running the Prince Rupert had altered his views on the supernatural.

'I was very sceptical about ghosts and spirits before I came here, but now I feel completely different,' he said.

In 1996, when he first moved into the hotel with his family, all the rooms had been occupied, so he put up two camp beds in the Prince Rupert lounge for himself and his nephew, who was working there at the time. The prince is said to have lived in the lounge in the 1640s. 'Around 2 a.m. we said let's call it a night and sat down on the beds and I said, "Let's have a drink before we go to bed." We popped down to the bar. When we came back, just sixty seconds later, our pillows had vanished. After more than half an hour of searching, we finally found them in the lift sixty yards away.'

Guests staying in room 6 would sometimes complain of a strange chill raising the hairs on the back of their necks – so much so that anyone appearing in reception in the early hours asking for hot chocolate would prompt the night porter to ask, 'Are you staying in room 6?'

People had also seen a Victorian gentleman walking the corridor carrying a lighted candle that cast no shadows. During filming of a 1984 remake of Dickens's ghostly classic *A Christmas Carol* in Shrewsbury, one of the directors who was staying at the hotel woke to see a ghost of a young man, who then vanished through a wall.

The hotel's reputation meant they often got amateur ghost hunters staying. Not long after Mike had bought the place and had begun renovation in the oldest parts, a guest left a message on checking out, warning, 'I'm a spirit medium and think you should know you are upsetting spirits with all the renovation you are doing.'

'I immediately got on the phone and delayed the bathroom refittings,' he said.

Over the years he had got used to strange occurrences, often putting something down in his office only to come back minutes later and find it gone, even though no one else was around. 'You live in a building and start to understand, and after a while you accept that's just the way it is,' he said.

Charlie and Jacki had always been sceptical. But one evening, a couple of years after Mez died, Charlie was doing the bill in the restaurant for a medium who was staying and had just enjoyed a fish and chips supper, when the woman said, 'Your son is here with me.'

'I thought, Oh God, she's off her rocker,' said Charlie. 'But then she said, "He wants you to know he's here, he keeps touching his hair." That was odd, as he did do that. Then she told me, "He says you have lots of big birthdays coming up" – I was going to be fifty, my mum eighty and Gabriella twenty-one – "and he wants you to know he'll be there." Lastly, she said, "He's with a dog and rubbing its head" – he had a boxer and used to pat it. How could she know all these things? It made me think.'

*   *   *

Among Shrewsbury's claims to fame was having both the country's tallest MP and the world's tallest town crier. The latter, Martin Wood, was seven foot two and he gave walking tours that often went down to the Prince Rupert's cellars, which he said dated from the twelfth century and had been part of the town's original stone walls.

Inside the cellars, Martin told tourists that he often felt the presence of a young Tudor lad called Thomas who had apparently drowned in a pond on the other side of the wall. On one occasion a woman visiting apparently felt the boy take her hand and lead her around, while another time a lady with a green necklace screamed and the necklace fell to the floor.

'Sometimes Martha the maid appears down there with a coachman who seems not to like me, as whenever I'm down there he tries to put his hands round my neck to strangle me,' said Martin.

As soon as the homeless heard about this, they were interested. 'Let's go down to the cellars,' said Chris Bennett.

'I don't think that's a good idea,' laughed Mike. He could just imagine what they were hoping to find and had no interest in disturbing any ghosts. 'I have no doubt there is a spirit of some kind,' he said. 'It lives within the building and is almost its protector. I am starting to feel it will never let me leave the hotel.'

17.

Sunday, 31 May 2020

Kim and Gabriella were making Michael Lambert's bed, when Kim's hand slid inside the mattress. 'What's that?' she exclaimed.

They removed the sheet and found holes all around the mattress, made by a knife. By now Gabriella recognised the fishy smell. Inside were packets of mamba.

The pair had become used to finding all sorts in the rooms: heroin rocks, cutting boards, socks over the smoke alarms and drawers full of syringes and needles. And the spoons that would disappear endlessly from the Darwin to be used for heating heroin with a lighter so the homeless could inhale the vapour, a process known as chasing the dragon. Once they'd found a razor-sharp machete under the mattress of a couple, who were quickly asked to leave.

Many of the rooms smelled, thanks to food that had been kept so long it had started to look like furry animals, toilets that had been used repeatedly and not flushed, and clothes left soaking in the bath for days until they smelled like wet dogs.

Samantha was one of the worst offenders. She seemed to spill coffee on her bed every day, so Gabriella and Kim would have to keep changing the quilt. As for Shaggy, they dreaded going into his room, with its needles everywhere, in drawers and awkward places, like down the back of the toilet, as well as hairballs from him combing his long hair.

Some of the alcoholics would try and stop them coming in to clean because they were embarrassed by all the bottles in their room. Mark Chapman would often have ten bottles of vodka under his bed.

Michael Lambert had been one of the tidy ones to start with, but had got more and more distracted by people shouting up at him from the front. Charlie had recently moved him to a back room, only to find him getting increasingly involved with Samantha.

Of all things, mamba seemed to cause the most immediate damage. 'Mamba is a horrible drug,' sighed Wendy from the Ark. 'The impact on people is terrible.' In the hotel they saw its effects for themselves almost every day. Just that morning Hannah had found Chris Bennett with his face sunk in his cereal bowl, blowing bubbles in the milk and Rice Krispies, and she had pulled his head up to make sure he didn't suffocate. Jacki, clearing plates from the Darwin, had found Derek Tyrer with his face in his pudding, then watched Stokesy playing pool with his rucksack on his back, sinking lower and lower until eventually he passed out on the table.

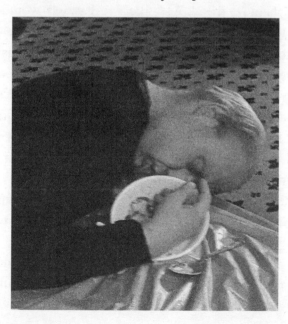

One day it seemed as if they were all off their heads. 'Where is everyone?' asked Mike when no one appeared downstairs or out on the steps. They were all passed out on the pool table and dinner tables, and no food was eaten for twenty-four hours.

The guests were often in one another's rooms up to no good. Shaggy, Chris Bennett and Mark Chapman would smirk like naughty schoolboys when Pam told them off and separated them. 'We were just watching Quest,' they would plead.

Now they had got to know Gabriella, they often chatted to her. She was pretty and easy to talk to and for some, such as Chris Bennett and Stokesy, she reminded them of their own daughters. They'd show her their pictures. She saw another side of some of the most difficult guests: Tracy FaceTiming her daughter, Derek Tyrer shouting 'Take it away, Tina!' and singing along to Tina Turner, Titch asleep on his bed with chocolate all round his mouth from the hot chocolate sachets he loved.

Richard Boffey would think it was funny to sneak up behind her and Kim while they were hoovering, or hide behind their trolley, tap one of them on the shoulder and run away like a child. 'It felt like *Fawlty Towers*,' she said.

Gabriella never judged, knowing only too well what it was like to harm yourself, thinking that somehow gave you control when everything around you was going wrong. She turned a blind eye to most things unless she thought they might hurt themselves. Although she would beg them to take the socks off the smoke alarms, saying they'd get her in trouble. 'Just go outside to smoke, guys,' she'd plead.

She told her mum and Jacki about Michael Lambert's ripped mattress but they didn't tell Mike, fearing he would 'loop the loop' as Charlie put it and threaten to stop the whole thing.

He was getting increasingly fed up with people shouting outside the hotel at night and calls asking, 'Is this one of yours?' Yet, as Charlie often remarked to Jacki, 'He only knows the half of it.' Just a few days earlier the police had called saying, 'One of yours is lying in the road outside Lloyds Bank off his face on something and stopped the traffic.' It was Stokesy. Charlie and Jacki had had to go and drag him back, Jacki still hobbling on her swollen ankle.

Mike kept complaining that the cleaners were not checking the rooms, as guests were smoking. Charlie pointed out that it was impossible for them to monitor when they weren't there at night. Some things couldn't be hidden. Samantha broke the desk trying to hide drugs behind it. Whatever chemical was in the mamba was eroding the enamel in the toilet bowls and turning them black.

One day water began pouring through to the restaurant from the hotel above. Mike, Charlie, Jacki and Pam ran around the corridors of the first and second floors, trying to find something overflowing or a burst pipe. Finally, on the second floor, they noticed wet carpet outside Donny's room and could hear water running.

One of their very first residents, Donny rarely came out of his room, living mostly on porridge pots, which he collected from the Darwin. Once Mike had smelled smoke and went in to find him blind drunk, smoking one cigarette with another lit.

Mike knocked on his door. 'Donny, are you running a tap?' he asked.

'No,' replied Donny.

'Can I just have a look in your bathroom?'

'I'd rather you didn't.' Mike went in anyway. There were three cartons of milk in the sink, the cold tap was running and water was overflowing all over the floor. From there it was pouring down through to the first floor and then through the lobby ceiling.

'Don't do it again,' said Mike. 'You can get milk from Darwin.'

But the leak kept happening. At least now they knew which room to go to. 'Donny, it's milk, isn't it?' they would sigh.

* * *

One day in June water started cascading through the wooden ceiling of the Royalist Restaurant. 'Oh my God, it's like Niagara Falls,' said Mike.

He called in an emergency plumber, who used high-pressure jets to clear the pipes, but to no avail. The hotel's pipes had always been a problem, starting from the week Mike first arrived when a sewage pipe had fallen through the roof of the restaurant just as a wealthy local businessman was about to host a dinner there for twenty-five people.

This time to try and locate the blockage the workmen sent an electrical line with a torch at the end through the pipe but that got stuck and to get it out, they had to thrust so hard that it damaged the cast iron pipe, making a four-inch hole. They patched this up with plumber's tape, thinking it would last two weeks while they decided what to do.

Before too long water started pouring through the ceiling again. Mike called in a team of plumbers, closed off the area and emptied all the rooms, telling the guests they would have to use the lobby toilet. One of the security guards was positioned on a chair at the top of the stairs and instructed not to let anyone back up for the next four hours.

The plumbers started work, cutting through the cast iron pipes with metal grinders to try and find whatever was blocking them. Suddenly there came an ominous gurgling sound. Someone upstairs was flushing a toilet. One of the plumbers yelled in horror – he was drenched. Then a noxious smell wafted through.

Mike ran upstairs. 'Have you let someone up?' he asked the security guard.

'Yes, four of them.'

'What?! Why?'

'They scared me,' he shrugged.

Mike had to run around the rooms and herd out their occupants, feeling like Basil Fawlty as he banged on doors yelling, 'Get out! Get out!' It was too late. There was another gurgle, followed by a yell from downstairs.

When the plumbers looked into the pipes, they found one of them jammed with newspaper. It turned out that, for reasons that were unclear, Stokesy had been using it instead of toilet paper. He had also just flushed. Fortunately, the plumbers had covered the restaurant carpet with protective rubber. But there was a disgusting mess.

Many of the guests came to help – Julie, Titch, Marianne and Leonard, and Chris Bennett, as well as recent arrival Bev, holding their noses as they mopped and swept the offending items into food-waste buckets.

Afterwards, when everyone had washed, Charlie brought out tea and cake. They put on music in the Darwin and Chuck Berry's 'You Never Can Tell' came on. 'Let's dance!' said Dave Pritchard. He grabbed Charlie by the hand and they recreated the famous Uma Thurman and John Travolta dance scene from *Pulp Fiction*, jiving and twisting. Mark Chapman joined in with his plastered broken arm, to much hilarity. Even Jacki hopped about on her ankle.

That night, once it grew dark, Mike and Charlie took the food-waste buckets to the churchyard to fertilise its garden, giggling like naughty children.

Mike was less amused when he got the £15,000 repair bill.

18.

Friday, 5 June 2020

'Lionel has disappeared,' frowned Jacki when Charlie came into the lobby. 'I think we better call the police.'

The police were in and out of the hotel so often that Charlie had them on WhatsApp. She pinged them a message. Ambulances also frequently arrived, particularly since Richard Boffey had checked in. Three nights in a row, he had come down in his pants in the early hours claiming there had been garlic in his supper and that he needed urgent medical attention because he was allergic.

It was always Charlie who the guards called and she bit her tongue when Mike came down looking rested and saying, 'Quiet night last night, I slept like a log.'

'Should I go and fetch Dave?' asked Jacki, looking at her two non-functioning watches. That morning Dave Pritchard had a Zoom appointment with a mental health worker. The council had set up a laptop in the lounge, as the tablet the Ark had given him had long disappeared.

He had been struggling more and more since the episode with his wife and the birthday card then the cancelled TV interview. He was starting on three-litre bottles of cider before breakfast, opening them before he had even got back from buying them, and they would often find him drunk on the floor of his room with the windows open. Afterwards he would be tearful, saying, 'I let you down.'

It was a major step for him to have agreed that he needed help and to talk to someone. Jacki was about to go up to his room when he walked into the lounge. By now they were all used to Zoom. Jacki pressed the link to start the meeting then left.

'Before we start, I just have to check whether you are adopted,' said the case worker.

'Yes, I am,' he replied.

'Then I'm afraid I can't help you. That's a different department. I'll have to rearrange the session another time with someone else.'

'What?' roared Dave. 'What difference does it make? This is nothing to do with my adoption, it's about my marriage and that fucking bastard who has taken my wife!'

He stormed off, furious. 'Dave is always a great one for walking off,' said Charlie, shaking her head.

Jacki was upstairs in her office and Charlie was in the lounge having a meeting with someone from the council and Rose from the Ark when Dave stormed back in. He was convinced the Ark didn't like him. 'All they do is send me back to jail,' he complained.

Snarling like a terrier, he went up to Rose. 'You've never helped me!' he shouted, his face right in hers. 'I'm gonna fucking kill you!'

Pam came through from reception to see what the disturbance was about. 'Get him away from here now,' Charlie urged her.

'Come on now, Dave, pack it in,' said Pam. 'Let's go and have a smoke.' She managed to shepherd him outside. But the damage was done. Mike came down to find Rose in tears. He had to go, said the council.

This time there was no arguing. 'Dave knew he'd gone too far,' said Charlie. She and Jacki were devastated. 'He was a pain in the neck but under it all he had a heart of gold,' said Jacki. He had given her a passport-sized photo of himself as a smiling ginger-haired little boy, 'before everything went wrong', as he said.

They'd put more effort into helping him than anyone, as other residents had noticed. When Dave was rattling, the sweat pouring off him, Charlie and Jacki had sat with him for hours giving him ice-pops to cool him down. 'I was always telling him, you could make things better for yourself but you won't,' said Chris Bennett.

A couple of days after Dave's outburst, they were asked to evict him. Although the weather was warm, there was no one on the streets at that time and it was forecast to rain that night. 'I couldn't see him sleeping on the street again,' said Charlie.

She gave Pam her car key and told her to take him to the car. Later she admitted to Mike what she had done. 'You're impossible,' he said, shaking his head, but then he went to the car park with her to take food and blankets. Dave was sitting in the car with the doors open and radio blaring. 'Keep it down,' they urged him.

That night he slept in the tiny Fiat 500. 'I was so squashed up I looked like I was having an orgy,' he said. 'You could have let me use your BMW so I could stretch my legs out,' he complained to Mike.

The next day they found him a tent, which he put up in the churchyard next to the hotel. Then he disappeared. After two days, Derek Tyrer told them he was sleeping under the English bridge. Jacki and Pam went down there with some food and found him in his tent on a sandy beach, a nice spot protected by reeds when the water wasn't high. He was sharing his tent with a tall aggressive-looking man called Scott who they had sometimes seen round the hotel. A few curious ducks swam by.

'Keep your head down for a while,' they warned him.

Dave didn't listen. Two days later he and Scott were outside the hotel shouting and causing trouble, smashing a bottle.

* * *

A couple of weeks after that, Charlie was getting ready around 7.30 a.m., when she heard howling. It sounded like a wolf.

'What on earth?' she exclaimed. She looked out of the window but could see nothing, so ran along the corridor. The noise was coming from round the corner, from Michael Lambert's room. Inside, the television was on at top volume and he was lying in a dying fly position with his arms and legs in the air, howling in anguish, with Samantha crouched next to him like a crab. 'I don't know what's wrong! I don't know what's wrong!' she was shouting, her eyes huge. 'I think it's a bad mamba attack.'

Charlie sent Samantha to tell security to call the police and an ambulance. Hearing the commotion, Jacki came to help from the Darwin Suite, where she'd been putting out breakfast. Pam ran up from reception. Mike appeared, having heard what he described as 'a terrible sound – I thought someone had taken dogs in the churchyard'.

Between them they tried to get Michael onto the bed but he rushed to the TV, hugging it and shouting, 'I can't save them! I need to save them!'

They turned it off, fearing he would pull the set off the wall. He ran round the room ricocheting off things in a frenzy. Fearful he would break something or hurt himself, Charlie started taking furniture out with Mike, first the coffee table and two chairs then the luggage rack.

The police and paramedics appeared in full PPE, but they refused to come in. 'Nothing we can do,' they said.

'Surely you can help,' begged Charlie.

'If we take him to hospital, they'll just send him back,' said one.

Eventually Charlie and Mike managed to get Michael on the bed and he started holding his crotch and thrusting back and forth. 'I'm going to fuck them all!' he shouted. 'I am going to fuck every woman in the town!'

'Sorry,' said Samantha to Charlie.

Then he leaped up again, trying to hug the TV. Chris Bennett appeared to help. 'Quick, turn the TV back on!' he said, grabbing for the remote. It was a Discovery Channel programme about Alaskan bush people going fishing and the boat sinking.

'The boats, the boats I've got to save them!' Lambert kept shouting. 'I must save the Alaskan boat people.'

'You save them, you save them,' reassured Samantha.

Eventually he began to calm down. 'I managed to save them,' he said, before falling asleep.

'Yes, you saved them,' said Samantha. She gestured to the bag of mamba on the side table. Charlie took it and gave it to the police, who then left.

When Lambert woke to a security guard outside his room, he was baffled. 'I didn't remember anything,' he said. 'When they told me, I was embarrassed.' He was not very happy about losing his bag of mamba.

'You seen this about Scottish John?' asked Pam. There was a story in the *Shropshire Star* reporting that John Patrick had been charged with raping a thirteen-year-old girl in his tent near the river in April. She had apparently come across his dog while on a trip to a supermarket from her care home and had been looking for its owner. Police later found her 'shivering' and 'incoherent'.

'Thank God we didn't let him in,' said Mike. While they were talking, the police arrived with Lionel who had been found at his mum's house in Wales. He swaggered in as stylish as ever, a bandana round his head like Johnny Depp.

'Same room, Lionel?' asked Jacki, smiling.

'New one,' he replied.

The next day he walked into the hotel with a surfboard. A local charity shop had been putting things out for people to take. He was always hoarding things. Another day he brought in a tennis racket, then a petrol can, which they found slightly worrying and had to get from him, not easy when his temper was like a light switch.

He didn't last long. Shortly after coming back, Lionel was in such a state, becoming so confused and aggressive, that they had to call a psychiatrist from the hospital. Within ten minutes of examining him, the doctor had Lionel sectioned.

Mike and Charlie stood at the door to see him off, feeling sad. 'Thank you,' Lionel said to them calmly, as he stepped into the ambulance.

19.

Monday, 22 June 2020

Mark Chapman was sitting under the twisty black locust tree outside the hotel, dressed in camouflage with his medal on his chest, straw trilby perched on his head, strumming a guitar some-one had donated and singing 'Moonshadow'. He loved Cat Stevens and would often start the day with a rendition of 'Morning Has Broken' while bidding good morning to passers-by.

It was a balmy night and gathered round him were Dave Pritchard, Stokesy, Shaggy, Martin and Michael Lambert. 'I liked the music but couldn't understand what he was singing,' said Lambert. 'I think he made up the words.' Occasionally, Shaggy joined in with a mouth organ that Pam had given him.

'Awright, soldier?' Mark would ask, tipping his hat, as each one joined the group.

At his side was Bev, who had arrived a few weeks earlier and he knew from the streets. A couple of years younger than him at fifty-three and a grandmother of eight, she had a soft pleasant face, long grey hair in a ponytail, and they had become such good friends that she called him 'Hubby' and he called her 'Wifey'.

Bev came across like a friendly pub landlady – in one rendition of her life she had been – and in a hotel of characters had quickly established herself as one of the most colourful. Every morning

Mike, Charlie and Bev.

she would come and sit on the doorstep in her dressing gown with a cup of tea and a cigarette, greeting everyone with 'How you doing, babs?'

She had, she told Charlie, spent fifteen years as a taxi driver – 'I was Shrewsbury's first lady taxi driver to work nights back in 1997,' she said. 'I liked the fact there were different people, different stories every hour.'

She had got into taxi driving following in the footsteps of her husband, who she started dating after his taxi picked her up from a Wham! concert when she was sixteen. 'I loved George Michael!' she exclaimed. 'That "Careless Whisper" gets me every time.'

Unfortunately, her husband was not as caring as he had seemed. 'I got hit a lot,' she said. Sometimes she even called the police. But she ended up staying fourteen years, 'for my children'.

The violence caused her anxiety attacks, which she tried to treat with alcohol. 'I found comfort in the bottle, which is the wrong way but the way it is,' she said. 'I would wake up with a mouth like Gandhi's flip-flop.' Unable to carry on taxi driving because of the drinking, she had gone on to work as an escort under the name Geneva and as a pub landlady. Eventually they had what she called 'a messy divorce', but she managed to bring up two sons, who were now in their thirties, and one of whom had eight children of his own.

At one point Bev's benefits were stopped so she couldn't pay her rent and the house was repossessed when the landlord failed to pay the mortgage. Just like that, she found herself on the streets. 'It's not something you ever expect,' she said. 'And when you are homeless you start noticing there are empty properties all over the place, which doesn't seem right.'

It was hard to understand why her sons hadn't taken in their own mother, particularly as the eldest was a social worker and the other a stay-at-home dad. 'They are lovely boys,' she shrugged. 'They just didn't have room.'

Her new home became the loading bay behind the police station – a place she had chosen because she preferred to be on her own and it was safer with CCTV. 'The police even used to bring me a cup of tea sometimes,' she said.

She had, she said, stayed there three years, going to the Ark to wash and eat, and bedding down in her sleeping bag when it got dark. 'People watch out for each other on the streets,' she said, 'but I kept myself to myself.' When the pandemic hit, she didn't have a clue until someone from the Ark came and told her she was being taken in. 'You don't get to watch telly on the streets,' she laughed, 'and I didn't have one of those smarty phones.'

Initially she was taken to the Travelodge in Battlefield, which she found 'very noisy – full of young people and fights', so much so that some of the homeless guests dubbed it Beirut. It was also far from town, in an industrial park near fields where one of Britain's bloodiest battles had taken place in 1403 – the Battle of Shrewsbury between King Henry IV and Harry Hotspur's rebels, when the sky was said to have rained black with arrows.

She was delighted to be moved to the Prince Rupert. 'It's a beautiful place with lots of history. Sometimes I dropped people off there in my taxi and I always wanted to see inside. Never in my wildest dreams did I think it would become my home. Sunday roast was amazing and afternoon tea and that thick pile carpet, and such a comfortable bed for my bad back after the cold hard concrete. It makes me feel like a million dollars.'

Bev liked to go to bed early in her pyjamas with a bottle of Magners cider and watch an episode of *Murder, She Wrote*. 'I love me Jessica Fletcher,' she said. She could also watch Arnold Schwarzenegger in *The Terminator* over and over.

When her Universal Credit payment came through each month, she would buy flowers for her room. She loved dancing. She and Mark would go into each other's room and find Magic FM on their phones. They loved songs like 'Brothers in Arms' and 'The Show Must Go On', and would dance, him on vodka, her on cider, though she did worry about his frequent falls. 'He would fall over his own foot,' she said.

Mike found her a welcome addition, as a grown-up who could impose some control on some of the others – at least until there was a fire in her room, something she claimed she knew nothing about.

Looking down from his third-floor balcony, the stars above and digital clock glinting on the Market Hall tower, which by night looked strangely beautiful, even if by day it was a sixties eyesore that had little connection with the ancient town, Mike smiled at the scene.

They had, as Lenny from the council had observed, become 'like a family', even if rather a dysfunctional one. 'If one of them didn't turn up for tea, others would notice, whereas on the street they could just disappear.'

From their rooms on the second floor, Charlie and Jacki also looked out of their windows. 'I love them,' said Charlie. Jacki rolled her eyes. 'I'm not going to say it, I'm not going to say it …' she laughed.

Earlier that day she had finally gone to the hospital, after almost two months hobbling around on her ankle. A doctor had X-rayed it and told her it had been broken and, having been left so long with her walking on it, might need to be broken again and reset. Fortunately, it turned out to have healed okay.

All three wondered how much longer this would continue. Shops had been allowed to reopen the previous week and around the rest of Europe, restaurants and hotels were once again open, as well as hairdressers, nail bars and cinemas. In the UK, coronavirus infections and hospital admissions continued to decrease and daily deaths had fallen to 130. That day the government had announced a further easing of lockdown and from 4 July, hotels, pubs, restaurants and beauty salons would be able to reopen.

There were lots of preparations needed to make the hotel Covid-safe for guests, as well as all the deep cleaning to remove the stains from carpets and the smell of smoke from rooms, and buying replacement pillows and duvets.

Many of the homeless were already asking what would happen to them. Mike didn't know but couldn't imagine sending them back out on the streets. They could be very frustrating with their overflowing baths, their fights and stealing from one another, their drug-taking when he was trying to give them an opportunity. As he was contemplating all this, he heard yelling – Julie was chasing round the churchyard after Andy, having spotted him with Hannah.

They'd been kicked when they were down throughout their lives, he thought, he couldn't do the same.

*　*　*

When his son James asked what it was like looking after the homeless guests, Mike would tell him, 'Remember that Burt Reynolds
film *The Longest Yard* where prisoners took on the guards at football? That's what it's like, taking on a group of hardened convicts
and shaping a team.'

That day they had played for real. The hotel staff and the various support workers had been looking for things to occupy the
guests and distract them from more nefarious pastimes. On several
occasions they'd held skipping competitions outside the front, one
of which had left Wendy from the Ark limping for days. One
evening the council had organised a quiz night, with questions on
the hotel, its ghosts, celebrities and current affairs. They were
astonished at how much some of the homeless knew – Derek
Tyrer turned out to be a real authority on politics. The winner
had been Martin the boxer, while Titch came second and could
barely contain his excitement. In true Titch fashion, the £10
Tesco voucher he got as a prize, he immediately spent on others,
buying Stokesy a banana milkshake.

Then Mike had suggested five-a-side football. He had checked
with the council that they could legally play as a family bubble
now that restrictions had been relaxed. They had been trying to
arrange it for weeks. Their guests would enthusiastically agree at
dinner the night before and they would set a time of 2 p.m. to meet
in the lobby the next day, then no one would appear. They would
wait half an hour or an hour, before walking round the rooms
trying to rally people to no avail, then wander round town looking
for them and finally give up.

It had taken four attempts to get them all to turn up. Even then
no one could find Michael Lambert, who was still recovering from
his mamba attack, or Shaggy. 'I prefer fishing,' he explained afterwards.

Finally that afternoon they had set off to Quarry Park by the
river. It was a scorching hot day. Walking them through town,

bare-chested with yellow bibs, carrying cones on their shoulders, they looked a motley crew, all of them talking loudly as if they were deaf. 'It must have looked like a prison day out,' said Gabriella, who was trying to marshal them all.

On the way they passed a disturbance near the statue of Robert Clive, better known as Clive of India and after Darwin perhaps Shrewsbury's most famous son. In military dress uniform, head up, hair tied back, he looked an imperious figure, as befitted someone who had almost singlehandedly secured the beginnings of the British Empire.

For decades people had walked past barely giving the statue a second glance, as with statues across the nation. But the previous few weeks had seen protests around the UK. They had started off as Black Lives Matter demonstrations to protest racism following the horrific murder of George Floyd, a black security guard killed in Minneapolis by a white police officer who kneeled on his neck for more than nine minutes while Floyd lay face-down in hand-

cuffs pleading that he couldn't breathe. The video had gone viral, even among the guests of the Prince Rupert, most of whom had little time for the police.

The demonstrations against racism had turned into statue wars as protesters in Bristol toppled the bronze figure of slave trader Edward Colston in the town centre on 7 June and threw it into the harbour. Activists had called for the removal of all figures who had prospered from slavery and colonialism, while others vowed to defend them. Even Churchill had to be boarded up in Parliament Square.

Clive of India, whose bronze likeness also stood outside the Foreign Office in London, was among those roundly denounced. In Shrewsbury, almost ten thousand people signed a petition declaring he must go, arguing that he had played a key role in Britain's colonial domination of India and in looting its resources as an agent of the East India Company.

In fact, Clive was controversial even in his own lifetime. A delinquent youth from nearby Market Drayton who was expelled by three schools and ran a local protection racket with a gang of youths, he was eventually packed off to India at the age of eighteen by his exasperated father to be a clerk in the East India Company. Caught up in hostility between English and French empire build-ers, he joined the company's private army and despite having no military training ended up commanding important victories over the French then toppling the French-backed ruler of Bengal, India's wealthiest province.

Clive became the first British governor of Bengal, where he was blamed by many for the Great Famine of 1770 that saw a third of its population die. In the process he amassed a considerable fortune, which on his return he used to buy up large tracts of Shropshire and to become MP for Shrewsbury and subsequently its mayor, despite widespread accusations of corruption. He was also an opium addict who suffered manic depression.

'A drug addict with mental health problems and a record of theft and violence,' chuckled Martin. 'Sounds like one of us!'

Clive ended up taking his own life in 1774, by then such a reviled figure that his body was buried in an unmarked grave without a plaque. Only much later, when all was forgotten, were statues of him made, such as that erected in Shrewsbury's market square in 1860. Now two groups of rival demonstrators were fighting over it. The small clutch of his protectors included Nick Griffin, former leader of the far-right British National Party. Insisting they were standing up for the town's heritage, Griffin said: 'He's been here longer than any of us.'

'Clive must go!' retorted the Black Lives Matter protesters. 'Clive's a racist! Boris Johnson's a racist!'

Bemused, the Prince Rupert guests left them to it and continued to the Quarry. The children's playground and the Dingle were still taped off, but the grass overlooking the river was crowded with people sitting on blankets or playing games, enjoying the sunshine and freedom of meeting outside.

The group divided into two teams, one captained by Mike, who before lockdown used to play football every Friday with what he described as 'middle-aged dads with fond memories of how we used to play in our twenties and determined to keep playing until our knees give in'. The other side was captained by Martin the boxer, with Charlie as his goalie. The referee was Antony Haycock, a tall man with big soulful brown eyes and legs calcified by years of heroin abuse, whose brother had died from alcoholism. Titch proved to be one of the most enthusiastic players.

'It was a great day,' said Martin. 'There had been a lot of fights in the hotel but that little game of footie brought us all back together.'

Somehow Dave Pritchard heard about the game and turned up drunk and shirtless, swaying and clutching a large can of beer.

Jacki was shading from the heat under a tree with Pam and he started chasing them.

Desperate to play, he begged, 'Can I come on, can I come on?' until Mike let him into his side. It wasn't clear that he was an asset. Running round like a maniac, he kept kicking the ball to the other side. At one point he fired at goal. Charlie made a great save, diving at his feet and he went flying over her.

After an hour, the scores were level at 5–5, so it went down to penalties. The first nine of them went in and then it was Mike's turn. His side were 5–4 down and he was taking the final penalty. Against Charlie. She dived to her right and saved, cheering wildly.

'I'm never going to be allowed to forget that,' bemoaned Mike afterwards.

Back at the hotel, Chez and Christian, the quiet Poles, were at reception looking distressed. The council had told them that they had to leave because as immigrants they were classed as 'no recourse to public funds', so were ineligible for government support. The good thing about Everyone In had been that all the normal rules around needing local connections had been dropped, yet now it seemed everyone did not mean everyone. 'That's terrible,' said Charlie. She wanted them to stay: they were so little trouble, and they kept their rooms so nicely, even with little mats by the side of their beds for slippers. But the council wouldn't pay for them any longer.

'I can't go against the council's wishes,' Mike told her. No one seemed to know what would happen to them.

They couldn't understand. 'Have we done something wrong?' Christian kept asking.

Outside, the music around the locust tree that evening went on late. Eventually Mike shouted from his window, 'Mark, you have a beautiful voice but it's 2 a.m. and we're trying to sleep!'

20.

Tuesday, 30 June 2020

All over town there was hammering and repainting, as cafés, restaurants, hair salons and bars got ready to reopen. Finally a feeling of hope and new beginnings had begun to replace the fear of catching Covid and the monotony of what had seemed like an endless lockdown. On Butcher Row, staff in the Libertine cocktail bar, the Bull Inn and Philpotts famous sandwich bar were all hard at work, scrubbing, cleaning and setting out tables that had been stacked away. The same was happening in shops that hadn't yet reopened.

Lockdown was finally ending. From that Saturday, people would actually be allowed to go out for a drink or a coffee, have a haircut and meet friends in a restaurant, activities once taken for granted that now felt so exciting. Newspapers were full of articles with titles like 'Are You Ready for Small Talk Saturday?' and fashion shoots of floaty dresses and high heels to replace the lockdown uniform of jogging pants and slippers.

Glorious organ music could be heard streaming out of St Alkmund's and Mike wandered over to greet the vicar. His team were also busy sweeping and cleaning, ready for its first service on Sunday after the church's longest closure in 1,100 years, having stayed functioning even during the Black Death. More recently they had survived near bankruptcy when the church's bells had to be sold off in 1990. These had summoned the faithful for centuries and rang out after victory over Napoleon at Waterloo, but had been threatening to bring down its soaring tower. They ended up in a church in Honolulu. This was much to the relief of hotel guests who often used to complain to Mike about the noise. The church had since gone through a £1 million renovation, becoming one of the first to install solar panels on its roof, cleverly hidden behind the parapets and providing all its energy needs. The vicar said he was delighted to be welcoming a congregation again, though no singing would be allowed.

Inside the Prince Rupert, however, the guests were worried. They all watched the news on TV. The hotel still had twenty-five residents and for the last couple of weeks many had been coming to Mike to ask if they would be thrown out.

He assured everyone that this would not happen but some had already packed their cases and bags. 'We were really worried,' said Bev. 'I'd gone from doorways to lying on a comfy bed, watching TV and having a bathroom next door where I could bath every night. It was like a dream and I was scared of waking up.'

When Mike asked the council what would happen to the homeless if he reopened, they told him they would have to disperse them. The number of people in temporary accommodation had doubled during Covid, with many sofa-surfers forced to move out of the homes of friends. 'It was as if everyone we ever had on our list had all come through at once,' said Tim Compton. There were not enough places in Shrewsbury, so some would be sent to Wolverhampton or Birmingham.

Mike was horrified. How could they send away someone like Bev who was so happy to be back in touch with her family – her eighth grandchild Henry had just been born and she had gone from the hotel at six in the morning to look after the other seven the day her daughter-in-law went in to hospital to give birth. 'I don't know who was the most shattered!' she laughed. If they sent her to a Travelodge miles away in Wolverhampton, she'd simply go back on the streets.

What about Titch? Just the other day Mike had paid him £5 to clean the windows and Titch had disappeared up the road, returning with a huge grin and five slips of paper. He had bought Charlie, Jacki and Mike a £1 bet each on the FA Cup final. 'He has a heart of gold,' said Mike. 'They are all marshmallows underneath.' Even Derek Tyrer had surprised Mike by asking if he could lend him a book to read. Not a great reader himself, the only thing Mike could find was Tony Blair's memoir, but the quiz night had revealed Dave's interest in politics and he seemed quite happy with it.

The three of them sat down over coffee and discussed what to do. They all felt that their mission had been to look after their guests until they had a home to go to. What they had expected to be a few weeks had turned into a hundred days, but they couldn't abandon them.

'If we break that pledge now, it would break the hard-won trust that they have developed in us and maybe lose their trust in humanity for the rest of their lives,' said Mike. 'These are some of the most vulnerable and misunderstood members of society and it would be like a guillotine coming down on them.

'Basically, the choice is everyone has to go or stay – we can't have both,' he added. 'If we have paying guests, then the focus will have to be on them.'

Mike had visions of telling people like Mark Chapman, Shaggy and Michael Lambert that they would have to use the back entrance.

To be honest, he also didn't know if the hotel would have much business. Shrewsbury Flower Show, the food festival, Let's Rock, the cartoon festival and the annual army reunion had all been cancelled. Would people want to holiday or would they be fearful? And if they could travel, wouldn't they go abroad to countries that were doing better at curbing the virus? Also, there had been little information from the government about how it would work. Rules for reopening included two-metre social distancing and sanitising surfaces between use, but it wasn't clear how to implement this in a hotel with all its comings and goings.

Mike sat in his office and pondered what to do. He still had a business to run after all. Charlie and Jacki had no doubts – they might have been working seven days a week and often eighteen-hour days doing all sorts of things they never imagined, and far from their own loved ones, but they didn't want to go back to being a normal hotel. They felt like a family, however dysfunctional, and wanted to carry on doing the same.

Not everyone would be pleased. The hotel rented out part of its premises to shops and a restaurant and one of his tenants had already called saying, 'I really appreciate what you are doing but how much longer have you got them for?'

Mike was polite but furious. Afterwards he wished he had said, 'I am waiting for Chester Zoo to reopen, then obviously they will take them.' He was beginning to understand the discrimination. The manager of the shop across the road also contacted him to say she was worried about the safety of her girls.

The Ark was ending its involvement with the hotel as it was reopening its day centre, to the delight of Charlie who had sometimes clashed with Wendy, like two lionesses protecting their broods. What Mike did not know was whether the council would continue paying for the homeless. Some local authorities had already said that as soon as lockdown was over, everyone would need to leave the hotels.

The daily £85 stipend they received for each guest was enough to keep paying the bills and the few staff he had kept on, but it wasn't enough to pay his mortgage and lease. By staying open, he had forgone government benefits other than business rates relief and pay for those staff he had furloughed.

Before he could decide anything, he had one key call to make – to his bank manager. His Swedish mortgage lender Handelsbanken was impressed by what the hotel had been doing and had allowed him a mortgage holiday, which had been a real lifeline. Without it he would have had to close and take government grants and a Covid loan.

'Really?' was the bank manager's reaction, when Mike told him he was thinking of not reopening. 'But we will support you with whatever decision you take,' he added.

As he mulled what to do, Mike's eye was caught by the portrait of Prince Rupert, the famed warrior who had won barely any battles. The tall long-haired prince had stayed in the Royalist town of Shrewsbury in 1644 with his white poodle Boy while rallying forces for his uncle King Charles I against Oliver Cromwell and the Roundheads fighting to oust him in the English Civil War.

Prince Rupert.

Rupert was the son of Charles's sister Elizabeth Stuart and Frederick V, Elector Palatine of the Rhine, who had become king of Bohemia in November 1619, shortly before Rupert's birth, but had been toppled within months. They fled to The Hague, where they were often referred to mockingly as the Winter King and Queen. After becoming a soldier when he was a teenager, Rupert had come to England in 1642 at the age of twenty-three to fight for his uncle Charles. The king had alienated his subjects and Parliament with his arrogant behaviour, ruling without calling Parliament for more than a decade, as well as angering the Church of England by taking a Catholic wife.

Charles appointed Rupert commander of his cavalry and then general of the entire Royalist army, to the displeasure of some of the king's advisers, who disapproved of what they saw as the young man's reckless cavalry charges. Battles raged across the land and towns changed hands. Shrewsbury fell to Cromwell's forces in 1645 after a Parliamentarian sympathiser let them through the medieval town walls at St Mary's Water Gate, which later became known as Traitor's Gate.

Six years of Civil War culminated in triumph for Cromwell, who had somehow transformed himself from East Anglian farmer turned MP with no military experience to the king's greatest military threat. Prince Rupert was banished and Charles was captured by the Scots and handed over to Parliament. In 1649, the king was put on public trial for high treason and executed outside Banqueting House on Whitehall, the grisliest end of any English king. Cromwell would eventually replace him as head of state, becoming the first commoner to rule the country.

The resulting republic or Commonwealth lasted just eleven years and in 1660 the king's son returned from exile in France to be crowned Charles II. His cousin Prince Rupert became commander of his navy, going on to lose more battles against the Dutch. These were difficult times: the Great Plague of 1665–6 killed almost a quarter of London's population and was followed by the Great Fire that raged for five days and destroyed many of its buildings, devastating St Paul's Cathedral. Before his death in 1682, Rupert spent his final years as governor of Windsor Castle. Mike had recently read that he fed the homeless from the castle's back door.

It felt like a sign. Mike's family would probably think he was crazy but his mind was made up. They would continue as a hotel for the homeless, whether or not the council paid.

'Yay!' whooped Charlie when he told them. Jacki simply smiled.

21.

Friday, 10 July 2020

It felt as if the whole town had gone wild. 'It's pandemonium out there,' said Mike to Charlie and Jacki. Looking out from his terrace, they could see people everywhere, lads peeing up walls, drunken yobs swaying on their doorstep, vomiting on the street.

Every night had been like that since bars and restaurants had reopened the previous weekend, the so-called Super Saturday, when people were released from eleven weeks of hibernation. Police vans kept coming and going. With nightclubs and discos still closed, everyone gathered in pubs. The Bull Inn next door was staying open till 2 a.m., its customers singing in the beer garden. Derek Tyrer ventured across the road to the Libertine and came back with a colourful cocktail decorated with paper umbrellas. But most of the homeless complained they couldn't sleep because of all the noise.

Such scenes in town centres all over the country terrified those familiar with the history of pandemics. Although Covid cases had fallen to six hundred a day, the lowest figure since the first wave in March, some were reminded of celebrations in the summer of 1918 after the first wave of the last great pandemic, the Spanish flu, ended. Instead a far deadlier mutated strain had emerged that was taken round the world by ships of soldiers. That autumn the death rate rocketed, no longer just young and old, killing many otherwise healthy twenty-five- to thirty-five-year-olds. Now, once again, people seemed to be celebrating the end of the pandemic instead of preparing for the hard winter that was inevitably coming. Far from reining people in, the government was encouraging fraternising: Chancellor Rishi Sunak had announced an 'Eat Out to Help Out' scheme through which people could enjoy half-price meals subsidised by the government.

One night a policeman came to the Prince Rupert about 12.30 a.m., pointing at the scenes of debauchery in despair. 'I can't do anything, I've got no back-up,' he said.

'Yes, you have here,' replied Mike. 'We have an army of people ready to help.'

Thank God he hadn't reopened. How could guests survive all this noise and chaos? He would have had to refund their money.

The council had agreed to continue funding the homeless at the Prince Rupert and sent them a bunch of new arrivals. One of the first was Robert Ligus, who had just come out of jail. 'I know that name,' said Pam. 'It's unusual.' She Googled and discovered that he was the son of Robin Ligus, a notorious local serial killer, a burglar who had killed the people he burgled. Robert was also a burglar and had appeared in court 40 times for 78 offences, most recently for stealing a coat.

He was a tiny guy and extremely polite, though he complained about the food. 'We got better food in prison,' he said.

'Well, you don't have to eat it,' Charlie replied.

He might have been a prolific burglar but shortly after he moved in, Samantha stole his trainers and phone. Within two weeks he had gone.

The chaos outside seemed to infect the Prince Rupert. Antony Haycock, who had refereed the football, got into a fight on Butcher Row with another guest whose girlfriend had apparently refused to pay for some drugs. The man started waving a broken bottle at him and Antony whipped out a Stanley knife. Both were moved out.

The hotel felt different – the new guests were more transient and much younger, and Mike felt 'treated it like Club Med from day one'. Up till then most of their guests had been rough sleepers and very challenging, and he and his staff had been winging it, trying to work out how to help them. But they had been more of their age, so easier to talk to. The new arrivals were a younger generation who tended to be sofa-surfers, victims of the country's lack of affordable housing, and the chemistry completely changed. It was, he thought, like going from playing Real Madrid every week to Derby County.

Among the new guests was Brendan, who waltzed in with a shock of peroxided hair, black-and-white houndstooth trousers and what he called his 'big boy' – a power iron for his clothes. His room was soon chaotic, with stuff everywhere. 'I don't know why people think gays are neat,' he said.

Brendan had never lived on the streets. He used to work in Tesco, but they kept cutting his hours because of Covid so he had quit, and then he was thrown out by the guy he lived with who he said 'kept abusing me behind me back'. He called the council and told them he had nowhere to go.

They had placed him initially in the White House in Telford, which he said was 'awful, full of druggies'. Then the Travelodge in Battlefield, where 'they just gave us pot noodles' and, like Bev who'd been there too, he complained there were 'too many druggies and fights'.

'I don't like druggies,' he said. 'I just smoke a bit of mamba and spliff and drink beer. It makes me feel chilled for an hour, not like I have to deal with every Tom, Dick and Harry. Then I get the munchies …' He would flounce in and out and was often in tears. Twice he told them he had taken an overdose and they had to call an ambulance. As before, such crises always came just as Charlie and Jacki were making dinner.

Several of the new arrivals did not look homeless. A twenty-something called Carl came in wearing £120 trainers and had a

£3,000 bike, while a pair of young men in skinny jeans and wraparound designer sunglasses arrived, trashed their room and left.

Most challenging was Jade, in her twenties with hair like rat-tails, who arrived lugging a huge ghetto blaster and said 'yam' all the time, a Wolverhampton expression short for 'you am'. 'One of yours,' Mike would tease Jacki.

'Yam don't know what I need,' Jade would complain. 'Yam just a wonderful world.'

'She's going to be trouble,' said Mike on her first day, when on the way back from the shops he saw her struggling with an enormous pack of lager cans.

Sure enough that night music started blasting out of her room and would be thumping night after night till 1 a.m. or whenever he could stop it. Large groups would gather there, including Chris Bennett, Samantha, Antony Haycock before he was moved, as well as Brendan and Natalie. The security guards refused to go in to disperse them, saying there were 'too many people'.

Most of their homeless guests had been male and they had always worried about relationships developing with the few female residents, given how vulnerable many were. Those who had arrived as couples tended to be tempestuous, such as Hannah and Neil, Andy and Julie, and Tracy and Randolph, the mood often depending on whether or not they had scored drugs.

Some of the single men complained they were lonely. Occasionally the staff saw them swiping on Tinder in the Darwin. It didn't take Jade long before she had got involved with Martin the boxer, as well as a recently arrived young man they called Liverpool Steve, a father of six who had been kicked out of his house by his wife and ordered by police not to see her.

One day while cleaning his room, manager Charlie emptied his bathroom bin, in which there was a tied blue carrier bag. When Liverpool Steve found out he was furious. The bag turned out to have contained what he said was £600 worth of drugs. Titch was so interested that he went through the rubbish trying to find it, but to no avail.

Another new arrival was Stacey, who told them she had worked as a travel agent. Initially Mike thought she was part of a new wave of people who had lost their jobs because of Covid. But it turned out that this was her fifth hotel, as she had caused trouble everywhere she went. She started drinking a lot, getting lippy with the guards and demanding a roast lunch after food was all finished.

Then there was Selina, who had dreadlocks and a colostomy bag that was always leaking, causing everyone to start complaining about the smell. She retreated to a cardboard box outside the hotel, like a wounded animal, only her head poking out, and began making strange noises. Eventually the police and an ambulance came, but she wouldn't let anyone near.

In the end it was one of their long-time guests Julie who persuaded her to get in. 'Don't mob-handle her or she will go mad and bite you,' she told the police. 'Selina, if I get rid of everyone will you get into the ambulance?' she asked.

Julie persuaded the other homeless watching on to disperse.

'I want that giraffe,' said Selina, pointing to a display in the gift shop opposite.

'If you get into the ambulance, I promise I will bring it to the hospital,' said Julie.

'Uh-oh – I think I know how she plans to get that giraffe,' said Charlie to Jacki.

'I love you,' Selina said to Julie as she lay inside the ambulance.

Later they heard she discharged herself and ended up back at the Ark.

*　*　*

Plenty of the old crowd were still there and they gathered in the Darwin at the end of July for Titch's thirty-second birthday party, to which he arrived sharply dressed in a black suit like a mini-gangster. Charlie had cooked a fabulous Victoria sponge with four layers, sandwiched with buttercream, iced and decorated all over with jelly babies, dolly mixture and lollipops. 'It's my first ever cake,' said Titch as he huffed and puffed to blow out the candles. When he tore off the wrappings of his present to find a shirt from his beloved Manchester United, he cried.

22.

Wednesday, 12 August 2020

Throughout lockdown people often talked about the joy of waking to birdsong for the first time rather than the usual hum of traffic, planes or the daily hubbub. A particular favourite was the cuckoo, its distinctive call heralding spring. In reality cuckoos are the bad guys of the bird world, so-called 'brood parasites' who never raise their own offspring. Instead they lay their eggs, one at a time, in the nests of other birds while they are off feeding, often gobbling down one of the host eggs to replace with one of their own. The nest owners are fooled into raising the infant cuckoo and when the chick hatches, it often ejects the host bird's own eggs or other chicks to claim the nest for itself.

Being 'cuckooed' was how several of the Prince Rupert guests had lost their homes. The first time Charlie and Jacki heard the expression was when a young woman edged into the hotel, her back to the wall, crying. With her long wavy hair and hurt-filled eyes, she seemed a walking embodiment of Edvard Munch's painting *The Scream*.

Her name was Charlene, but had quickly become known as Big Charlie to differentiate between Charlie the manager, as she was tall as Charlie was petite. She had, she told them, been 'cuckooed'. A man had befriended her, she explained, and wheedled his way into her affections, eventually moving in. He turned out to be a drug dealer and started using her flat as a base until in the end she left.

Those looking for someone to cuckoo generally identify lonely and vulnerable people and target them. Charlene was ideal. She had been abused by her father from an early age, but been told by her mother that she was the bad girl. Later her mother left her dad and remarried, but by then she had got in with the wrong crowd and into drugs, moving quickly from weed to heroin and crack pipes.

She was a simple girl, eager to please, desperate for someone to love her, and she had two sets of twins who had all been taken away. 'I was pushed from pillar to post,' she said. 'People were always taking advantage of me.' She had lived on the streets in London then Telford, after which she had moved to Shrewsbury, finding it 'nicer and safer' until the drug dealer ousted her from her own flat.

The day after Charlene was brought in, she disappeared. Hannah, who had talked to her the night before, was worried. 'I could tell she was in a mad place so I put a note under her door saying, you are loved and if you ever need someone to talk to, I am here.'

Charlene had taken the note and gone to the Welsh bridge, from where she called Hannah, crying. 'She said she was on the bridge and had nothing to live for and was going to jump,' said Hannah. 'I was telling her not to, there's always hope.'

A police officer eventually found her and managed to lead her away. Shaggy, who had been watching from his hangout near the bridge, said she really looked like she was going to do herself in. Back at the Prince Rupert, Charlie and Jacki sat with her and persuaded her to give them a chance to help her.

Within weeks, Charlene would be transformed. 'They took me from the dark to the light,' she said. She went from being terrified to helping out with cleaning, calling people for dinner, and going and introducing herself to new arrivals. 'I like to show them the ropes,' she smiled.

For the first time she began to have hope. 'I'd like a nice house, a bungalow with a garden I could do up nice and sit in, with flowers in pots, and maybe have a poodle,' she said. 'I want to be a carer, to look after people the way I would like to have been.'

Charlene was not their only guest to have been cuckooed. Later a pudgy man called Ivor from Basingstoke would arrive with a much younger associate, who they assumed was his grandson. When they asked, the younger man laughed and lifted up his shirt to show his vest – he was armed and explained he was a police escort. Ivor's home had been taken over by a drug dealer who had moved in and started using it as a base to store and distribute drugs. Unlike Charlene, his home had been taken forcibly, the dealer walking in with a knife and announcing, 'I am going to use this house from now on.'

Gabriella was lifting the plastic bag from the bin in Chris Bennett's room and tying it when she felt a sharp prick on her hand. 'Ow!' she exclaimed.

There was a used needle in the bag and it had pricked her under the nail of her middle finger. She was used to guests leaving needles lying around in their rooms, but they all had sharps boxes to dispose of used ones so she had not expected one to be in the bin bag.

'What's happened?' asked Kim.

'Don't be angry but I may or may not have been pricked by a heroin needle,' she said.

'Oh my God!' gasped Kim.

Gabriella did not want to tell anyone but eventually was persuaded by Kim to tell her mum. Charlie was livid. 'I couldn't believe this had happened,' she said. 'They all know to use the sharps box and Chris has two daughters of his own.'

Gabriella refused to be cross with Chris. 'I'm sure he wouldn't have done it intentionally,' she said. 'I don't know what state of mind he was in when he left it there.'

Charlie called 111, who advised her to wash Gabriella's finger well then take her to the hospital for a hepatitis test. At the Royal Shrewsbury, Covid restrictions were still in place and everywhere seemed to be cordoned off with red 'No Entry' signs. Charlie was not allowed in and had to wait in the car park.

Inside the hospital, Gabriella was left waiting for more than two hours before a doctor gave her a hepatitis injection and did a blood test. Charlie sat in her car stewing and Googling hepatitis on her phone. One of its possible side effects was infertility. For this to happen after all Gabriella had been through to recover her health seemed so unfair.

Other guests were furious with him, but Chris Bennett refused to go for a test. 'You have daughters of your own. Don't you feel guilty?' asked Charlie.

'I was absolutely devastated,' he said later. 'I always put my needles in a box. The only people who did gear in my room were Lambert and Shaggy, so it must have been them.'

Gabriella's brothers were also extremely angry. 'Maybe this job is too risky,' Callum told Charlie. Gabriella was having none of it. Though she missed having her mum at home to look after her and Fraser, and it was hard work juggling cleaning up after the homeless and keeping house for her younger brother, working with such troubled souls had helped tame her own demons. 'Of course being pricked was scary,' she said. 'But doing this work has really brought out my confidence. Before, I couldn't walk through town without having a panic attack.'

'Chris has definitely got hepatitis,' Titch said helpfully.

23.

Monday, 17 August 2020

Perhaps because they weren't used to having their own doors, the homeless guests were always losing their room keys. It was one of Mike's biggest frustrations, along with all the spoons that went missing. 'After the pandemic there will be Prince Rupert keys all over Shrewsbury,' he sighed.

Whenever Derek Tyrer lost his, he told them, 'He'll let me find it when he wants to.'

'Who will?' they asked.

'God,' he replied.

In the end they always had to give him a new one. Michael Lambert had lost his key one too many times. Rather than ask for a new one, being a burglar he tried to take the lock apart. When that didn't work, he enlisted the help of Stokesy, who barged against the door to force it open and broke the frame. Titch helpfully told Mike, who was furious, and they had to inform the council.

Lambert knew it was almost certainly the end of his nine lives. 'I let you down again,' he said.

He desperately wanted his own place. 'Being with so many druggies was making it hard for me to be clean,' he said. Shaggy kept stealing his methadone, which was supposed to stop withdrawal, so he had ended up doing heroin again. He stared at the encrusted scars and purple blotches on his calves from circulation problems caused by the drugs and worried he would lose his legs.

Moving on was not so easy. One reason for there being so many homeless was the lack of affordable social housing: its availability had decreased dramatically in recent years. In the 1970s it's estimated that nearly a third of homes across the UK were council houses, but since the 1980s, when Prime Minister Margaret Thatcher's Housing Act launched a 'Right to Buy' scheme, numbers had plummeted. The Act enabled council tenants to purchase their homes at reduced prices, while at the same time limiting the amount of money councils could borrow for capital expenditure.

The number of new affordable homes being built had decreased, causing social housing in England to fall from a peak of 5.5 million homes in 1981 to less than 4 million by 2020. At the same time, need had increased enormously, for not only did the population rise by ten million, wages did not keep pace with house prices. More and more people were left having to rely on the private rented sector. Caught between the rising costs of renting privately and falling housing benefit payments, many had been left struggling to pay rent.

A parliamentary report released in July 2020 by the Housing, Communities and Local Government Committee* found that fewer than 7,000 new homes had been built in England in 2019 for social rent, compared to the minimum 90,000 that were needed, and that one in every 200 people were without a home. It described the housing system as 'broken'.

Anti-poverty charities such as the Joseph Rowntree Foundation argued that this housing crisis was one of the biggest

---

* 'Building More Social Housing', report by Housing, Communities and Local Government Committee, 20 July 2020.

drivers of the UK's high levels of poverty. 'It's disgraceful that one of the world's most affluent countries has such high rates of homelessness,' said Darren Baxter, head of its housing policy division. 'Rough sleepers are the most visible form and draw the most public empathy, but they are just the tip of the iceberg – homelessness is a whole spectrum and there are millions of people living long periods in small cramped temporary accommodation, sofa-surfing, or inadequate housing not fit for human habitation.'

In Shropshire, like most of the country, there was a shortage of council housing and able-bodied single white men like Michael Lambert came lowest on the list. Every council had its own system and in Shropshire eligible applicants were assigned a band, such as platinum, gold or silver, depending on priority, and they could bid for properties in that category on a computer system called HomePoint. New properties were released on HomePoint every Wednesday. In Lambert's case, he was not even bronze.

'The council would not give me accommodation because I had got into debt before and lost a place so they said I had intentionally made myself homeless, that's how they see it,' he complained. 'But if you don't have a home, how can you ever get a job and pick yourself up? You can't even get a bank account without an address.'

Lambert's only option was to go to estate agents to find a private rental. He wanted to live in Market Drayton where he grew up, 'even though it's the town where I got into trouble', because his two eldest daughters were there and he was hoping to become part of their lives. 'I know I can't just walk back after what I did,' he said. His sixteen-year-old had recently asked him for money. When he asked how much, she replied, 'As much as possible, as you've never given me anything', which made him cry.

With the encouragement of the hotel, he had got back in touch with his mum, who had abandoned him when she moved to

Germany, as he had heard she was ill. 'She's never said sorry and still won't talk about why she did it,' he said. He did not want his own daughters to feel the same.

Private landlords often did not want to take people on benefits, particularly those who have been homeless, and the shortage of rental accommodation meant they could afford to be picky. But he eventually managed to find a one-bed flat in Market Drayton, helped by Mike vouching for him, though the rent was a bit more than his housing benefit. His brother-in-law gave him work as a painter and decorator. 'I've done it in the past and fucked up and went back to jail, but am hoping this time will be different,' he said. 'I'm getting too old and tired, I'm almost forty.'

Charlie always felt conflicted when guests left. If they were moving on to their own place, like Michael Lambert, that felt like a success story, but she would miss them.

That summer suddenly felt like an exodus. Not long after Lambert left, Chris Bennett decided to go. The council had opened a new facility near the station called Number 70, with ten rooms, and he had asked to move there without telling them. A former night shelter, it was far from the luxury of the Prince Rupert, but they could cook for themselves in the kitchen and it had a keypad to enter so no one else could get in.

'I needed to get away,' he explained. 'I was getting a headache from all the fights. Shaggy knocking on my door all the time.'

He too complained that Shaggy was stealing his methadone so he had to go back to drugs.

Richard Boffey was moved out after the council saw him begging one too many times on Pride Hill and also because of a conflict with his ex-partner, who had moved in. Boffey went to the Travelodge at Battlefield, though he soon ended up back on the streets. He frequently came back to blow kisses through the lounge window.

One they would not miss was Derek Tyrer and his endless mutterings. 'My brain's too big,' he would shout if they asked him to quieten down.

'He's the one individual I just can't warm to,' said Mike. 'He's so aggressive and unpredictable.'

When Dave Pritchard was there, the pair were always having fights, as Tyrer hated alcoholics. He had disappeared a couple of times after collecting his benefits and was with a woman who would become known as the Black Widow, as one boyfriend after another would die of drug overdoses.

One time Mike got a call from security in the middle of the night. There was another cascade of water in the lobby. 'Not again,' he groaned.

He dashed round the corridors and came to a first-floor room where the carpet was soaked and he could hear a movie playing loudly inside. He knocked and knocked, but there was no reply. Eventually he used his master key to go in. Inside, he found Derek Tyrer in the overflowing bath, completely stoned.

When he asked him to stop running water, Derek became very aggressive. 'I hate the hotel!' he shouted.

Shortly afterwards he packed up and left. He also ended up in Number 70, though afterwards they often saw him in doorways looking filthy. His room was littered with dog-ends that had been ground into the carpet, which even deep-cleaning could not remove.

Nor were they sorry to see the back of Jade and her ghetto blaster. She did not go quietly. Even though Liverpool Steve had been moved out, he kept sending messages to Martin, taunting him. 'It all started because I'm a Villa fan and she's a Wolves fan and they were playing each other, so I invited her to watch on my tablet and we were just chilling,' said Martin. 'When he saw us, he said, "You're dead." I said, "You're threatening to kill me?"'

A few days later Liverpool Steve turned up with a bunch of flowers and Jade threw them back at him, then went to Martin's room. Shortly after that he and a friend turned up at the hotel in a taxi. The security guards heard from the taxi driver that they were carrying knives and sent them away. A couple of nights later, Mike passed Martin on the stairs after dinner, heading to his room. 'I hope you're going to control everyone tonight,' he told him. 'I want a quiet night.'

Not long after, Martin heard someone outside shouting, 'Pippy! Pippy!'

It was Liverpool Steve again. Martin had had enough. He went out and started punching him and kicking him by the tree. 'The problem with me is if my head is provoked, I can't control it,' he said. 'I'm bipolar and ADHD, which is a bad mix. I only hit him three times,' Martin added. 'I could have done a lot worse.'

Security called Mike, who went out and found Liverpool Steve in a pool of blood. They dialled 999 to get an ambulance and the police, and Martin was charged with actual bodily harm.

Jade was told by the council to leave for her own safety. As she went, she cursed Charlie, the hotel manager, and the council, calling them 'c**ts' and threatening to 'do them over'.

Next to go was Stokesy. Like Lambert and Bennett, he was supposed to be on methadone to stop taking heroin but it was clear that he was back on drugs – Gabriella found his mattress ripped and stained with blood. Charlie told Wendy from the Ark and together they knocked on his door and asked him. He started to cry, saying, 'I'm clean – look, I am doing mindfulness drawings', holding up colouring sheets they had been given by the Shropshire Recovery Partnership.

In fact he was doing so many drugs with Samantha that Charlie was scared they would hurt themselves. Following them up the stairs one day, she had picked up what she thought was a red tissue only to realise in horror that it was something bodily. The council moved them both to the Travelodge, from where Stokesy would eventually go to join his old friends Chris Bennett and Derek Tyrer in Number 70.

Not long after, they heard that Samantha had fled town. She had stolen a ring from a house on the river near the weir where every autumn salmon returned from the Atlantic, leaping upstream on their way to lay their eggs at the end of their adult life – salmon always return to the place where they were born. It was a popular spot for tourists from the hotel.

Unfortunately for Samantha she had chosen the house of one of the most powerful families in town and they had let it be known that she was a dead woman walking.

One person who was relieved that Samantha had left was Hannah. 'Samantha was always trying to put her key in my lock, all her pills and everything falling out of her bag, and yelling at me when I kept telling her it was my room,' she said.

By the end of the month there were only ten guests left. Most of the noisy young ones had gone, as well as the complex older individuals, and those still there were discreet about their addictions.

With Covid numbers going down and the town starting to calm, Mike began to wonder again about reopening. Chancellor Rishi Sunak had urged people to go back to cafés, pubs and restaurants with his 'Eat Out to Help Out' scheme, offering customers 50 per cent discount. Now the government was encouraging people to return to offices. Maybe we could even hire some of the homeless, thought Mike. Neil had been a chef. Titch was desperate to be kitchen porter. Someone like Charlene could be a hostess.

He wandered round the closed-up parts of the hotel with Charlie. Chambers Bistro had been closed so long that snail tracks glistened all over the floor. Camellias Tea Rooms were smelling musty. Maybe it was time.

24.

Saturday, 5 September 2020

'A large Chardonnay please, Charlie,' asked Hannah, standing at the bar and tossing her hair as if she owned the place.

Hannah, Julie and Charlene were unrecognisable. They had all dressed up and, with their hair done and faces made up, looked glamorous in clingy dresses and high heels, adorned with jewellery and different shades of shiny metallic nail varnish. 'You look like the bees' knees,' smiled Mike as they came in.

Hannah was soon holding court, telling people how she used to be a ballerina and about living in Chicago with her jazz singer father. She recounted hanging out with stars like Jude Law and Martin Kemp and living in the south of France, cycling past walnut-picking gypsies, stories that may or may not have been true.

Only her rotting teeth were a clue that all was not as it seemed.

Julie watched Hannah in shy wonder, her own hand shaking as she lifted her glass, hoping no one noticed the scars under her bangles from self-harming, awed at Hannah's confidence speaking to paying guests who looked like they might run the country.

'I'm a chameleon,' Hannah shrugged. 'I can sit with the Queen or sit with a c**t.'

'They keep telling us we're guests here,' she added, 'so let's act like it.'

'Except not paying for the wine!' laughed Charlie.

Having new people to talk to was a breath of fresh air. Hannah had admitted that she and Neil were 'snobbish about the others – we've never been on the streets. My house was the place people stayed: we sat round the fire-pit playing drums and guitars. Never in my wildest nightmares did I imagine ending up in a situation like this.

'Some days here it's like pulling teeth,' she complained. 'Mamba attacks, window lickers, pulling them out of their cereal in the morning ...'

Mostly she was bored. 'I have nothing to do, just my art,' she said. Her osteoporosis meant even after lockdown had ended she barely went out. 'I struggle to put on my shoes or get into my bath. I'm scared I'm going to end up in a wheelchair with a blanket over my knees.'

Sitting in the bar telling stories was a rare escape. Mike breathed a sigh of relief to see the women fitting in with the guests, even if occasionally Hannah did veer off into a rant, such as why should inheritance tax go to the Queen and not be used to fund air ambulances.

When he had told the homeless that the Prince Rupert would be reopening on 4 September, he'd said, 'Please be respectful. Don't walk round in pyjamas and flip-flops, wear proper clothes. And don't smoke just outside the front,' he added. 'I don't want to be sweeping fag ends from the doorway.'

He also spoke to some of them individually. 'No more breakfasts of cornflakes and vodka, Mark!' he said to Mark Chapman. For the last couple of months, Mark had been entrusting his vodka supply to reception and usually came down for his first shot of 'medicine' from the guards at 6 a.m. That would have to move to the Darwin.

Mike urged Bev to change her normal routine of going and sitting in pyjamas and dressing gown on the doorstep in the morning with a cup of tea, saying 'Hi darlin'' to anyone who passed. Chapman often sat with her. As for Titch, who would stride through the hotel yelling 'Where's my mum?' while looking for Jacki, he pleaded, 'Keep your foghorn down!'

Though he told them he was happy for them to integrate with other guests, Mike knew it was a risk. 'I wasn't sure what would happen,' said Charlie. 'They'd had so much freedom during lockdown – it was totally and utterly their hotel and their town.'

Donny still rarely left his room. Jamie was a hypochondriac and always claiming to be ill, and he was paranoid that people would hear what he was talking about, so he also tended to stay in. When he did open his door, however, as Gabriella had learned to her cost, he was often naked.

The biggest concerns were Martin and Shaggy. Martin had been on a downward spiral since his fight with Liverpool Steve, getting drunk every day on his cheap rosé. 'I felt like I was getting back on track but now I was facing prison again, all because of a girl I didn't even really care about,' he complained. 'Women have caused me nothing but problems.'

Liverpool Steve had twenty-eight days to withdraw the charges and Mike and Charlie had initially been confident they could persuade him, yet now he had disappeared. Unfortunately for Martin, his last sentence had been for assaulting a copper. 'Hitting a policeman, they don't forget,' he said. 'I knew I'd go back to jail. It was just a question of when and for how long.'

As for Shaggy, he was not the best at personal hygiene and they worried about his smell. Most of all they had urged him not to go begging on Pride Hill. 'Please, guests can't see you in the bar then begging in a doorway,' said Mike. Shaggy was not happy: now that tourists were back, he could easily net £80 in a day.

The staff had one final request: everyone had to wear masks in public spaces.

'We were told to be polite,' said Bev. 'I had a chat with a couple about local history for an hour. I told them how Shrewsbury has lots of history and to visit Shrewsbury Castle, which was never inhabited by a king but stayed in by Henry VIII and Anne Boleyn.' Mike, standing nearby, was pretty sure that wasn't true, but the tourists seemed to take it all onboard.

Mark Chapman passed by with his medal proudly displayed on his chest, bidding them good morning. Mike hoped they wouldn't look too closely and realise it was for a half marathon.

The first group of guests were trainspotters, twelve of them on a railway tour. The Royalist Restaurant had been reopened for them to dine in style and Charlie found herself having to prepare a proper three-course menu, offering French onion soup, poached halibut or steak au poivre, followed by crème caramel or cheese and biscuits.

Jacki served out front, Charlie and Mike in the kitchen. The first evening there was a bit of a wait between starter and main, as some had ordered the steak, which took longer. When the guests began to grumble, Mike found it hard not to be irritated. 'I thought, Oh my God, is that all they have to worry about? I had forgotten how annoying real guests can be!'

Most new residents were very understanding – they were just delighted to get away for a break after so many months stuck at home.

It had been hard work cleaning everything up after five months of housing alcoholics and drug addicts. Gabriella and Kim had scrubbed like mad, and they brought in professional carpet cleaners to try and erase the smell of smoke from the carpets. Some of the rooms on the third floor hadn't been used for months, so were very dusty. Being Covid-safe meant lots of extra work – they were constantly sanitising banisters, door handles and public toilets, and disinfecting tables and chairs after each use. In the rooms, the TV remotes were sanitised and wrapped in plastic.

Before their arrival, guests had been sent a letter, which Mike had modelled on one the Hilton group had been sending out, informing guests that staff wouldn't service their rooms during their stay unless they asked. 'It was clear no one read them,' he said. 'People were coming back at 5 p.m. and complaining, "My room still hasn't been serviced", so later it was changed to we would service unless they asked us not to.'

They also couldn't valet park guests' cars, so had to let them drop off their luggage then explain how to get to the car park through the town's narrow winding streets.

The hotel didn't feel the same. Before Covid, the lounge would have been buzzing with mostly ladies meeting up for coffee, but now it stayed virtually empty. In the Royalist Restaurant every other table was blocked off to maintain social distancing, and condiments, sugar and sauces such as mustard, mayo and ketchup all had to be in little packets.

They didn't open the tea rooms but got planning permission for tables outside. Staff all wore masks and guests had to use them in public areas.

They couldn't put out a buffet as they used to for breakfast. Some hotels were simply leaving a brown paper bag outside each room with a Danish pastry and drink. Mike didn't want to do that, so everything had to be ordered and cooked individually. They hired Neil as breakfast chef. He was delighted, though he found it hard work. 'I hadn't done it for twenty years and suddenly I was doing thirty or forty covers in a morning, turning out eggs benedict, full English with black pudding, avocado on toast ...'

Occasionally he panicked and Jacki would find him standing in front of the walk-in fridge with glazed eyes and had to encourage him to get on.

*　*　*

The hotel had reopened on Friday 4 September and by the following weekend, they had forty rooms occupied with seventy guests. The chef came back to work from furlough, as did one of the receptionists and porters and it felt as if the team was dribbling back.

Neil sometimes worked in the evening, though he complained he was worth more than the £8.72 an hour they paid. He spent the money on hot chocolate, Refreshers and buying trainers on eBay. 'I have an addictive personality,' he said.

They did not tell guests there were still homeless residents. A few had read about the hotel in the media and were intrigued, asking if they still had any homeless they could meet. But most guests had no idea. There were some tell-tale signs, however. One corridor stank of weed so Gabriella and Kim had to keep spraying it with disinfectant and air freshener.

Donny had to be picked up from the corridor a couple of times because he had overdosed.

The security guards could be a bit brusque, bidding 'All right mate?' to guests coming in and out the door. One visitor questioned on TripAdvisor, 'Why do they have so much security?' Eventually Mike decided to move the guards from the front to upstairs in the Darwin, where they were only too happy to spend the day watching TV.

One day a lady asked for teabags and Shaggy grabbed a handful from the Darwin to give to her, which not only were cheap ones, rather than the individually packed Twinings English Breakfast and Earl Grey placed in the rooms, but it was as if Covid didn't exist. Another night they were serving guests in the restaurant and they could hear banging from upstairs – it was Mark, Bev and Hannah dancing. Generally, however, Mike felt like a proud father. 'They really made an effort,' he said. 'It felt like they elevated their game.'

If anything, some were a bit too enthusiastic about helping out. Hannah kept offering to do the bar, saying, 'You don't need to pay me, I'll just have a few drinks.'

Charlie smiled. 'We were like, no!'

Occasionally some of their previous guests, such as Chris Bennett, Michael Lambert, Stokesy and Boffey, would pass by to say hello or bang on the lounge windows. During the first month just one man complained that he had booked on booking.com and was not paying to stay in a hotel with the homeless.

'They're not homeless,' replied Charlie. 'They all have an address and that address is here.'

In the end it was the homeless who complained most. They didn't like having to wait for their dinner until the paying guests had been served or when Gabriella gave them sheets and towels to change their own beds. 'We're being pushed to one side,' they would complain to her. 'They'd got to expect silver service,' said Charlie.

'Actually we are paying guests,' Neil pointed out. 'It's just the council is paying for us.'

One day, to Mike's fury, he saw that Jamie had posted a stinging review on the hotel's Facebook page. 'Ever felt you've outstayed your welcome?' it asked.

25.

Saturday, 12 September 2020

Julie ran into the hotel waving Mark Chapman's guitar and crying. 'Come quickly!' she said. 'It's Mark.'

Eventually they calmed her down enough to discover he had fallen over on Pride Hill between the cross where executions used to take place and Tesco Express where he bought his cheap vodka. He had hit his head on the pavement. 'He didn't get up,' she sobbed. 'I held his hand and he told me, "I love you."'

Charlie and Mike sprinted there and found a large group had gathered but an ambulance was already disappearing up the road. There had been no fight, according to Julie. He just fell over. A vodka bottle lay shattered nearby. Bev told Charlie that Mark's family lived just twenty minutes away in Whitchurch, so she found their number and spoke to his brother and told him about the fall and where he had been taken.

After that the family updated them, saying Mark had been taken from the Royal Shrewsbury Hospital on to the Royal Stoke for surgery. A day later they learned he had died.

Charlie and Jacki were devastated. 'My angels,' he had called the two women. The timing seemed so unfair. Mark had really wanted to go into rehab to get off alcohol and had written all his appointments with the addiction services on the calendar in Jacki's office so she would remind him. He had recently started talking for the first time about getting his own place, though he complained bitterly about the bidding process. Rather than being seen as a priority as a long-time rough sleeper, it was hard to get on the housing ladder if you had no evidence of previous accommodation.

It seemed so sad that his father, brother and sister had been living so near all that time and apparently did not even know he had a daughter, by then in her late twenties. Mark had told Bev and Hannah that he also had a son in France from when he used to live there, but they had no idea where or how to contact him.

'They came to the hotel and they seemed a lovely middle-class family and so appreciative of what we'd done for Mark,' said Mike. 'How could they be so near and not have reached out?'

'He was very private,' said Chris Bennett. 'It was clear he had lived a life. But he never talked about his family.'

Charlie and Mike told Mark's brother that he had wanted to donate his organs, as they had talked about it one night. They also knew his favourite music and suggested 'The Show Must Go On' by Queen for the funeral.

All the homeless guests were shocked – it was the first death from their community. Martin and Dave Pritchard had been particularly close to Mark, hanging out in one another's rooms, all being alcoholics, though each with their different tipple: Martin with his rosé, Dave on cider and Mark vodka. Once they had found Mark sleeping on the sofa in the Darwin and stuck one of Samantha's dummies in his mouth.

Sometimes Martin had lost patience with Pritchard. 'I don't like bullies,' he said. Mark would always intervene to calm things down.

Martin used to play pool with Mark, Mike unlocking the snooker room downstairs to let them use the proper table. 'We'd play pissed out of our heads at 3 a.m.,' he laughed.

He told others off for bullying Titch.

Hannah told of the night she, Mark and Martin had been outside the hotel and a Romanian had tried to buy her. 'We'd all been sitting there and this guy asked if we had any baccy as he had vodka,' she said. 'Mark had a full pouch, so we went round the corner with him to his flat and he said he wanted to buy me. Martin told him, "She's our friend, she's not for sale", but the man pushed me downstairs and locked me in the room. It was Mark and Martin who got me out.'

Chris Bennett was sad but not surprised. 'He was a nice guy, clever, with a really dry sense of humour. But from the day I met him he told me he was on his way out. He was drinking a litre of vodka a day, plus anything else he could get.'

The memorial to Mark Chapman.

His 'wifey' Bev was the most affected. 'He had been like a family to me,' she sobbed. 'He always said he never wanted to leave this place. I guess he got his wish.' She couldn't believe she would never again hear him say 'Awrighty then' and dance in his arms, or listen to him strum his guitar and talk late into the night of how he loved living in the woods and building fires before bidding him 'Ta-ra'.

Charlie and Jacki were worried about her. Since arriving, Bev had already taken one overdose and had to have her stomach pumped and she'd always been threatening to do it again, though others were cynical. 'She took four tablets – it wasn't even a good night out,' said Neil. 'It was attention seeking. We used to call it her monthly suicide note.'

They made a memorial for Mark under the twisty tree where he loved to sit and sing, with a photo above a wine bucket, which seemed fitting. Word on the street spread via the bush telegraph. Homeless people started coming from all around. One after another went to the memorial, touched the photo and bowed their heads. 'See you along the way, mate,' they said.

Dave Pritchard was devastated and refused to leave, sleeping under the tree. 'I want to feel near Mark,' he said.

Gabriella and Charlie were in tears when they cleared Mark's room with all its empty vodka bottles and evil-smelling slow cooker in which he used to keep food for days.

The council also told them to clear Julie's room. Andy had got to her again and she was spending most of her time in his flat round the corner, so they refused to keep paying for her.

'I know what he is and I know you disapprove, but I need to be with someone,' she told Charlie the day she came to collect all the toys and teddy bears and clothes she had 'amassed'.

She would sit all day outside the pizza shop where he worked, waiting for him to finish. Every so often they would see her running down Butcher Row, screaming at him about sleeping with another woman, and they'd shake their heads. She had torn up a sign that Hannah had painted for the Darwin asking people to throw their rubbish in the bin, accusing her of flirting with Andy.

Martin was the next to move out. The council had found him accommodation in Yew Tree House, a shared house beyond the station. He was in tears when he got the call. 'I'd still be homeless if not for the pandemic,' he said. 'You helped me get on my feet again,' he thanked Charlie, Jacki and Mike as he left, and they wished him luck.

There was still a cloud hanging over him, however, because of the impending assault case from Liverpool Steve. His new accommodation was a room in a house meant for six, but for the time being he was the only resident. 'It's lovely,' he said. 'I keep it tidy as fuck.'

He often came past to visit, usually at mealtimes. 'I miss your cooking,' he told Charlie.

Shaggy also decided to leave, though without informing them. One of his friends had got out of jail and he went off to join him, leaving his room full of his rosary beads, Lee Child novels and needles.

When Chris Bennett heard Shaggy had gone, he was annoyed. 'I would have stayed if I'd known he was going,' he said. 'I left the Prince Rupert because I was trying to get away from it, then I get to Number 70 and who's there – Stokesy and all the idiots. I went from a bad place to a worse place.'

As for Titch, left on his own without his gang, he started to lose some of his swagger.

The hotel was slowly getting back to normal when, on Tuesday 22 September, the government announced a 10 p.m. curfew for pubs, bars and restaurants across England, starting from that

Thursday, to try to prevent alcohol-fuelled breaches of social distancing and halt the growing second wave of coronavirus.

Cases were doubling every week, according to Sir Patrick Vallance, the chief scientific adviser, who warned in a Downing Street briefing alongside Professor Chris Whitty that the UK could face fifty thousand new cases a day by mid-October and 'two hundred-plus deaths per day' again by November if no action was taken. 'Next slide please' had become the familiar phrase, as they called up a graph showing a dramatic incline, and the pair had been dubbed Professor Gloom and Dr Doom.

The government's SAGE advisory group of scientists was calling for a two-week 'circuit breaker' lockdown to slow the spread of the virus. 'Not acting now will result in a very large epidemic with catastrophic consequences in terms of direct Covid-related deaths and ability of health services to meet needs,' they warned in a newspaper.

The prime minister insisted he did not want to put the country in a second lockdown, his chancellor warning it would have a devastating effect on the economy. The previous evening Boris Johnson and Rishi Sunak had sat in Downing Street on a Zoom call with medical experts, including Anders Tegnell, Sweden's leading epidemiologist who had masterminded his country's controversial policy of avoiding lockdown and trying to build up herd immunity. Sweden had experienced far more deaths than its neighbouring countries.

Afterwards, instead of a lockdown, the government simply issued more restrictions – the 10 p.m. curfew adding to the so-called 'rule of six' limiting gatherings to six people.

For Mike, like other hoteliers, the new rules were very confusing. 'We'd have to hurry guests out of the restaurant at 9.55 p.m., then they would try to come into the bar for a nightcap or Irish coffee thinking that it was fine because they were staying. When we said no, you'll have to take it up to your room, they would say you're having a laugh. One night we had a big group celebrating an anniversary who had spent a lot of money and didn't want to leave. But we had no idea what we were supposed to do. I was asking other hoteliers: no one knew.'

From what he could see, the curfew simply led to big gatherings outside pubs and restaurants as people were turfed out and bought beer or wine from Tesco to drink on the street.

The end of the month saw Bev's birthday. Even though they were busy with the return of paying guests, Charlie decided to lay on one of her cream teas to cheer Bev up. She did the whole works: crustless cucumber sandwiches, scones and cream, served on fine

Charlie, Bev and Hannah at the afternoon tea.

china, with glasses of prosecco. Bev wore a slinky silver dress. 'It's like a Queen's tea!' she exclaimed.

They raised a toast to Mark.

A few days later they got a call. It was Bev. 'I took some pills again,' she said.

26.

Wednesday, 21 October 2020

It had been a while since the spate of media interviews back in the spring, so there was excitement when a producer called from BBC's flagship chat show *The One Show*, wanting to send a reporter, intrigued that the Prince Rupert still had homeless people staying alongside regular paying guests. The producer was even more impressed when Mike told them that the hotel was not only providing beds and meals but also helping them find homes and jobs.

Mike thought the filming could be a distraction from Mark's death and the growing second wave of Covid. For almost three weeks the daily death toll had been higher than in March, when the first national lockdown had been brought in. Belgium, France and Germany were all back in lockdown.

Boris Johnson, however, was adamant that he would not do the same in the UK. Putting the country back into lockdown would be the 'height of absurdity', he raged in Parliament during Prime Minister's Questions on 21 October, when opposition leader Sir Keir Starmer called for a two-week 'circuit break' over school half term to bring the virus 'back under control'. Johnson accused him of wanting to 'turn the lights out' on the economy.

Instead a three-tiered traffic light system had been brought in and local lockdowns introduced in the worst-hit places – Tier 3.

Shrewsbury was in Tier 1, which meant the hotel could stay open, carrying on with the same 10 p.m. curfew and rule of six, but it felt like more restrictions were coming. It was all very tiring.

'Who wants to be a TV star?' asked Mike. 'Let's put Bev up to cheer her up, and Titch,' he told Charlie. 'I'm going to offer him a job.'

They got Titch to dress in his black suit, which made him feel sharp even if the others teased it was from Mothercare. Told that he would sign a contract on camera, Titch was beside himself with excitement. 'Thank you, Dad,' he kept saying.

Charlie and Jacki went home that evening. They had both finally moved out of the Prince Rupert a few weeks earlier, on 3 October, which had been their first day off all year. Jacki had used the day to clean her cottage after seven months away, finding spider webs everywhere, while Charlie had moved house with Gabriella, Fraser and the two cats into a pretty three-bedroom terraced cottage with a dormouse in the back garden. 'I didn't have much choice,' she said. 'The kids insisted, we're not moving unless you come.' Even then she had still worked in the hotel in the morning. Her new house was soon filled with love and fairy lights, the biggest bedroom for Gabriella, a den for Fraser and, in the front lounge, black-and-white photos of Mez and the angel wings.

On the day of the filming, Jacki arrived first to oversee breakfast for the regular guests and lay out food in the Darwin for the homeless. There was no sign of Titch. She was not too perturbed. But when she went to knock on his door to get him up, there was no reply.

When Charlie arrived, they opened the room to find him flat out. He had been on the mamba.

'Oh no, Titch!' said Charlie. His eyes were lolling, his body floppy. Desperately, they tried to revive him. They used Chris

Bennett's trick of orange juice but it dribbled out of his mouth. They managed to dress him then Jacki walked him round and round in the courtyard outside, but he was like a red-eyed zombie. 'Sorry, Mum,' he slurred.

'The crew has arrived!' said Charlie. 'There's no way he can do the interview. What are we going to do?'

To fill in a little bit, they introduced the reporter to Bev, who was in a flowery dress, looking like a friendly pub landlady, as she talked of being a grandmother of eight and three years sleeping in the police loading bay. 'We're still human beings,' she said. We're not bad-mannered. We deserve respect as well.'

Mike was interviewed next, talking of their round-the-clock commitment and how his own attitudes towards homeless people had changed. Even though the hotel now had paying guests, he said he was committed that no one would leave until they were all provided with secure and safe houses.

It was clear that Titch was not going to be in any state to talk sense. In desperation they asked Neil to step in. He had already agreed to be filmed in the kitchen and they had organised him a new black chef's uniform, but he did not like being in the limelight – 'I'm the sort of person who does my shopping at 3 a.m. at the twenty-four-hour Asda to avoid other people,' he said.

'I felt I had no choice,' said Neil. 'They were always saying they were going to kick us out. Jacki used to say to me, "I think you're the kingpin of the hotel."'

Asked about finding himself homeless, he told the reporter, 'It was scary. It was like, what happens? You got a lifetime of belongings and nowhere to go.'

Mike said they had discovered that Neil had been a chef twenty years ago and had been trying him out in the kitchen, where he was 'absolutely excellent'. Neil talked of how working there had given him new confidence. 'I get up in the morning and get a spring back in my step,' he said.

Neil getting the contract from Mike.

'Even when Neil moves out, he will still be coming back to the hotel,' the reporter intoned. 'Today his job in the kitchen is being made permanent.'

'Congratulations, Neil, you deserve this,' said Mike, handing him a contract. 'You are now a full-time employee of the Prince Rupert.' Neil was filmed signing while some of the others looked on, clapping and shouting, 'Woo hoo!'

'It's a weight lifted off my shoulders,' he said afterwards. 'I'm excited to have been given the responsibility, the trust, and I've just got to repay my part now.'

When the programme went out, he got a message from his parents. 'Well done, son, we're so proud of you.'

27.

Wednesday, 28 October 2020

Mike drove to Heathrow feeling nervous. This was the day his life could change for ever. He was meeting a British Airways flight from Los Angeles. On board was Rita, a Californian interior designer who he had first met five years earlier in St Lucia. Although things were already strained with Diane at the time, he hadn't been looking for love – his mother had just died and he had taken his youngest son Alexander on a trip down memory lane to the Caribbean, showing him the places where he and Diane had lived and his elder siblings had been born.

They stayed at a spa resort that Mike had managed for several years back in his thirties and were due to leave the next day for Sandy Lane, which now his eldest James was running. On his last day Mike was taking photographs of various parts of the hotel and grounds, when an attractive blond woman stopped him. 'Excuse me,' she said in an American accent. 'Can I ask you a question? Everyone else takes photos of the beautiful beach and the sea but you have your back to them.'

Mike laughed. 'I used to be manager here twenty years ago and I planted these trees,' he said. 'I want to show my family back home how they have grown.'

They chatted for perhaps two minutes, then he went to find Alexander. That evening they went to a beach deli for their final dinner and there on a table was a lively group of women from Orange County, including the blonde he had met earlier. They got talking again and he learned her name was Rita and she introduced him to the woman next to her, who was a travel agent and interested to hear that his son was manager at Sandy Lane. 'Maybe he could give me a tour one day,' she said, proffering a business card.

Back in his office at the Prince Rupert after he arrived home, Mike kept picking up the business card on his desk. He and Rita had only spoken briefly but he had felt a spark, he was sure. Eventually he emailed her travel agent friend, asking if she might pass on his contact. Shortly afterwards he got a message back. Soon he and Rita were FaceTiming almost nightly.

After about six months they decided to meet up, settling on the Mexican resort of Cancún as a sort of halfway destination. He had never done anything so crazy in his life, flying across the world to holiday with a woman he'd met so briefly. As soon as he saw her, he knew he had done the right thing. Those ten days together flew by as they got to know each other. After that they met in a series of places a couple of times a year. He went to visit her in Los Angeles and they met up again in St Lucia and Barbados, where they stayed with James. Rita had come over to the UK three times too. Over time she had met all of his children.

They were at a similar stage in life. Rita was slightly older at sixty-seven but looked younger with her gym-honed figure and long straight blond hair. Both had three grown-up children of similar age and were estranged from their partners – Rita had gone to St Lucia to reflect on the end of her marriage and finally divorced in 2018.

'It felt like we were looking for the same thing,' said Mike. 'To find someone to enjoy our twilight years with and a settled future and happiness.'

He would never have left Diane while the children were growing up and they were building the hotel up together. Even when the children were small, it was she who had chosen curtains and cushions for the rooms, often driving for hours around the country to source fabrics, and once they were older she worked full-time overseeing reception and the tea rooms, as well as conference and private dining bookings. 'I could have drifted on but I was not happy,' he said. 'I had fought it for years but we had grown apart.'

With Rita he felt he had found someone who could also be his best friend. They both enjoyed good food, fitness and health and sport – she loved the ocean. Both loved their family 'to bits' and she had devoted her life to bringing up her children. She was more studious than Mike: she loved reading and listening to audio books whereas he was more interested in sport and politics, and also so tired by the time he got to bed that there was little time to read.

More than anything she made him look at things differently. Usually when he went on holiday or to new cities, Mike liked visiting hotels. Whenever he went to London, his favourite thing was to sit in Claridge's, the Ritz or the Savoy with a cup of tea and just take in the atmosphere. When she asked him what he wanted to see in LA, he had said the Hotel Bel-Air and the Beverly Wilshire.

Rita loved history, particularly British history, and also architecture, which she had studied in Seattle before moving into interior design. She had ended up only really dabbling in it, mostly devoting herself to being a good wife and mother, as well as helping out her husband in his accountancy practice.

When she came to stay, she wanted to visit cathedrals at Salisbury and Winchester, which felt like the sort of things his parents might once have dragged him to yet he found himself astonished by the soaring beauty. One weekend she insisted they went to a garden open-day at Cerne Abbas in Dorset and Mike protested he would rather watch the football, but he ended up loving it, particularly the cold beer in a country pub at the end.

'They were things I would never normally have gone to but made me look at my own country in a new way,' he said.

He took her to Cliveden, the ancestral home of the Astor family, where she was 'gobsmacked' by the walled garden and he was able to show her the button that opened a secret cupboard in which Lord Astor used to keep his whisky, a trick he had learned from James who had worked there.

They explored the Cotswolds in winter, walking the fields and going to village antique shops, then enjoying glasses of claret by a roaring log fire in the Lygon Arms at the end of a day.

Most of all she loved Shrewsbury, where they had stayed in an Airbnb and wandered the streets, Rita marvelling at the preponderance of churches, as well as the black-and-white Tudor buildings, which she had read were of a design peculiar to a local

carpenter. She even pointed out rooftop figurines that he had never noticed. He showed her the recently restored Traitor's Gate through which the Roundheads had taken the city and the last remaining parts of the city walls. Her favourite place was the square with its weekly stalls selling delicious honey and cheese from Church Stretton and the grand stone Market Hall dating back to the sixteenth century – a bit of a contrast to back home in Orange County. Mike told her how in front used to be what was known as the Bishop's pool for dunking dishonest traders and nagging wives.

He had shown her the Prince Rupert and taken her in a couple of times for a coffee and a salad lunch in the courtyard, but they had spent little time there. Mike felt slightly awkward taking his girlfriend into the place he had built with his wife.

In between the trips, they spoke almost daily. Yet something had changed that year. The pandemic and its heavy death toll had brought home how easily life could be cut short at any time. In a way it had also forced an end to Mike's marriage by him moving into the hotel. He sensed that Diane was happier without him, and he felt less and less comfortable each time he returned home to do his laundry.

Even their children had started asking, 'Why don't you just get on with it, Dad?'

He had also found Rita a real support during the hardest times of lockdown and looking after the homeless. He would FaceTime her from his terrace late at night to tell her stories of the day and found her a calming influence from seven thousand miles away. 'I don't know how I would have got through this without you,' he told her.

Gradually they started talking about trying to make it work permanently. He wasn't sure who had first brought it up. Over the summer, with the hotel reopening and things getting back to some kind of normality, it had seemed like more than a possibility.

Now she was walking into arrivals with a big smile and five suitcases piled high on her trolley and he wasn't sure what he'd done, not least as Covid cases were back on the rise.

The US was on the government's red list of high-risk countries, which meant Rita had to self-isolate for ten days on arrival. Mike drove her down to the flat in Bournemouth, where they had stayed on one of her previous visits.

That night he cooked her salmon and roasted vegetables, and they sat on the sofa and watched *The Crown*, having seen the first series together on her previous visit to the UK. Under government rules she was not allowed to leave the flat but they worked out that ten circuits of the driveway round the block of flats was equivalent to one mile, so they did twenty circuits every morning. 'Not quite California,' he laughed.

He was happy to see her. Then Charlie called with an issue at the hotel. Almost immediately he felt torn. He had left Charlie and Jacki in charge.

It was also hard to ignore the news. The numbers were spiralling out of control. The famous R number for transmission of Covid was above 1 and there were warnings of hospitals running out of capacity. In a heated meeting, Boris Johnson was said to have raged, 'Let the bodies pile high in their thousands!' He was, however, becoming increasingly isolated from ministers and advisers, leaving him little choice but to climb down.

By Halloween, cases had reached a daily record of 21,915, with 326 more deaths reported that day, taking the overall death toll to 63,000. That evening the prime minister held a hastily arranged press conference, announcing a second national lockdown from Thursday 5 November, telling everyone once again to stay home. The only difference from before was that schools would remain open.

The lockdown was to last four weeks, until 2 December, the idea being to reduce coronavirus cases in time for families to gather for Christmas. Watching on TV, Mike felt his heart sink. The Prince Rupert would have to close to guests again. By now they only had eight homeless residents, which was not enough to make running the hotel economically viable.

He would have to go back to the council to ask them to send more homeless. He worried that his bank would not stay patient about delaying the mortgage payments. He called Jacki to contact those with reservations for the next few weeks to cancel them and refund deposits.

What would he do with Rita? She had been expecting to stay in a normal hotel getting ready for Christmas. He made sure she was well stocked with food at the flat, then headed back to Shrewsbury, taking some of her suitcases. It was 3 November, the day of the US presidential elections, which Rita was hoping would see the end of Donald Trump, and he had promised to be back in a couple of days for the final stages. From the car, he called Charlie. 'Please be there when I come back,' he said.

'Sod's law,' he cursed when he got a puncture about forty miles outside Oxford. He tried to make it slowly to Alexander's house, but eventually a breakdown lorry picked him up and towed him back. It was 4 a.m. when he got to Shrewsbury.

28.

Wednesday, 4 November 2020

As Mike emerged bleary-eyed that morning in the kitchen, seeking coffee, Charlie was hopping from one foot to the other, eager to introduce him to a new guest. 'He looks like Father Christmas,' she said. 'He's adorable!'

'You say that about all of them,' laughed Mike.

Jacki rolled her eyes. 'I'm not saying anything,' she said.

Mike had left three of Rita's cases in the lobby and he noticed Charlie and Jacki raise their eyebrows. They led him into the Darwin, where an old man was sitting in one of the armchairs in front of the TV. He did indeed look like Father Christmas, with his long white hair and beard, twinkly eyes and bobble hat.

'Mike, meet Simon,' said Charlie. 'Simon, this is Mr Matthews who owns the hotel.'

Simon shook his head. 'You people are always rushing around trying to own things,' he sighed. 'The biggest education we all have is life. If people sat down for a minute or two and just watched, they'd learn a lot.'

'You're very right,' said Mike.

Charlie and Jacki had found Simon a couple of nights earlier on Pride Hill, in the doorway of Cotswold Outdoor with a sleeping bag, a radio and three bottles of red wine. It was a frosty night and they had coaxed him indoors.

He didn't remember the last time he had slept in a bed. 'It's years and years,' he said.

At sixty-two, he was the hotel's oldest guest so far and, unlike most, had chosen to spend much of his life on the streets. 'I don't like the expression "on the streets",' he said. 'I think it's degrading. The same with rough sleeper. I am not rough. Nor do I sleep much. For me it's about freedom. I have lots of friends round the country so like to travel around and meet them.'

Perched in front of the TV in the Darwin Suite, he took a swig of red wine from the bottle in his pouch and rolled some tobacco with his long dirty fingernails. 'It's luxury, warmth, a roof over

Simon.

my head, food and these lovely people,' he smiled, 'but I won't stay long.'

He had, he told Mike, come by train from Wells in Somerset, where he had spent lockdown living under a yew tree in a church-yard for six months. 'Don't eat the berries, they are poisonous,' he warned.

'When I first heard about the virus, I went under a tree in St Cuthbert's churchyard in the fresh air and didn't mix with anyone,' he said. 'That's a nice church, thirteenth century. It looks like a cathedral really. Though of course, Wells has a pretty cathedral, which was why I went there.'

Simon particularly liked cathedrals. 'I am not a religious person but I just appreciate the architecture and that they have taken generations to build: someone starts it and never sees it completed. I like a high spire like Salisbury, that's a good cathedral. Whereas Shrewsbury, you could say, is insignificant. Though it has some fine churches.

'Churchyards are the best places to sleep,' he added. 'Those strange folk living behind walls and windows don't tend to go because they are frightened of ghosts, but it's safe. I often talk to the gravestones and always read them. Each one is the life of someone with a story.'

Throughout lockdown he would get one meal a day from an organisation in Wells called Connect, run by the church. 'There was a garage across the road to buy a pasty, so if I played the spoons I could get enough – and a bottle or two of red wine.'

People often called him Simon Spoons, for he was a talented spoons player and a number of videos had been posted on YouTube of him playing to rave tracks near London's Borough Market, as well as to Tom Jones's 'Delilah' in Henley. He had even played at Glastonbury Festival, where he was known as the Dude with Spoons. 'I go most years and sometimes they drag me on stage,' he said.

Simon had taught himself to play when he was a student. 'I used to play guitar at a folk club in Carmarthen and thought I wanted to do something different. One day I was at home in my bedroom listening to the Chieftains on my old Dansette record player and for some reason started to play the spoons, then it went from there.'

Born in Swansea, Simon was proudly Welsh and loved rugby. 'I think when you're born in Wales, they put a vaccine in your arm to like rugby.'

Mike laughed. 'We have something in common,' he said. 'I love rugby. I used to play.'

As a child, Simon's family had moved around a lot, starting with Birmingham. 'Dad was a probation officer in prisons and always moving, and my brother and I were shoved from pillar to post,' he said. 'Every time we changed school, I was bullied as a new kid – kids are so cruel – so I had to develop armadillo skin.'

One of those schools was Carmarthen Grammar, where a fellow pupil had been Mark Drakeford, who ended up as the first minister of Wales. A talented painter, Simon had gone on to do a fine arts degree at Winchester Arts College. 'That's a place with a fine cathedral,' he said.

For a while he ran his own business framing and selling antiquarian prints, and for seven years was married to a woman he met in Winchester 'over a bag of potatoes at a friend's birthday'. But he became increasingly concerned about what was happening to the world around him. 'We weren't taking care of the planet,' he said. He did a second degree in environmental studies in Swansea.

'I'm the black sheep of my family,' he said. 'Once I got 81 per cent on a paper and told my dad and he said, "Well, that's nineteen points lost."' Simon had not seen his family for thirty-five years. His parents were dead, he had heard, and he had no idea what his elder brother did.

Simon's life in the open air started as an environmental protester – he was, he said, on the front page of the *Sunday Times* in 1996 during the Newbury bypass protests, one of an army of eco-warriors who set up a series of tree camps, chaining themselves to the trees, rigging up a sound system belting out songs like 'I Shot the Sheriff' and digging tunnels to try to stop the construction of the road. Among them was his friend Daniel Hooper, who became known as Swampy and the country's most famous eco-warrior.

'It was not easy, being a bitterly cold winter,' said Simon, 'but we were trying to protect nature and local villagers brought food and let us use their bathrooms.'

More than seven hundred people were arrested and six hundred security guards were brought in. It was the first such protest in the UK and unsuccessful in its immediate objective, as the road went ahead and ten thousand trees were felled, but it changed transport policy. When the Labour government came to power the following year under Tony Blair, it scrapped the road-building programme.

Simon started a relationship with a fellow tree-dweller. 'It first seemed fine but turned out she was paranoid schizophrenic and had been in and out of institutions since the age of five. I managed to get her back to her parents.'

After the Newbury protests ended, he went to Exeter and met up with a woman he knew. 'We went for a drink in the Cavern Club and had a chit-chat and there on the table was the local rag, so I started looking through.'

He turned a page and there was a photograph of a parish councillor next to a river in Teigngrace, near Newton Abbot in south Devon, complaining about the recent granting of planning permission to one of the world's largest clay companies. The project involved diverting the Bovey and Teign rivers so that they could extend a quarry and excavate untapped deposits.

'I didn't like the sound of that at all,' said Simon. 'We decided to go to the library to see the environmental impact report and found a map of the area from 1836. Then we got the train to have a look.'

They found locals bitterly opposed to the quarry, fearing their village would be flooded, as well as destruction of the habitat of animals such as otters and badgers. For a year they had been writing letters to Devon Council and the Environmental Agency, but to no avail.

'As we walked over the hill, we saw a fox by the river so decided to start a protest,' said Simon. 'We recruited some others and when they came, they magically saw the same fox so called everyone from Newbury and got about forty people, including Dan [Swampy] and Plymouth hunt sabs we called on the radio.'

The protesters moved in on 17 July 1997 and began building tree houses to stop the development. They also contacted the media. The quarry company came with bulldozers but could do nothing with people in the trees. The locals who had got nowhere writing letters were delighted and took the tree-dwellers food, clothes and daily papers. 'They even brought us chocolate cake,' said Simon.

Having learned from their experience in Newbury, the protesters brought in lawyers and public figures such as David Bellamy, the jolly bearded TV botanist, who warned about the loss of otters and badgers. An American hydrologist, Phil Williams, founding president of the International Rivers Network, showed that the company's figures had understated the impact of changing the rivers' course.

Eventually they organised a 250-mile march to London, along with villagers holding banners proclaiming 'Save Our River' and someone's pet Jack Russell. When they reached the capital, they held a demonstration outside the Department for the Environment in Whitehall. Deputy Prime Minister John Prescott ordered a temporary halt to the quarry expansion and in 1998 a public inquiry blocked it altogether.

'Local villagers were overjoyed and brought us more chocolate cake,' said Simon in tears, as he recounted the victory. 'It was the start of a whole campaign to save our rivers.'

After that he never went back to living within four walls, apart from the occasional stays with friends, and any time there was an environmental protest, he was there. Once he had helped stop an Underground train going to an arms fair at London's Docklands.

Over the next twenty years, the kind of people living on the street had changed a lot, he said. 'There are far more drug addicts and because of that more theft. And also they closed so many mental institutions and pushed them out – they call it "care in the community".'

Attitudes of passers-by also changed, he found. 'People have become more hostile. They walk past without so much as a good morning or kick you and say, "Wake up and get a job." I also saw more nationalism – all this British exceptionalism palaver – so I knew the Brexit vote would win.

'The majority of time people are good but unfortunately you get idiots. I always tell young people new on the streets, never do up your sleeping bag because people will kick you, set fire to you or urinate on you. You've got to keep your eyes open and wits sharp. Once when I was kipping out in Cambridge, a mob came to do what they call tramp-bashing.'

Even in the genteel town of Wells during lockdown some teenagers had thrown bricks at him. 'That wasn't pleasant,' he said.

Simon had heard about the Prince Rupert in a report on the radio. 'I've got a digital and listen to Radio 5 Live,' he said. 'I like to hear the persiflage these politicians come out with – that's a good word – and how they keep changing the goalposts.'

The report gave him the idea of getting the train to Shrewsbury. 'I'm a fan of trains,' he said. 'I always pay for my ticket.' But he had not been intending to go to the Prince Rupert. 'I'd been to Shrewsbury before – someone I knew was here. When I arrived the weather was a bit dank, so it was a case of looking after yourself and I found a deep doorway next to Cotswold Outdoor. Then police arrested me because they said I was blocking a fire hydrant.'

Eventually he was allowed back to the doorway, which was where Charlie had found him on that frosty night. She promised warmth, a comfy bed and a hot meal, yet he wasn't keen to come initially. 'I'm not one for taking handouts,' he said. 'I'm more inclined to give than take.'

Of all their guests, he was the only one to have chosen the life. Tim Compton from the council told them he was very unusual. 'In twelve years of working with homeless, I've probably met four Simons at most,' he said.

A philosopher of life, Simon quickly became one of their favourites, though he drove them mad refusing to change into clean clothes they provided and leaving his dinner under an armchair all night to eat in the morning.

He would be up with the larks at 5.30 a.m. and if it was a fine day, off out, walking round the churches or sitting on Pride Hill 'watching the hoi polloi', for he had little time for most of his fellow guests, particularly the drug addicts. 'Disgusting habit,' he complained. He reserved his greatest disdain for those he said 'pretended they were not addicts like that Hannah and Neil'.

As for his own drinking, Simon got through three bottles of red a day but insisted, 'I'm not an alcoholic. You'll never see me drunk. I just sip my wine through the day.'

When Gabriella went into his room to clean, he was embarrassed. 'So sorry about all the bottles,' he'd say.

'I'm not here to judge you,' she replied. 'I've seen more bottles than you can imagine.'

Simon was desperate to get back on the road again. 'I follow the birds,' he said. 'I am just waiting for spring then I'm off, the world's my oyster. I'll find a nice tree to sleep under by a cathedral – it could be Durham, could be Aberystwyth, Lichfield or Salisbury. There are only a few I haven't seen. A really nice one is Ely, that's brilliant.

'When I die, I don't want a funeral, just a bench for people to sit and watch,' he said.

29.

Saturday, 7 November 2020

'I feel like bloody Doctor Dolittle,' said Bev. 'When I get up at 7 a.m. crowing for the birds and having my tea and smoke, there are ducks on the green and magpies and squirrels in the garden.'

She was calling from her new house. Like most of the homeless guests in the hotel, she had been bidding on HomePoint every week. Then one day she'd got a message to go into the dining room to meet someone from the council who greeted her smiling with the news 'You've got accommodation!'

Bev's new home was the ground floor of a little house opposite a green on an estate in the north of the town. There was a kitchen, a front room cum bedroom with TV, a bathroom and a small over-grown garden that Titch had promised to come and clear, and where she thought she might put a table and chairs in the summer.

She had put pink covers on her bed and had taped up drawings from her grandchildren on the walls. 'I love those babbies with all my heart,' she said. 'If I don't see them for three days, I miss them.'

In the front window she had placed a picture of Mark Chapman, the card from his memorial service. 'I miss him,' she said. 'He was lovely.'

Some of the homeless, like Hannah, had possessions in council storage, but Bev had lost everything when she was evicted. For her new home, the council had provided furniture as well as a

£300 Argos voucher to buy a kettle, toaster, duvet and other things. The newly housed used to get cash but too often they would spend it on drugs or alcohol instead, so the council had switched to vouchers. Even these they would frequently use to buy a big screen TV and DVD player, which they could sell for drugs.

Bev, however, craved some normality. A council support worker had helped her sort out bills and the water supply and arranged for her to pay the money owed from her last flat in easy monthly payments from her Universal Credit. She missed her room on the first floor of the Prince Rupert and Charlie's Sunday roasts, but since Mark died it had never been the same.

'It's wonderful to have a door of my own I can shut and say it's mine,' she said. 'And also a place my grandchildren can come, even if it's small. And I can lie in bed in me pyjamas watching my *Murder, She Wrote* with a bottle or two of Magners and no one to disturb me.'

Sometimes she took the card down from the window with Mark's photo and remembered how they danced in her room. 'I can't say thank you enough,' she told Charlie. 'Being at the Prince Rupert gave me a goal. I got sorted because of you and Covid. Maybe it would have happened anyway but Prince Rupert was my stepping stone.'

While Charlie was catching up with Bev, Mike and Jacki wandered up Pride Hill to collect out-of-date sandwiches from Marks & Spencer. The town centre was once again deserted. With the country back in lockdown and shops and restaurants all shuttered, it felt like they had gone back to the same as before in the hotel, except now it was autumn and they had a mostly new cast of characters. From the first intake, only Titch, Hannah and Neil remained, as well as Shaggy, who had moved back as suddenly and quietly as he had left, perhaps drawn there by the colder nights.

With Bev moved out and the Prince Rupert closed again to paying guests, the council had quickly begun sending in other homeless to boost the numbers, as Mike had asked. Among the new arrivals was Paul, who was fifty-two and walked in wearing a fleece, jeans and cowboy hat. He was carrying a bottle of sparkling Lambrini, which he called his 'mouthwash', and a golf club that to his dismay they confiscated as a potential weapon. He had been living in a tent on the golf course.

'Golf is my passion,' he said. 'As a kid I spent all my time on the golf course, caddying for people and collecting lost balls and selling them.'

The money he made, he spent gambling in a local arcade. 'I grew up with gambling,' he said. 'Both my parents were addicted: my mum on the bingo, my dad at the bookies. My nephew hung himself because of it. I used to be a bookie's runner, taking bets for people from the pub and running to the betting shop.'

Teased at school as 'Dumbo' or 'Flapper' for his big ears, at home Paul was beaten with a belt by his dad. 'He was very strict, like a brigadier – it was "my way or the highway". Eventually I had enough, went down the Welsh coastline and never came back.'

He left school at fifteen and worked on a building site until someone there died. 'Whatever I did went pear-shaped,' he said. For a while he sold printed T-shirts in a market and rented a bedsit but then turned to drink. 'I lost everything and started robbing places and cashing stolen cheques and ended up in prison.'

Paul liked to talk and over time told them a meandering story involving him falling madly in love with a woman with five children, stealing a car to take them on holiday to Weston-Super-Mare and finding a dead body in the stairwell of her apartment building, which led to him being arrested on suspicion of murder, though he was then released. His girlfriend was the daughter of an alcoholic, so she could not tolerate his drinking, and although they had four children together and 'ducked and dived for twenty years', he lived most of it on the streets.

'I used to drink anything and everything,' he said. 'Each has its own kick. Give me Bell's whisky and I'll fight anyone. Then one day I only had £2 and all I could find was Lambrini, which cost £1.50. Since then I've drunk nothing else. I wake every morning, put the kettle on for tea, then once my body is feeling all right I start on my mouthwash. It does make me quite loud,' he warned them.

He was overjoyed to be in the Prince Rupert. 'It's fucking brilliant,' he said. 'My brother won't believe me.'

Next came Rob, a tall man of forty-three in a blue Smurf hat, jeans and Nike trainers, with a loping walk and a Cockney accent, who had come from hospital and before that prison. 'Everyone told us he's the biggest thief in town,' said Mike. 'As soon as the manager of Tesco heard he was here, he called and warned me.'

Mike almost asked Rob to leave but then remembered Michael Lambert, about whom they had received similar warnings yet had ended up one of their success stories. Besides, Rob was recovering from heart surgery and told them he was also suffering from post-traumatic stress disorder.

Once he started talking, he didn't stop. He was, he said, from Tottenham, born on the Broadwater Farm estate and a lifelong Spurs supporter, and thought he had been in prison thirty-two times, 'though it's all a bit of a blur, darling'.

Mostly it had been for cash and car theft. 'I've done cars all my life,' he said. 'It's in my family on my mum's side – my uncles are a right johnny bunch. They all grew up in the East End in the fifties. My nan thinks she's Barbara Windsor, the Krays' moll.

'One of my uncles had a couple of scrapyards that made a lot of money, more than you should if you know what I mean. We would get exclusive cars for order: he'd pay us £2,000, then re-register them and send them to Spain, where he sold them for £35,000.

'Another had a couple of bent charities doing fake rubber duck races – he'd tell companies there was a duck race in aid of a hospice and they could put their business name on one for £40. I used to go round with a list and leave a little teddy and collect the money. I felt terrible, as often they would say, "Thank you so much for doing this and we were so moved that over the weekend we held a raffle and raised some extra." Those duck races never existed.'

Rob left school at sixteen with five GCSEs and went to college to do A Levels in psychology and communications, but he was playing guitar and vocals in an indie band called Big Long Now and 'thought we were going to make it big', so left. Instead he ended up in Feltham Young Offenders Institution by the age of twenty.

He also had a son with a woman who left him because of drugs – by then he was addicted to heroin and crack cocaine. In and out of jail, when he was twenty-five he entered rehab for the first time – in a town just outside Shrewsbury, his first experience of the area. Ever the charmer, he was soon in a relationship with the assistant manager's daughter, who was doing research in forensic psychology. 'It felt like a turning point,' he said. 'We rented a two-bedroom Tudor cottage in Shrewsbury and I fell in love with the place. I'd never seen cows or sheep before, or such countryside, I'd never even been to Essex.'

Rob had done an accounting course in prison and 'really had a taste for it', so moved on to an advanced diploma and started an Open University degree.

The couple split up after seven years and he 'went on a bender and made some bad decisions'. With nowhere to live, Rob ended up sofa-surfing with friends in Bath and Bristol who were doing drugs and he was unable to resist going back on them. Soon he was back in and out of jail, as well as doing a couple of stints on the streets in Southampton and London's Cardboard City by Waterloo station.

Eventually he ended up back in rehab. There was obviously something about rehab and relationships for Rob. At his next one he got involved with his counsellor, who was reported and struck off for 'taking advantage of a vulnerable person'.

'Losing her career wasn't the best way to start a relationship, particularly as she had been in a long relationship with a guy she'd been doing a house up with and left him for me,' said Rob. 'But we leant on each other and I felt I was really punching above my weight. Lots of girls may be very pretty but if you want to talk about literature and poetry, forget it.

'I was staying clean but then saw a pal from Bristol who was doing heroin all the time and of course I couldn't resist. My girlfriend was trained to spot this and lied to herself to start with, but in the end she couldn't ignore it and in 2015 we split up after two years. I didn't think I was capable of missing someone so much and just let myself go.

'Loneliness and guilt are the worst emotions. When I was using [heroin] I could numb them but when I stopped I was so raw that I cried at Christmas adverts.'

So he turned to more drugs. This time he started selling for a gang in Liverpool, picking up his supply from a young guy in Shrewsbury who divided heroin and cocaine into £10 bags, selling him a hundred of them for £600, which he would then sell for £1,000.

One day on the way home to his flat in Sundorne on the edge of Shrewsbury, Rob had just passed Morrisons when a van mounted the pavement behind him. 'Someone hit me with a crowbar, broke my jaw and took out my bottom teeth, then threw me in the back and kept beating me,' he said.

They drove him to a derelict estate in Liverpool and for the next three and a half days kept him prisoner, beating him over and over, and torturing him. 'They tied me to a chair, poured water on the floor and kicked me over, then used a cattle prod to electrocute the water and give me shocks. I felt like I would rather die. They thought I was trying to escape so smashed a chest of drawers against both my ankles and broke them. It was agony.

'Then these two lads poured petrol on me and started flicking matches, though they blew out. If one had stayed lit, that would have been it.

'They were discussing whether to throw me in the Mersey or set fire to the house when a man came who was clearly the boss. He threw some clean clothes at me to change into, as mine were all bloody, then they carried me into the back of a car and drove me back to Shrewsbury. They stopped near a car dealership on the outskirts and kicked me out.

'I lay there and eventually a woman who worked there walked past, I remember her screaming. She called an ambulance, which took me to the Royal Shrewsbury. I had thirty broken bones, as well as compound fractures of my ankles and a bleed on my brain, for which they had to drill into my skull. It was all quite messy.'

Rob lifted his shirt and took off his hat to reveal vivid scars on his chest and the back of his head. 'The stupid thing is, it was all a misunderstanding. I only owed those guys £120. But it turned out that the young guy I'd been getting the gear from had been siphoning off thousands of pounds and blamed it on me.'

Once Rob had recovered, he ended up back in prison. The kidnapping left him with PTSD, but that wasn't all. His drug use had damaged his heart and he needed a stent. It took three attempts at different hospitals before it worked and then he got an infection, so he had spent fifteen of the previous eighteen months in hospital, where he worried about catching Covid.

He now took a daily cocktail of drugs – gentamicin, methadone, which he said had a horrible sweet sticky taste, and Temazepam for his PTSD. 'The upside to all this horror story is it puts me in a high band of need, so I get PIP and quite a lot of benefits, and am high on the list for a flat,' he smiled.

Rob had come to the Prince Rupert straight from hospital and described it as 'literally life-changing'. 'I couldn't have gone on the streets from hospital, as I was susceptible, and also the doctor said if I use again, I might as well sign my death certificate.'

He was spending his time in his room, listening to the radio, mostly indie music, going the long way to the chemists to get his daily methadone and watching movies on Film Four. Usually he liked watching news but he complained, 'There is too much Covid!'

He also liked to read, ordering books on Amazon. 'I am a bit of a nerd about graphic novels. I love horror films and zombies, like *Night of the Living Dead.*'

Though Rob did not believe in ghosts, he said he'd been 'creeped out' at the hotel several times while having a shower when he thought he'd seen a flash of movement. 'Once I was brushing my teeth and kept hearing a noise like kicking under the sink, then saw another flash of movement toward the window. I felt a really malevolent vibe.'

Occasionally his brother would come down from London and they would share a bottle of wine. Rob did not socialise that much with the other guests. 'They are not my type,' he said. 'Some here are institutionalised about being homeless. Even if they get a house, they will end up back on the streets. I'm not like that, though trust me, I'm no better than anyone else. Now I'm trying to make a genuine effort to be nice to everyone. It's good for my soul.'

He was back in touch with his son, who was twenty-four and working at a Premier League football club as a physio, to his great pride, and they would regularly FaceTime. 'I'm trying to have a beautiful resurgence,' said Rob, 'but I've got to be pragmatic. I'm no spring chicken, I'm never going to be CEO of my own company. That doesn't mean I can't have a better life. My son will be proud if I don't hurt myself or go back to prison.'

Yet Rob was not entirely reformed. One day he walked in with bags of rump steak as gifts. 'My girlfriend gave me them to cook,' he said. Charlie and Jacki looked at each other and raised their eyebrows. The security guards took care of them.

Even though the government would end up spending more than £70 billion on its furlough scheme to help businesses keep on staff throughout lockdown, by helping to pay the wages of millions of employees, coronavirus had led to many people losing their jobs. The service sector had been particularly hard hit: around 355,000 people in hotels, restaurants and pubs had been laid off.

Among them was Peter, a forty-one-year-old chef with a broad Scottish accent and a talent for writing poems and songs, which spilled out of notebooks and folders in his room at the Prince Rupert, written in coloured felt-tips along with elaborate menus for venison and foie gras, beef wellington with ginger, cinnamon and garlic jus, Isle of Mull scallops.

Back in March he had been living in a three-bedroom house with his wife and two children, a nice car and a good job earning £34,000 a year. 'Eight months later here I am,' he said. 'What a fucking curveball life sends us.'

He seemed walking proof of Hannah's theory that everyone was just two paycheques away from the street. Though that was not the whole story. 'I do have a bit of a drink issue,' he admitted.

From an early age Peter's dream had been to have his own restaurant. 'I've been passionate about food as long as I can remember,' he said. His mother abandoned him and his two elder sisters shortly after he was born and went to Saudi Arabia, and his father married again. Then his dad also upped and left, leaving them with their stepmother. She was a catering manager and Peter started helping out in kitchens at the age of eight. 'I loved chopping cucumbers and vegetables to help her,' he said. 'Maybe it was trying to win her love after my real mum had gone, I don't know.'

Around that time, his biological mother returned and started fighting for custody in the high court to get her children back. 'Every couple of months we had to traipse to London for hearings,' he said. 'Finally the judge decided we should stay in Scotland but spend holidays with my biological mum, which I resented and stopped when I was sixteen.'

While at school he worked washing pots and pans in an Italian restaurant, where he learned how to make pasta, then studied catering. After that he got a job at Norton House, a luxury hotel in Edinburgh that was part of the Gleneagles Group. 'Days were often seventeen or eighteen hours and not easy, but I was working with great Scottish produce and great chefs and I learned all I could,' he said.

From there Peter headed south to be commis chef at a four-star resort hotel in Berkshire built in the style of an Alpine chalet. Over the next few years he worked his way up to head chef and fell in love with a fellow chef, who he married in 2002.

He then got a job as director of dining for the pharmaceutical company AstraZeneca (later to become a household name for the Covid vaccine), where he cooked for directors and important guests, including Tony Blair and Gordon Brown. He also got to meet Heston Blumenthal, who would work with scientists developing menus for his famous restaurant the Fat Duck.

After three years there and a divorce, Peter worked at various companies and banks in Canary Wharf. At one he met a woman who worked out of Market Drayton and he fell in love. In 2009 he decided to move north to be with her and got a job as head chef at a pub called the White Lion. They had two children.

Life seemed good until mid-2018, not long after Peter's daughter was born. 'Both the wife and I liked pound signs, so I took a job for lots of money which I wish I hadn't or I probably wouldn't be here ...'

The job was head of catering for a large dairy plant that operated twenty-four/seven, feeding as many as 1,200 people. 'I was getting calls day and night, working fourteen-hour days and weekends,' he said. 'Clients were often difficult. I'd get pulled up because they had found a crumb on the table.'

Peter had always drunk socially but started to drink to numb his problems. 'I was getting no sleep and drinking too much, everything, beer, wine and vodka,' he said. 'My wife was getting annoyed I was out so much then drunk when I was back, and the worse the arguments got, the more I drank.'

In the end, in January 2020, she could take no more and kicked him out. First, he stayed with friends nearby, then rented in shared accommodation. By the beginning of March his company could see Covid coming. 'I was highly paid and had been there seventeen months – at eighteen months they would have had to pay me redundancy – so they got me out. I went to the Citizens Advice Bureau but they said there was nothing I could do.'

To start with Peter wasn't worried and didn't even apply for Universal Credit. 'I'd had jobs since I was thirteen and was confident with my talent and experience I would easily get work. But then the pandemic came and no one needed chefs.'

Then his landlord told him he was going to renovate, so he would have to move out. 'I couldn't go to friends because of Covid. My mum and stepdad couldn't take me, as they run sheltered housing for elderly people so were locked down. My wife wouldn't take me back.'

He ended up going to London and sleeping in an alleyway near Paddington station, drinking from a bottle. 'I felt like a loser,' said Peter. 'I'd worked my way up to head chef at top places and now I was on the streets. It's somewhere I never want to be again. It's horrible the way people look at you and the derogatory comments they make. I had a little money so I would get the bus to Euston or Waterloo and pretend I was going to work as normal. Eventually I had nothing left.'

Peter was a type 2 diabetic and with nothing to eat, his blood sugar fell so low that one day he fainted and bashed his head. He ended up in St Mary's Hospital, where he was diagnosed with blood poisoning and he was in for a month. In August he was taken to a rehab in Wolverhampton. 'I hope someone is proud of me,' he posted sadly on Facebook a month later. Finally in November he was moved to the Prince Rupert. 'I didn't know anything about it, I was just happy to be nearer my kids, but Charlie and Jacki welcomed me and helped me adjust.'

He had started doing what was called a 'Walk and Talk' with someone from the Shropshire Recovery Partnership to help with depression and alcohol addiction. 'I'll be fine for a few weeks then there will be a trigger, usually from my ex, and I binge again,' he said.

Sometimes he would start raving about Chinese people hiding in the cupboards. 'The little people are trying to take my kids again!' he would shout. Another day he insisted Neil had his wife hidden in his room and tried to barge in.

'When he was on his vodka he was quite mad,' said Hannah.

Mostly Peter stayed in his room, writing his notes in coloured pens, only going to the Darwin for his meals. 'I try to have a rhythm,' he said. 'I get up, make my bed, check emails – and avoid triggers like my ex ...'

Peter also liked walking round the town and looking at all its old houses and watching the swans glide under the weeping willows on the river. 'It's such a beautiful place,' he said. Sometimes he would write poems about it. His latest was called 'The Covid Streets with No Names'.

He usually came up with the menus in the middle of the night. He was hoping Mike would use some in the hotel. 'I am still reeling at how you can go so quickly from one day having a family, home and a job and the next day nothing,' said Peter.

On his phone were photos of two gorgeous children on a slide, a smiling blond boy and a curly-haired girl. 'My son just got Star of the Week at school, so I am very proud,' he said. 'Now I want to be the best I can for them.'

Mike told Charlie to prepare the Princess Charlotte Suite, where she had previously been staying, for him and Rita to share. Then he set off back to Bournemouth to collect her. He'd been away longer than he planned, what with getting the car fixed, but at least she'd had the elections and all Trump's shenanigans to keep her occupied. The president was refusing to accept the results.

What was she going to think? California might be one of America's wealthiest and most liberal states, but Mike knew from his trip to visit her that many Californians didn't have a very positive view of the homeless, referring to them as vagrants, and there was growing anger there at the spread of vast encampments of people living under plastic and tarp, which locals said attracted rats and spread disease. But he thought Rita was open-minded and she'd told him about a friend of hers who worked at their local food bank and thought what they had done at the Prince Rupert was 'remarkable'.

He was sure she and Simon would get on, with their love of cathedrals. He just hoped Shaggy washed for a change, that Titch kept off the mamba and that Rob didn't flirt with her or Peter start raging about the little Chinese men in the cupboards.

30.

Sunday, 15 November 2020

Mike liked this time of year, with its misty days and crackling fires in the pubs and restaurants. It suited the town, giving the cobbled streets and timber-framed buildings a Dickensian feel, even if this year because of lockdown there were none of the usual stalls roasting chestnuts. Dickens had loved Shrewsbury, giving a talk at the Music Hall, which was now part of the town's museum, and staying in the Lion Hotel, from where in 1858 he wrote to his daughter, 'I can look all downhill and slantwise at the crookedest black-and-white houses, all of many shapes except straight.'

Not surprisingly the town had been chosen as the location for the 1984 remake of *A Christmas Carol*, much of the filming taking place around the Prince Rupert in Fish Street and by the Bear Steps. The gravestone the production had erected for Ebenezer Scrooge in St Chad's churchyard was still there and had become a tourist attraction. George C. Scott, who played Scrooge, had stayed at the Prince Rupert and framed black-and-white stills of the production hung in Chambers Bistro.

Inside the hotel, Charlie and Pam had already put up Christmas trees in the lobby, lounge and Darwin. Rita seemed to be adjusting to life in what was essentially a homeless hostel, however upmarket. Mike had warned her that no one wore masks and that the homeless wandered around and about them meeting who knows who so they could easily bring Covid into the hotel, but she too had discarded her mask.

He found her in the Darwin, chatting to Simon about cathedrals, and who she found fascinating, or Hannah who had lived in America.

'They're adorable,' she said.

He wasn't quite sure what they thought of this perfectly groomed Californian with all her luggage. It hadn't started well. They had arrived in the evening when he had thought the guests would all be at dinner. But it was fine weather and as he drove up, some of them were sitting outside. 'Is that your daughter, Mr M?' asked Hannah, as this trim blonde got out of the car.

He didn't know how to introduce Rita – it seemed odd to say 'my girlfriend'. He also felt awkward having her in the hotel he had created with his wife – Diane had even chosen the furnishings of the Princess Charlotte Suite, where they were staying and where Charlie had lived the past seven months.

'We were confused,' said Hannah. 'We thought his girlfriends were Charlie and Jacki. And there was a wife in the background. Then this American arrived holding his hand.'

Most of all he felt torn. Normally he would be working day and night, ending the day with a late supper and glass of wine with Charlie and Jacki, their entire focus on the homeless. Now they were wearing themselves out as usual and he was entertaining his girlfriend.

But Rita was his visitor and if he didn't take her out, he worried she would wonder why the hell she had come, particularly as she could not wander round shops or cafés because of lockdown. On fine days she walked to the Quarry Park and along the river to feed the ducks. Otherwise she stayed in her room, reading, knitting and doing yoga.

She insisted she didn't mind but Mike took her out whenever he could. On crisp autumn days they went for walks in the Shropshire

Hills, such as the Long Mynd, which was splendidly clad in purple heather. One day he drove her to Ludlow: the ancient market town was as deserted as he had ever seen it. They walked along the beautiful Georgian streets, round the old castle from which Wales was once ruled and down to the river, sitting by the watermill to eat the sandwiches he had prepared.

When they got back, Jacki and Charlie made them supper, serving them a spread of tapas and wine.

That day a little Welsh woman called Deb had been brought in under police protection, which usually meant domestic abuse.

Charlie was surprised to see her smiling. 'I put my smile on every day like lipstick,' Deb told her later. 'If I cry, I know I'll never stop.'

Behind that smile, most of her teeth were missing and it was clear she had been through a terrible ordeal. Over the last eight months they had heard some horrific stories but Deb's was beyond anything.

Now fifty-three, she had, she told them, been married at sixteen to a Welsh farmer called Leslie who had kept her prisoner in his bedroom for almost thirty years, tying her up, raping her and breaking almost every bone in her body. She had given birth to six children, every one of which had been taken away. Leslie had been her first boyfriend and she had met him in the local saloon bar. 'I knew he was the one,' she said. 'He was very good looking and assured.'

Eighteen months older, he was controlling from the start, but Deb initially thought he was being protective because she was so young. 'I thought it lovely,' she said.

An only child with a tyrannical father and having been bullied at school, she'd been only too glad to get away. 'I had no happy childhood memories – my mum hated me because she didn't want his kids and my dad hated me because he didn't believe I was his.'

Deb gave birth to her first child at eighteen. But the problems really started, she said, when she had her second two years later. 'Leslie was taking drugs and got paranoid and kept saying the boy doesn't look like me so you must be cheating on me. He left for a while but when he came back things started going downhill. He was beating me, raping me, sometimes for days. He was on amphetamines, so didn't sleep. I wasn't allowed to go to the toilet or eat or anything. He was a strong, strong man and I couldn't do anything. Then he would tie me to the bed and lock the door and go and get drunk. I would shout for a while but then give up. Sometimes he put a blanket over me to muffle me. I could hear the kids crying but couldn't do anything.

'Even when I was pregnant he hit me. He kicked me out of the car once when I was pregnant with my second daughter.

'Sometimes police came because neighbours called at all the commotion. What was I going to say? He was in the front room and I still had to stay with him after they went. I never told anyone. I didn't have the kind of relation with my mum to tell her. Also, they had a bad marriage so I didn't know any different.'

Deb did try to escape. 'I left him three times but he found me,' she said. 'The last time he dragged me out of the refuge and back home and threatened to kill the kids. He broke my arms so many times and when I was pregnant the scans showed the walls of my womb so thick that the doctors thought I had something wrong with me.

'In 1998 they came and took my kids away from me for neglect. I felt guilty but I was locked in a bedroom, tied to a bed for days and days, and the kids didn't get looked after. People told me it was not my fault, but of course I feel guilty. My youngest daughter was just five months then and I was pregnant – that baby was born in care and they took her away at two days.

'When they took my kids, I was suicidal. I tried to kill myself four, five, six times, because I had nothing to live for but nothing worked, so I realised someone must be watching over me and picked myself up.

'The hardest thing is the kids. I signed them over for adoption, as I was told it would be better for them so they didn't keep moving them, but it meant I have no contact with them apart from my eldest. Twenty years on, it's still painful. I don't even know if they are alive or dead.'

In the end Deb stayed, trapped in her abusive marriage, until 2011, when her husband was arrested. Yet it was not for what he had done to her. 'He went to jail for paedophilia,' she said. 'When the police came to take him, he kept me hostage to stop them. He held me for three days with a nail-gun at my head, then shot himself in the chest and tried to shoot me, but the police broke down the door and dragged me out.'

Finally being free of Leslie was not the end of Deb's problems. 'A year and a half after he went, I was in such a mess on drugs. Not only had I lost my kids but at the age of forty-five I had to learn how to handle money, how to be alone. For twenty-four hours a day, for all those years, if he moved, I moved – everyone called me his shadow.

'When someone sexually and physically assaults you for such a long period, they fuck with your head and you don't know what's true. I think the sky is blue but I have to have someone reassure me it is.'

To start with, Deb even went to visit Leslie in jail, until one of the girls at the refuge where she was staying informed the staff. 'I promised I'd just go one more time to say goodbye, then cut up my sim card so he couldn't contact me. Then he started sending letters to me, so they contacted the jail to stop them.

'But I had to keep moving because my son came after me. The first time he held a knife against my throat and demanded £10. I didn't even know that was wrong because of my past, but later told my support worker and she was shocked. They moved me but he found me again. I'd gone to college in South Wales to study cookery and English and loved it, but unfortunately one of the girls at that refuge told my son where I was. She didn't see the danger – he can be sweetness and light, a real Jekyll and Hyde.

'Now I'm very fast with packing,' Deb laughed wryly. Police had decided to move her out of Wales. 'I don't hold it against him,' she added. 'He was twelve when he was taken into care, so he saw some of the things his dad did, that's why he's messed up and also has bits of his dad in him. He also takes drugs – smack, crack and weed to take the pain away.

'I didn't walk away when my husband hit me,' she added. 'How could I when it was my child?'

She still cared for Leslie, even though he had caused her so much pain and anguish. 'No matter what he did, he was the love of my life and that makes it even worse. I still love him and if I look at a picture of him when he was young, I cry. I am hoping once I start divorce proceedings and change my name back, I can put him out of my head, I want him out of there.'

She was also planning to lay charges against him, though she was worried about having to relive everything in court. 'I've always got a smile on my face,' she said. 'It might be false but it's a smile.'

Though she put on her brave face, it was hard for Mike and Charlie to understand why Deb was not getting counselling. Apparently she had been told there was a delay because of Covid. 'I've spent my whole life walking on eggshells, at home then in my marriage,' said Deb. 'I have so many years of anger balled up in my stomach and when I let it out and cry, I cry like a baby.'

At the Prince Rupert, Deb soon drifted towards the most damaged souls, such as new arrival Fanny, who'd just arrived at the hotel with a broken shoulder and had apparently been trafficked. 'We discuss our broken bones,' laughed Deb. 'I am loving and caring and help people all day, it takes my problems away: it's come on, give me your problems. And I can always tell if people are hiding something – you can't bluff a bluffer.'

31.

Thursday, 26 November 2020

Rita had been slaving away in the kitchen for two days. Roast turkey, stuffing, garlic mash potato, cranberry sauce, carrots cooked in orange juice, broccoli with lemon butter, sweet potato casserole with pecans and marshmallows, pumpkin pie with candied pecans and whipped cream – a proper Thanksgiving feast.

Charlie had prepared a festive table in the restaurant, its crimson tablecloth decorated with garlands of pine cones and dried orange slices and candlesticks, and Rita brought out dish after dish of food. 'Nice to see you served upon for a change,' said Mike to Charlie and Jacki.

The meal was delicious – Mike particularly enjoyed the turkey stock gravy. 'Even better than yours,' he said to Charlie, who smiled tightly. But he felt guilty. Rita was trying so hard but his head was swirling with so many 'what ifs'. Would there be lockdown or no lockdown? Would his business survive? Would they be able to reopen? And what about the long-term effects even if they did – would people be put off because they had been housing homeless? The internet didn't forget, he knew: whenever they Googled Prince Rupert, this would always come up.

In the short term he needed to decide what to do about Christmas. The town had just switched on the Christmas lights but without the usual gathering or carol concert. In theory lockdown was due to end the following week, yet the government was still not saying if hospitality would be able to reopen. Boris Johnson was still insisting they would allow mixing at Christmas even though other countries had cut back religious festivals and many scientists were warning that allowing festive gatherings would be calamitous.

December would usually be the Prince Rupert's best and busiest time, its restaurants packed for Christmas parties, the tea rooms at their most crowded and the highest revenue coming in for the hotel. Profits from December would keep them going through the fallow months of January, February and March. After lots of toing and froing, that day Mike had phoned the company that usually printed their Christmas brochure and menus and said, 'Let's do it.'

On top of everything Pam had suddenly resigned. She had not been as integral to the project as Charlie and Jacki, but she had worked for Mike for two decades. His shelves in the Bournemouth flat were full of knick-knacks she had given him over the years.

They were also having issues with Titch, who remained devastated about not getting the contract on *The One Show*. 'Mr M promised me,' he told anyone who would listen. Neil, who had been given the contract, felt 'the whole thing had been done for TV – once lockdown came back, they wanted me to work for nothing'. Without guests, there was no need for a breakfast chef. He did not really want to go back to cheffing anyway.

With so much on his mind, Mike had not wanted to think about him and Rita. However, she knew things were not right and had written him a beautiful six-page letter saying, 'I know you are struggling to communicate with me.' But he had not opened up, feeling it was wrong to burden her with his problems.

He had moved out of the Princess Charlotte, back to his third-floor eyrie, ostensibly because she was not sleeping well. One day he asked her if she was missing her family and friends back home. 'Obviously,' she replied.

'Maybe you would sleep better if you go back home,' he said.

They weren't teenagers, he thought, they could handle this in a grown-up manner.

The atmosphere had changed in the hotel because for the first time they had families staying – single mothers with children who had found themselves homeless because of bad relationships or job losses rather than addictions. It was lovely to have children running round the corridors and watching Titch play dinosaurs with them. Their presence seemed to change the behaviour of the rough sleepers. As Mike now knew, many had children.

One of the single mothers was Emma, a quiet girl in her twenties with two children, who was always immaculately made up with fake eyelashes and dressed in expensive clothes. 'That's a £400 North Face coat,' exclaimed Charlie after she arrived. Emma had split up with the children's father and moved in with another man but it proved a mistake and after nine months he had kicked them out. She seemed so aloof that at first they assumed she thought herself above the others, yet afterwards they realised she was embarrassed to be homeless.

They even had a budding romance. A young woman called Jess, thirty-one, who was a waitress but had lost her job because of Covid then got kicked out of her accommodation, had left her little girl with her parents. Soon she became very friendly with a quiet unassuming man called Keele. He'd also lost his job as a delivery driver due to Covid and split up with his girlfriend, so had nowhere to live and had been staying in the Travelodge. 'Maybe we will have our first homeless wedding!' said Charlie.

As always there were complicated issues to deal with. Ivor, the man who had been cuckooed, had to be told to leave after he propositioned Deb and Charlene. Only then did they discover that he was a sex offender, just like Andy. Mike was furious that they had not been told. 'How could this happen twice?' he asked the council.

Julie had finally split with Andy and tried to come back to the Prince Rupert. 'Everyone had said you don't need him and one day I just thought, They are right,' she said.

He had been caught selling drugs and trying to pin it on her. 'He told me we can go down together and spend Christmas in jail together,' she said. 'He also got control of my bank account and had been taking my monthly Universal Credit and PIP, then using it for buying drugs and spending the day with Charlene.'

But the turning point was something else. 'When he went to jail before, everyone had told me he was a paedophile and it was even in the papers, but he told me it wasn't true so I defended him and supported him through court and went to visit him every day,' she said. 'Only when he is asleep can I have a proper conversation with him, so one night I asked, "Just tell me if something happened as I'm still getting abused about it." He turned round and said, "She asked for it." I woke him and said, "What?" "It was just a one off," he said.

'No,' she replied. 'I supported you, told everyone to fuck off when it was in the paper and they said you were a paedophile and you lied to me. That's it,' she said. 'You're going back to jail and I can't be with you any more.'

'I hope you die while I'm inside,' he replied.

Although the Prince Rupert was happy to take Julie back, the council did not think it a good idea she stay so near to Andy and instead sent her to the Travelodge at Battlefield.

The next thing they knew, Deb had suddenly disappeared. Knowing her background, they were worried something had happened but she called to tell them she had taken the train to Wales, even though she had been warned to stay away. After a week she came back again.

When she arrived, Simon started shouting at her for breaking lockdown. He kept having arguments with people, insisting on searching them for weed and mamba when they came into the Darwin.

Soon after Thanksgiving, packages began to arrive. Many of their residents ordered things on Amazon or eBay – Rob liked zombie books and Neil seemed obsessed with trainers, for example – but this was on an entirely different scale. 'What is all this stuff?' asked Mike, watching more brown boxes be brought in.

'It's Hope,' said Charlie. 'Her room is full of it. Kitchen appliances, £60 griddle pans. Just not clothes, sadly.'

'Where's the money coming from?'

'She gets lots of benefits from the Danish government,' said Charlie.

Hope was Danish and her real name was Agata, though she had been living in England for the last twelve years. When she had arrived at the Prince Rupert, the morning of the Thanksgiving dinner, her grey complexion, long grey hair and teeth like fangs gave her the look of a ghost. She was dressed in dark trousers and a black and grey Wolfskin parka, which she never took off. The council had warned them that she was very vulnerable – she had recently tried to jump off the English bridge.

She had grown up in Jutland, the only child of a single mother who she described as 'stifling'. She left home at eighteen and trained to be a dietician, but ended up working as a croupier in a casino, 'dressed in tiny dresses – it was very uncomfortable'.

Now forty, Hope had moved to the UK after striking up a relationship online with a man named Alan, a customer service representative in Liverpool. The following year, they had a daughter, Mica, 'such a loving girl'. But at the age of six the little girl started vomiting and complaining of stomach aches. She was eventually diagnosed with leukaemia and had to have chemo-therapy, spending months in hospital. She died at just eight years old.

Alan never forgave himself. When Mica was four, they had lived on the streets for a few desperate months after he lost his job. Then they'd been given accommodation infested with rats and moved to a place with 'a schizo upstairs screaming'. A long-time sufferer of irritable bowel syndrome, Alan didn't work again after Mica's death, living off benefits.

For a while they stayed in a caravan and were somewhere between Shrewsbury and Wales when its electrics blew. After that Alan's health deteriorated, and he ended up in the Royal Shrewsbury for stomach surgery. But his kidneys failed and 'at ten to five on 25 February' he died.

Hope was inconsolable and headed to the English bridge. 'I wanted to be with Alan and Mica,' she said. 'It was too much to lose both of them.'

She was stopped by police and taken to rehab, where she had spent the last seven months trying to come off drugs and alcohol. 'It was horrific,' she said. 'Near to me was a woman screaming all night.'

She also missed her cats, which had been put into a shelter by the council.

Hope was glad to be in the Prince Rupert and kept herself to herself. She went out early every morning down Grope Lane to Costa Coffee. 'The hardest thing I drink now is hot chocolate,' she said with her sad smile. Sitting outside with her paper cup on the bench in front of the church, she spent most of her time smoking and scrolling through her phone. They thought perhaps she was looking at photos of her little girl but these had all been lost, she said. Instead she was searching for gluten-free recipes. She didn't eat in the Darwin – a carer brought in her food. 'I have to be very careful,' she said. 'Rice can make me suicidal.'

Hope was an easy guest, always polite in her accented English. But she never changed her clothes and, according to an exasperated Gabriella, never flushed the toilet.

As the end of the second lockdown neared, Mike kept turning over and over in his mind what to do about Christmas. Even if they did reopen, there were going to be so many restrictions. And above all he didn't want to negate all they had done with the homeless. They still had twenty-eight residents and there was no way they could look after them and open, as they had in September, because this time of year would be too busy. But how could they turn them out on the eve of Christmas?

One morning, while Rita was knitting in her room, he talked it over one more time with Charlie and Jacki. 'You know what, let's stay closed and focus on making it a Christmas to remember for the homeless,' he said. 'Call the printers to cancel the menus,' he told Jacki. 'Let's make it a hell of a day!'

Jacki smiled and Charlie beamed. 'Yay!' she shouted.

32.

Thursday, 10 December 2020

Mike sat in his car at Heathrow's Terminal 5 car park and reflected on what he had done. It was a cold miserable day, low grey cloud, rain pitter-pattering in that English way that made him yearn for the bright blue skies and seas of the Caribbean. The airport was desolate and he wondered what that was all about. How could you think someone was so right, then in a flash it was all over and they were gone?

He shook his head, turned on the engine and took out his phone to put on charge. But there was a phone already there. Rita had left her phone! What could he do? There was no point in ringing her. He grabbed the phone, jumped out of the car and raced back to departures.

Inside the terminal, a sign read 'Passengers Only' and a security guard blocked his way. 'Are you travelling today, sir?' he asked.

'No, I'm trying to find someone.'

'Well, you can't come beyond here without a ticket. Covid restrictions.'

'You don't understand. My girlfriend is flying back to LA and she left her phone.'

'I can give it to Lost and Found and we can message her over the tannoy.'

'No, there's no time! Please just let me go to the check-in.'

Eventually the man agreed. Mike looked at the board for the British Airways counter for Los Angeles and ran. Please let her still be there, he prayed.

He spotted the familiar bob and svelte figure from behind. Rita was at the desk, handing over the last of her five cases.

'Rita!'

She turned and looked at him, eyes stained with tears.

'I've got your phone!' He was waving it.

She smiled in relief. 'I'd just realised and didn't know what to do,' she said. 'I only have your number in the phone, so I was thinking I would have to call the Prince Rupert to get them to phone you, by which time you're probably forty miles down the motorway.'

'Ma'am, you need to go through,' said the man at the desk.

Rita stood looking at Mike. He took her in his arms and kissed her and for a fleeting moment he thought about saying something, then he let her go and watched her walk away. She turned just once before disappearing through the security gate. Wasn't that phone fate? he wondered. Should he have told her, just grab your luggage, don't get on the flight?

He had no idea what she would have replied. All the way along the motorway back to the Prince Rupert, he was thinking he had done the wrong thing. He had found someone special he shouldn't have just let go.

33.

Monday, 21 December 2020

Normally this time of year would be manic: Christmas lunches for ninety or a hundred people, office parties that often ended in drunken disarray – the worst of all were lawyers and surgeons – and Christmas shoppers pouring into the tea rooms and the hotel lounge to rest their feet over a cuppa or a glass of mulled wine.

Instead the hotel was closed to all but the homeless, and Mike, Charlie and Jacki were in Millets telling an assistant dressed in a Father Christmas outfit, 'We need twenty-eight warm waterproof jackets and scarves.'

Donations had been pouring in. A British diplomat based in the Middle East had sent a cheque for £1,000 after reading an article about the hotel in the *Sunday Times* and a local businessman had sent £500. A woman from the West Bromwich Building Society had phoned to ask how many residents they had as they wanted to arrange presents for them. The Food Hub was still sending food. Local companies had donated everything from turkey crowns to vegetables. An anonymous donor had sent bubbly from Tanners and scores of pigs in blankets had arrived from Blakemans sausages.

Every time Mike went into the Darwin, there were children zooming around in reindeer hats and flashing noses. Perhaps because of the families, the homeless were surprisingly excited about Christmas.

'Are we going to have presents on Christmas Day?' they kept asking.

'You'll have more than you ever had in your life,' he told them.

'Oh my God, it's like having twenty-eight children!' exclaimed Charlie.

Every spare moment they kept discussing what to buy, what they would do on Christmas Day, what to cook, how the day would pan out. They went to Card Palace to buy Santa sacks for the presents and spotted Julie helping herself to cards and paper, winking at them as they passed by.

Everyone was going to get a new winter outfit, as well as some goodies, and there would be toys and books for the children, though the families would not be there on Christmas Day as they were allowed to meet relatives.

The government had brought in new restrictions the previous day after a new more infectious strain of coronavirus had been identified, the so-called Kent variant (later known as Alpha). Much of the country, including London and the South-east and East, as well as Scotland and Wales, was back in lockdown and not able to meet at Christmas.

Shropshire, however, remained in Tier 2, which meant three households could meet on Christmas Day, and shops, beauty salons and churches were open, as were restaurants. But pubs were not allowed to serve alcohol unless it was with a 'substantial meal'. No one knew what that meant until the Cabinet Office minister Michael Gove proposed a Scotch egg. Mike doubted whether police would really be going round pubs checking.

Mike did not regret his decision to stay closed. Although, in the end, hotels in Shrewsbury could open, there would have been so many restrictions, those lucrative Christmas parties would have been impossible and he could not imagine many people would be wanting to risk travelling. Some of his hotelier friends told him they were getting round the rules by having twenty-five tables of two instead of a party for fifty, but he did not think it was worth the risk.

All the Christmas preparations made a welcome distraction from his sadness over Rita's departure and the feeling that the distance between them was just too hard to overcome. Indeed, he told Charlie he had never enjoyed Christmas so much.

Finally it seemed there was some positive news on the pandemic. A vaccine had been developed in Germany by a team led by a Turkish husband and wife, Dr Uğur Şahin and Dr Özlem Türeci, for the pharmaceutical company Pfizer and been found to be more than 90 per cent effective. UK regulators quickly approved it and at 6.31 a.m. on 8 December, early riser Margaret Keenan, a ninety-year-old grandmother in Coventry, had become the first person in the world to receive it.

V-Day, as it was dubbed, was the start of the biggest vaccination programme in the history of the NHS. The Royal Shrewsbury had also started vaccinating that day, one of the first fifty hospitals chosen around the country to start vaccinating those aged eighty and over, as well as front-line staff. Another vaccine had been developed by a team at Oxford University for AstraZeneca. Maybe there was going to be a way out of this.

The only bad news was a call from a distraught-sounding Michael Lambert, saying he was going to be kicked out of his flat because his landlord had caught him hosting a group of friends.

'Are you sure that's all?' asked Mike.

'Well, maybe there was some mamba ...' he said.

'Let me talk to him,' said Charlie. 'I'm sure if you say you were confused by the rules and won't do it again, it will be okay.' She also called the council, who told her to tell Michael to stay put and they would sort it.

A few days later, Julie came by in tears. Her father had died from a heart attack, she said, and her mum wouldn't let her go to the funeral. 'I was a daddy's girl,' she sobbed. 'He was there for me with the kids, he took my eldest to school, brought me food and money. But my mum won't let me come because she says my younger sister would then refuse to bring her babby and it would upset her.'

As usual Julie's hands were fluttering like caged birds as she spoke and Charlie caught sight of some tracks on her wrists. 'I think she's self-harming again,' she told Jacki.

They knew that for some of their guests it was going to be hard at Christmas, like Peter who for the first time would not be seeing his children and had recently taken an overdose. When he disappeared on Christmas Eve, they were worried, but he came back telling them he had been to Shrewsbury Abbey.

'The priest said a prayer for my kids and I lit a candle,' he said.

34.

Christmas Day, 2020

'Look at you!' exclaimed Charlie.

Shaggy had come down super-smart in a nice tracksuit, his hair all washed and smelling fragrant.

Christmas songs were playing and all the residents had dressed up, and around 11 a.m. they had started coming down to the lounge, where they were greeted with a 'Merry Christmas!' and a glass of prosecco from Mike, Charlie and Jacki in Santa hats. Everyone was excited when they saw the sacks of presents. Titch could barely contain himself. Soon they were ripping off the wrapping like children, pulling things out and trying them on, swapping items with one another.

Each had a warm jacket, a gilet, socks, pants, a *Keep Calm and Carry On* T-shirt and chocolate and biscuits. There was a zombie book for Rob, the latest Lee Child for Shaggy, folders for Peter to keep his poems and recipes in, a golf book for Paul and a Man United dressing gown for Titch.

Some of the old-timers like Shaggy and Titch also had gift bags from the Ark, and there was hilarity as they pulled out gravy granules, packs of sage and onion stuffing, jars of bolognese sauce, colouring books and plastic signs saying 'Santa Stop Here'.

'Where are they supposed to put that?' asked Jacki. 'In the door-ways?'

Mike opened up the bar and the men were soon drawing pints. Shaggy downed eight. Titch was drunk after one and a half. Rob pocketed a bottle of prosecco.

Even Hope came down. She was carrying presents for the hotel staff – sparkly Christmas mugs from Costa Coffee and a sandwich maker for Charlie. 'It feels wrong homeless people giving me gifts,' said Mike.

They left the residents in the lounge while they went to prepare lunch. Soon they heard Simon shouting. He was having an argument with Neil and Kieran, a young guy who had arrived recently announcing, 'I was the tough nut of the Travelodge and anyone who takes me on, I'll floor.'

'That's not going to happen here,' said Mike. He had taken an instant dislike to the 'gobby little lad', particularly after he upset Gabriella by telling her 'you weren't fed at birth, that's why you're so short'.

They soon saw what Simon was shouting about. 'It was wicked,' said Mike. 'I walked through the lounge and these sacks, which had been bulging with hats, fleeces and gloves, were half-empty, so I realised what was going on.'

From what he and Jacki could see, Kieran was rifling through and had some kind of a system. Jacki spotted Hannah going through the bags and asked her what she was doing. 'Nothing,' she replied. 'Well, you've got a present in your hand,' said Jacki.

Hannah insisted this was all a misunderstanding. 'The sizes were all wrong and Charlie told us to swap,' she said. 'Neil got a T-shirt that was tiny and I had a sweatshirt that swamped me so we were looking in other bags to find the right size. Why would we want more than one?'

It was a sour note but they had been through enough over the past year not to let it spoil lunch, which this time took place in the Royalist Restaurant. Charlie and Jacki had perched Santa hats on the knights standing by the fireplace and between them they had produced a huge spread: prawn cocktails to start, followed by turkey that Mike carved and all the trimmings – roast potatoes, carrots, sprouts, cranberry sauce, stuffing and pigs in blankets. He teased Jacki, who was doling out the vegetables and seemed to be counting the carrots, calling her 'Mrs Money', much to everyone's amusement.

On the tables were crackers, which they all pulled with each other, shouting out the dreadful jokes and sticking them to their hats. Finally, even though they were all stuffed, came Christmas pudding, doused in brandy and set aflame, along with mince pies and brandy butter. There were lots of tears. 'In my whole life I never had a Christmas like this,' said Titch.

'It was wonderful,' said Peter afterwards. 'I never expected anything like this. I particularly loved the Brussel sprouts. I ate three plates piled high, then collapsed in my room.'

The only one who didn't eat was Hope. She never ate on the twenty-fifth of the month as it was the day her husband died. 'I

don't celebrate Christmas or Easter or any holidays because my daughter loved them so much and seems no point in celebrations without her,' she added. 'And seeing people around me laughing and happy is hard.'

Apart from the families, a few others were absent, such as Bev, who had gone to visit her son and grandchildren, and Deb, who was staying with a friend she knew from a refuge. When everyone had finished they cleared up, helped by a drunken Titch. In the afternoon the guests all just vanished and went to sleep.

They had cooked an extra ten lunches for their former residents who had moved to Number 70, including Chris Bennett and Stokesy, which they packed up and asked the security guards to deliver. Later, to Charlie's fury, they would discover it never arrived. Indeed Chris Bennett told her Dave Pritchard had tried to sell them Christmas dinner.

For the evening they put out an array of sandwiches and nibbles in the Darwin for those who might be peckish after their sleep. With that done, Charlie and Jacki had planned to leave around four that afternoon to join their own families, but they came across Simon in the lobby in tears. He had brought all his belongings down and said he was leaving. He hadn't touched his own presents. It turned out that Kieran had been picking on him all afternoon, annoyed that he had accused them of stealing the presents and teasing him about his appearance. Simon had hated bullies since he was at school.

Mike was livid. 'He's an old man who is gentle, frail and wise. You should be talking to him about his experiences in life, not making fun of him.'

'How would you feel if that was your grandad?' asked Charlie.

'Horrible,' replied Kieran.

'Well, that's what you've done,' she said.

She and Jacki sat with Simon, hugging him as he cried and cried, then Mike had an idea.

'Simon, would you like a glass of port?' he asked.

'Yes, please,' he nodded.

Mike opened a bottle of vintage port. After three generous glasses, Simon was smiling again.

It was after six and dark when Jacki and Charlie finally left to see their own families. Mike walked them to the car park then went home himself for a bottle of bubbly and dinner and presents with Diane and Alexander. It felt like going on vacation, being away from the hotel, but he also felt proud to have seen so many of their residents so happy.

He couldn't help remembering a few years before when they had lots of food left over from Christmas lunch at the hotel and it was a particularly cold day, and thinking, This is crazy, all those guys out there in sleeping bags, we should be wrapping the remainder up and giving it to them. But then he thought there was probably an organisation doing that. And if he did do it, the homeless might want to come back and start coming to the hotel all the time. So he had done nothing. He knew better now.

Next day they all came down wearing their new coats and hoodies and went into town to show them off.

Simon's presents remained wrapped up in the gift sack.

35.

Wednesday, 6 January 2021

The phone call came around 4.15 p.m. Mike and Charlie had gone to Marks & Spencer, so Jacki answered. It was the mother of Nicole, an eighteen-year-old who had arrived recently. Her mum was hysterical. Nicole had texted a friend to say, 'Goodbye, look after my family', and the friend had called her.

Jacki grabbed the master key and ran to Nicole's room, calling one security guard to go with her and the other to phone Mike and Charlie. Inside, Nicole was standing on a chair, a noose round her neck made from two pairs of bootlaces strung from a hook on the Tudor beam.

'Nicole! What are you doing?' Quickly, before she could kick away the chair, they got the noose down and just as quickly Nicole grabbed a belt from the drawer, but the security guard swooped and snapped it. Charlie ran through the door, panting.

For the next two hours she and Jacki tried to talk Nicole down, then the police came. At that point Nicole went wild, banging her head on the wall and pulling her hair out furiously. It was clear she needed twenty-four-hour monitoring.

'Get her out of here,' said Mike. 'I don't want her in here.'

'Listen to me,' said Charlie, as Jacki tried to restrain her, which was not easy as Nicole was a big girl. 'What's this all about?'

All Nicole would say is that something had happened to her when she was young. Charlie was mystified. She was clearly from a good family and bright – Nicole had told her she wanted to be a vet.

Finally an ambulance arrived. 'Please walk to the ambulance,' pleaded Charlie. 'If they carry you, you will be sectioned.' She knew this from her own experience with Gabriella.

Nicole did as she said and they took her to a mental health facility. Later Charlie spoke to her grandmother, who explained that when Nicole was twelve she had been abducted after school by a sixth-former. He had taken her to the local woods and raped her. For the next two years he did it repeatedly. Nicole told no one but became anorexic. She tried to kill herself at home and her mother had been unable to cope, so Nicole had been taken into care. There her anorexia had been replaced by compulsive eating. 'Poor kid,' said Charlie.

It was a dramatic start to the year, which had otherwise begun with a bit of a whimper.

To Mike's surprise, after the success of Christmas none of their residents had wanted to celebrate New Year. When he suggested a party, Titch said, 'Don't bother, it's just another day.' Most of them drank every day anyway. None even seemed to acknowledge the new year. From his window, he stared at the leaden skies and the rain sheeting down. It felt like an anti-climax.

Charlie had gone home and played games with Gabriella and Fraser. Jacki spent it with her mum. Mike had driven home and had a drink with Alexander, only the second time he had been at home for New Year's Eve since he was nineteen – working in hotels, Mike was usually on call or hosting events for guests.

Everything was closed again. On 5 January the country had gone into its third national lockdown. 'I must be the only woman in Britain looking forward to it,' said Charlie.

Daily Covid cases were up to sixty thousand and, according to the Office for National Statistics, more than 2 per cent of the population were infected, over a million people in England alone. All this, said Boris Johnson, meant 'we have no choice'. He warned that the weeks ahead would be 'the hardest yet'.

Hospitals were filling up, faster even than during the previous highest peak in April, one admission every thirty seconds, according to the chief executive of the NHS, and this time many of the patients were younger, fitter people. The military had been drafted in to help. Mike felt for the nurses and doctors who had worked so hard all year with barely a break, risking their own lives.

Like the first lockdown, schools were shut and they had no idea how long it would go on for. Certainly at least seven weeks, as the government had said the roadmap out was to be announced on 22 February. 'One Last Push' said the front page of the *Sun*. 'Lockdown 3: The Worst Sequel Yet' in the *i*. 'Hope and Fear' was the headline on the *Evening Standard*, referring to the vaccine.

As front-line workers, Mike, Charlie and Jacki had been called for their first vaccine, which were being carried out in the local bowling alley. Mike fervently hoped the vaccine would mean this lockdown would be the last. Business, particularly retail and hospitality, couldn't survive much more of this. Some of the shuttered shops and cafés in Shrewsbury would never reopen. The UK economy had shrunk by a record 9.9 per cent the previous year, worse than predicted and more than twice as much as the previous largest annual fall on record. Indeed it was the worst since the Great Frost of 1709. Not only had the UK suffered the highest death toll in Europe but it had experienced a steeper slump than almost any other major economy apart from Spain.

* * *

One cold night in late January, Titch took umbrage at the security guards telling him not to go in the kitchen and he started shouting and swearing at them. He threw his keys on one of the glass tables and it broke, leaving them no option but to report him. The council had ruled that anyone who did damage to the property had to be moved, so his funding was stopped and they had to put him out in the freezing cold.

Later, watching *Match of the Day* in the lounge, Mike saw Titch's little face pressed up against the window. 'I could see he was pleading to come in, but I ignored him as we have given him so many chances and he has to learn,' he said.

To his irritation, Charlie and Jacki went out to talk to Titch. 'I can't see him out there, he's part of our family,' said Charlie. 'I would take him home with me if I had a spare room. It breaks my heart this poor kid.' She said to Mike, 'You've been parading him in front of cameras and social media and now you won't help him.'

The next day Charlie saw Titch walking up and down Butcher Row with his case, trying to get attention and asked him, 'Where are you sleeping?'

'Outside Tesco,' he said. She shook her head. Without talking to Mike, she told him to come back to the hotel and called the council to get their approval for him to return temporarily. She told Mike the council had asked them to take him back.

'What else could I do?' she said afterwards. 'Otherwise, he'd be taken somewhere where there isn't the support and fall back into bad habits and through the cracks, after all we did for him.'

The next morning they all woke to muffled sounds outside and a sky lighter than it should have been. Mike opened the curtains to see postcard-like scenes of the church and twisty tree blanketed in snow, which was coming down in thick flakes all around. Charlie had always loved the snow and would normally be excited, out building snowmen with her kids. Now she thought of all the

Titch and Charlie.

people shivering on the streets. 'Thank God we took Titch back in,' she said.

36.

Wednesday, 3 February 2021

'Ow,' grimaced Charlie, chopping onions in the kitchen for that night's chilli con carne. 'That knife is razor sharp. Look, I've sliced my finger.'

The offending item was a knife that had been ordered online by Hope, who had told Charlie she was thinking of killing herself with it because people kept stopping her jumping off the bridge. Charlie was horrified. 'We can't have a knife in the room,' she said, sitting with Hope for a while, trying to talk things through and improve her spirits.

After she and Jacki had served the homeless supper, they were eating roasted salmon and vegetables with Mike in the lounge when they heard banging on the window. One of their ex-guests Richard Boffey was outside blowing kisses. 'I love you!' he shouted.

'I miss him,' said Charlie. 'I liked him, even though he was smelly.'

'Hmm,' said Jacki. 'Don't you remember him coming down with his pants halfway down his legs, scratching his bottom, then calling an ambulance three nights in a row saying he was allergic to garlic?'

'He just wanted attention,' said Charlie.

Jacki shook her head. 'Look, Boffey's with the Black Widow,' she said. The Black Widow was what their homeless guests called a young woman always dressed like a goth who had been with a number of their mates when they had overdosed and died. Among these was one of their former guests, Antony Haycock, who had left in July for the Battlefield Travelodge and died there a month later.

Boffey had also left around that time and ended up sleeping outside Barclays for a while, but had come back to the Prince Rupert for a few weeks in the autumn. He was then moved again to the Holiday Inn Express in a business park outside town, where there was nothing to do so he often came back.

'Let's send some food out to him,' said Charlie. She prepared a tray and got Hannah to take it to him.

The next morning they came in to shocking news. Police had found Boffey dead in the early hours behind the church, along with their plates of food and a dirty needle.

He had been taking drugs with Neil and Titch, who was in a terrible state, yabbering away so fast he was hard to understand. 'It was me who told the police,' he said. 'Neil was washing cocaine and Boffey smoking heroin in a crack pipe. He offered me some and I said no. He said, "That's strong", and was falling over on me. Hannah came with the food and Neil said he was going. She said, "You can't just leave him", but he did. I said to Boffey to sit up but next minute he was on his hands and knees snoring. I went to get a drink and came back with Bevan [another local homeless]. He said, "You all right, Boffey?" but there was no answer. Boffey didn't move, so I went to call the police.'

As the news quickly spread, there was consternation among the guests, as well as some of their former residents, who gathered near the twisty tree. The bad heroin had come from a dealer known as Frumpy, who most seemed to know. Many were angry with Neil for leaving Boffey because all the addicts should have had naloxone kits to reverse an overdose. 'We had the kits in reception, which could have saved his life,' said Jacki. Neil insisted Boffey had been fine when he left him. 'Boffey was his friend,' said

Hannah. 'It's very hurtful to Neil that anyone would say such a thing.' Others claimed Titch had emptied Boffey's pockets before the ambulance came, pointing out that he had not called 999 until hours after Boffey died.

The sad reality was that deaths from drug misuse in the UK were at record levels that year – Boffey was one of 4,561 drug deaths in England and Wales, a number that had nearly doubled over the previous quarter of a century and was three times the EU rate. The majority were, like Boffey, aged between forty and fifty, and almost half from heroin. Many went unnoticed – people walking past the empty doorway where the person normally slept.

It seemed no coincidence that numbers had risen starkly the previous decade, at the same time as government austerity programmes had seen cuts in addiction services and particularly since 2013 when responsibility for their provision had been shifted from the NHS to cash-strapped local councils. An independent review by Dame Carol Black published in July 2021 found that spending on treatment for drug abuse had fallen 17 per cent since 2014 and for young people by 28 per cent, and that provision for treatment urgently needed repair.

While they were all talking about Boffey, the fire alarm went off – someone else running their hot shower too long to create a sauna for faster absorption of drugs. Mike shook his head. It was all very dispiriting.

Titch, who he had invested so much in and who called him Dad, was once again red-eyed, his head drooping from mamba. Titch was also upset. He knew he was on probation since breaking the table. 'Mr Matthews and me have these fall-outs,' he said. 'He lets people get too comfortable and close but doesn't understand that people who are desperate will do anything for drugs.'

Later that day Boffey's father came by. He seemed a nice man and to Mike's astonishment, he lived just two miles away. 'All the time he was at the hotel, we'd had no idea his dad was so near,' he said. 'If your son was living in the doorway of Barclays just up the road, wouldn't you go and find him? What's that all about?'

Boffey's death seemed to Mike the culmination of the past few weeks, in which he felt like they were losing control. He was on edge. He lost his temper with the security guards, who seemed to do nothing but watch football and wrestling on their phones. It irritated him seeing more and more Amazon packages arriving. He complained to Gabriella about all the fingerprints on the glass entry door – why couldn't people use the handle?

It wasn't just Mike feeling the tension. Deb left, saying she couldn't stand Titch running round the corridors and Simon shouting at her. 'He pretends he is deaf but he watches everything,' she said.

Maybe they had been wrong not to establish rules like other hotels that had taken in the homeless. For the first time, Mike decided to 'bolt the door' a bit. 'It was, if you want to stay here, fine, but I am not engaging.'

When Kieran, the mouthy young man who had so upset Simon at Christmas, overflowed his bath and water started dripping through the ceiling, Mike called the council and got him out. He had never done that before. 'That gave them all a kick up the bum,' said Charlie.

Mike, Charlie and Jacki often talked about how they missed the characters of the first lockdown. 'They had been more our age and were people you could talk to. They had life experience,' said Mike. 'Even Dave Pritchard, for all his volatility, was someone you could laugh and cry with.'

'It was easier with hardened rough sleepers,' said Charlie. 'You could shout at them more and they would listen.'

Mike also felt like the tide was turning against them. If people saw anyone begging in a doorway, they'd ask, why isn't the Prince

Rupert keeping these people under control? The hotel had even had abusive messages posted on its Facebook page. The only bright spot was Paul with his Lambrini and hats, which he changed weekly, depending on what his son wanted him to wear. Paul had recently run into his old headmaster, who was widowed and lonely, and started walking his dog, which he said had given him a new purpose.

Normally this time of year they would be doing renovations. With a hotel that age, they were always updating. There were another sixteen bathrooms to renovate, thirty-four bedrooms needing new furniture, the bar lounge furniture and decor looked tired and in want of upgrading, and they needed a new kitchen. 'There are always things to do in an old hotel,' said Mike. 'You never become a millionaire!'

The day after Boffey's death, Julie came by. 'Too many deaths,' she said. She had been in the Travelodge when Antony Haycock died. 'I'd only seen him ten minutes before,' she added. 'He was with the Black Widow.'

Julie now had her own room in Wem, a quiet town about eleven miles away, but she did not know anyone there. She said she got the bus into Shrewsbury most days. She had started cutting her arms again.

'While I was in the Prince Rupert, I reduced a lot of drugs because they gave me the opportunity to do TV interviews and talked about a cleaning job, so I wanted the opportunity to prove myself,' she said. 'When I talked to Charlie I wasn't judged or condemned like most people do. Sometimes I'd wake up in a bad mood and think, I need a bag, but then I'd walk down and see Charlie and talk to her and do something else, and then I wouldn't want it. Now in Wem I don't have anyone like that.'

Her daughters were also living in Wem, with their foster mum, less than ten minutes away, just the other side of the railway line, which was both good and bad. Julie was tearful as she had seen them that morning and had to turn away because she was not allowed contact, just one letter a year.

'My eldest has just turned eleven,' she said. 'She is the spitting image of me and still has her curly hair.'

'You have lovely hair,' said Charlie.

Julie smiled. She had brought a red bag of beautifully wrapped gifts for Charlie's birthday, which was in a few weeks. 'I wonder where they were stolen from,' Charlie laughed with Jacki after she had gone.

Dave Pritchard also came in, dressed in a white Pierre Cardin T-shirt and grey strappy jeans, and sat on the sofa, trying to squeeze close to Julie who quickly left. He was shouting as usual. He had just been thrown out of Number 70. 'They wouldn't let me use the phone as someone was using it to make drug deals and I wanted to speak to my mum and was upset, so I punched the wall,' he said. 'No matter what I do I am screwed.'

He too was tearful as he had just seen his little girl in the Co-op and she had called 'Daddy!', but he was not allowed contact. He had to watch her walk away with his ex and her new partner. He was, he said, still waiting for mental health support. He told them he had taken lots of pills the previous week to try and kill himself. 'Welcome to our world: you're a minority not worth bothering with,' he raged. 'That's how society view things.'

Charlie and Jacki calmed him down and called the council to arrange for him to stay in a new place known as the Pods. 'You'll like it,' said Charlie. 'It's country, near the river, where I run every morning. I can come by.'

Later Chris Bennett told them that Dave Pritchard had not just punched the wall in Number 70 but smashed all the TVs. 'And Derek Tyrer took all the pans from the kitchen and sold them ...'

Michael Lambert also popped by. He was still in his job and flat, and now had a girlfriend. He still did the occasional mamba, he admitted, but only to forget things when he wasn't working. 'I'm still waiting for my mum to say sorry,' he said.

Sitting on the sofa, sipping from his bottle and watching on, Simon was philosophical. 'The lunatics have left the asylum,' he said. 'One lunatic leaves, another comes ...' He gestured towards Tyler, a twenty-two-year-old who had arrived from the Travelodge and was impeccably dressed in a turquoise peacoat and grey trilby with a green feather, carrying a cane, and spoke in an elaborate drawl. He went off walking every day and lived in his own world. 'I go which way my feet and the wind take me, towards my palace,' he said. 'I walked in the woods and a swan bit me,' he told Gabriella, 'but only on my left hand because the other one is magic.'

Most days Tyler went and sat in the Dingle, which had reopened and he had taken a liking to, perhaps because of the name. 'I like to sit and eat with the fairies but they run away when children come.'

It was unclear how he had ended up homeless. 'I liked school but never had the chance to get on with it, not being a happy person,' he said. 'I woke up one day at five to ten in the morning and police were on my mum's sofa, waiting to take me away. Now I want to get back to my mum's, but it seems like mission impossible. I am, you could say, stuck in something of a predicament.'

Then there was Rebecca, a twenty-year-old who shortly after arriving handed over to Charlie a plastic fork with three nails embedded between the prongs that she had been using to self-harm. She lifted up her sleeves to show scars all over her arms. 'How long have you been doing this?' asked Charlie, horrified.

'Since twelve,' replied Rebecca. 'It's my life now. It's my own fault,' she added. 'My stepdad abused me. He was a crackhead.'

'No woman is to blame for being abused,' Charlie told her. 'You must never ever think that.'

'It was either me or my little sister. And she was only five.'

Rebecca showed Charlie a photo of four children in a country lane – her, her brothers and sister. 'They looked so sweet and innocent,' said Charlie afterwards. 'They could have been my children.'

A few days later Rebecca called Charlie to her room, saying she was thinking of self-harming again. 'Look, I can do it with anything,' she said, taking a rubber out of her handbag and showing the tracks she had made on her arms.

'Can I ask you next time to stop and think, I'm better than this?' asked Charlie.

The council had insisted that Titch move on and finally, on Friday 19 February. he agreed to go to the Holiday Inn. Charlie settled him in. Within a day they spotted him back on Pride Hill in a filthy sleeping bag and begging for cash to buy drugs. 'It's so frustrating,' said Mike. 'I don't believe we could have done more for him. But it shows how difficult it is to change someone from what they have known all their lives.'

That same weekend Mike broke up a drug deal behind the church. He'd been having a glass of wine in the lounge when he spotted the man known as Frumpy, the same dealer as had supplied Boffey, waiting nearby to supply some of their guests. Mike called the police, then went out to stop the deal. When they got there, the police told him off for intervening, saying he could have got hurt. 'If I had waited for them to arrive, the drugs would have changed hands and someone else could have died,' he shrugged.

That night he contacted Rita. 'If I had asked you to come back that day at the airport, would you have come?' he asked.

'Yes,' she said.

37.

Friday, 19 March 2021

'A hotel is something very personal,' Mike always told new staff. 'It's not a factory or a card shop. It creates memories — people celebrate christenings, birthdays and weddings in hotels. Our job is to make them as special as possible.'

Over the past year, some very different memories had been created, not just for their guests. Never in his wildest dreams had he imagined that he would spend a year living with the homeless — people with nothing more than the clothes they stood up in, perhaps a plastic bag with a few items.

Normally, however much you tried to offer personal service, hotels could be quite anonymous. People brushed past each other in lifts or the breakfast buffet without exchanging a word, many not wanting to interact. Instead they had been able to get to know their unusual pandemic guests as people, to laugh and cry with them, be with them in their darkest moments and witness improvements.

'We saw them late at night when they were crying, arguing, rattling, overdosed,' said Jacki. 'We saw it all. At the end of the day we've all got issues, just theirs are fuelled by drink and drugs.'

Though it had been frustrating having so little information about them from the council or the Ark, in a way it had enabled the staff to get to know them with no prejudice. All would always look at homeless differently now, having learned how so many had been made to feel like throwaway children, beaten, abused and left to think themselves worthless. Mike hoped they had created a family for many who had never had one.

Yet he felt humbled and he knew that more than anything it was he, Jacki and Charlie who had benefited – yes, they had given shelter at the inn to those with none, but it was their own lives that had been changed. 'We gave them hope but they gave us something much more,' he said.

In so many ways it had been a terrible year, a year of plague that had taken more than 3.5 million lives around the world, a time of not being able to hug or even see loved ones, when for so many schooling and university had been disrupted and for the most part, people had been prisoners in their own homes, with no socialising or travel.

It would have been easier not to do this, just to stay home, sit in the garden and take the government money, but he couldn't have closed a hotel that had been open for centuries.

Schools had reopened on 8 March and people were allowed to meet one on one outdoors. From 12 April, shops, gyms and beauty salons could reopen and outside dining could restart. Yet when the government said hotels would not be able to reopen till 17 May, Mike realised he was relieved.

'So why did you do it?' asked Paul, their Lambrini-guzzling gambling addict who had been living in a tent on the golf course.

'Good question,' said Mike, who was standing in the lounge, trying to make a speech.

It was a year since their first guest had arrived. Mike had been planning to invite all their old residents back and hold a big anniversary party with a buffet for sixty or seventy. But he realised it would breach Covid rules. Instead he had set up a table in the lounge bar with bottles of prosecco from Tanners and platters of smoked salmon and prawn canapés, and had rounded up their remaining guests, never an easy task. The offer of free alcohol had helped.

Hannah sashayed in looking glamorous in a dark clingy dress and heels, face made up and adorned with silver jewellery. Simon was ensconced in front of the TV, watching his beloved Wales take on France in the rugby Six Nations. They had already beaten England, which was a shame because Mike had finally got him to promise to change his clothes if they lost. 'That'll do nicely,' he smiled as Mike opened him a Châteauneuf-du-Pape instead of his usual Tesco plonk.

Gradually Rob, Shaggy and Paul drifted in. Even Hope joined, though she refused to eat, mostly scrolling through recipes on her phone. Tyler popped his head through to announce, 'I will not be attending this gathering as I have matters to attend to.' He was upset, he said, because the guards had made a comment about his personal hygiene.

Once they were gathered, Mike stood up with a glass. 'This is to a year of looking after homeless – I don't like to say homeless, for you have a home here – a year of looking after wonderful human beings.

'The hotel business is very demanding and challenging – it becomes your life and a way of life where all your focus is on your guests, so when the government said last year we had to close we fought against it and were desperate to keep this place open. It's been open for centuries. When the opportunity came to stay open by taking in homeless, we celebrated.

'We thought it would be for a few weeks but fifty-two weeks later we are still here and I can honestly say without a shadow of doubt it has been an incredible period. I am sixty-two and if someone told me when I was nineteen and first said I wanted to work in hotels, you'll spend a year looking after the homeless, I would never have believed it.'

It was not easy to speak as he kept being interrupted. 'What's up, Mr M? You won the lottery or something?' called John, a previous resident, who was passing by and spotted the festivities through the window.

'Can I pull a pint?' someone asked.

'Shut up!' shouted Simon, who was trying to watch the rugby.

Mike continued. 'We thought it would be an experience we'd never forget and it has been.'

'It was a hell of a risk you took,' said Paul. 'Couldn't you have just closed and taken government handouts?'

'It would have been a different ballgame,' replied Mike. 'We would have taken government grants and Charlie and Jacki furloughed. This hasn't been for financial gain,' he added. 'The government has been incredibly generous … But the experience has been life-changing.'

'It opened your eyes,' said Hannah.

'Well, I raise a glass to you, sir,' declared Paul.

'How did it start?' asked one of them. 'Did you go and get people from the street?'

Mike explained about the council. A phone call made. A scrap of paper almost lost. 'We were last on their list,' he laughed. 'I couldn't have done it without Charlie and Jacki,' he added.

Everyone agreed. 'They are angels,' said Simon.

'We had one day off in 365,' said Charlie. 'Me to move and Jacki to clean her house.'

'Do you look at the homeless differently?' asked Hannah.

'It's been very humbling,' said Mike. 'It made us think of others less fortunate.'

'It's been trying at times,' laughed Hannah.

'You went through this dealing with the lowest of the low,' said Rob.

'Speak for yourself!' she said.

'We never ever came to the point we didn't want them here,' said Charlie. 'It could be any of us in their shoes. I know after my Mez died I could have taken that very route.'

Paul had one last question. 'When this is all over and we are rehoused, will this affect guests coming?'

Mike smiled. 'I knew by doing this that there is judgement in the world: the internet doesn't forget. Whenever people Google Prince Rupert it will come up, but I think the majority are understanding and will think this was an interesting project when the whole world closed down. And if they are not, then are they the kind of people we want staying?'

A few days later, on 23 March, the anniversary of the first lockdown arrived. At midday a national one-minute silence was held in memory of all those who had died in the pandemic, followed by the tolling of bells, including from the many churches across Shrewsbury.

That afternoon Hope left to go to sheltered accommodation, needing two taxis for all her Amazon purchases. She seemed happy. 'There is too much noise here,' she said.

While they were seeing her off, a phone message came from Dave Pritchard. 'Please say thank you and goodbye to Mike, Charlie and Jacki,' it said, which left them worried.

Hannah and Neil were finally on a housing list, as Neil had negotiated with the council to pay £80 a month towards their debt, and when his Universal Credit had come through he'd immediately transferred the £80 to Jacki so he wouldn't spend it.

Upstairs in the Darwin, Simon was sitting with his bottle of red, watching *Escape to the Country*, one of his favourite programmes. 'You watch all these property programmes,' said Charlie. 'Wouldn't you like a house of your own?'

'No,' he laughed. 'Give me a tree and a river. Spring is coming and I'll be gone soon,' he added. 'This is the longest time I've been under one roof in thirty-five years.'

But he was looking frail. His dinner from the night before was under his chair as usual, but these days he barely pecked at it. He refused to be vaccinated against Covid, as had most of the homeless guests. Always suspicious of authority, they seemed convinced that it was a government plot to insert microchips to control the population.

'They want to turn us into zombies,' said Tyler.

As more and more people were vaccinated and daily Covid deaths came down to single figures, they couldn't ignore reality. It was time to start preparing for reopening the hotel and there was lots to do. Painting, new drains, deep cleaning of the rooms to get rid of the smell of smoke and weed. Plants for the courtyard, where from the following month they could do outside dining. A request to the council to have tables outside the front of the tea rooms. Mike asked Charlie to do an inventory of all the china, glass and cutlery – by now there were 150 missing spoons. They also needed to order replacement duvets and pillows.

'In a way we got off lightly,' said Mike, as they assessed the damage. 'In normal times we don't go a whole year without a chair being broken, lampshades, taps and towel rails destroyed. We get bedwetters, red wine on the carpet.

'Real guests can be very annoying – you get people saying, "I don't want all those Tudor beams in my room – I don't like history." Once we had a single room booked and could hear a lot of strange noise, like gas escaping, so were worried and used the master key to open it. Inside, there were five of them doing laughing gas and crack cocaine, and one more jumped out from the wardrobe.'

There was also something else he was preparing – he got plans drawn up to convert part of the townhouse into a three-bedroom apartment. Over the last few weeks he had spoken more and more to Rita and eventually put his cards on the table. 'It wasn't 100 per cent successful before for whatever reason, but you can't bury feelings and I miss you,' he said.

She had agreed to try again and would be flying out a month after her son's wedding in June. The apartment could take a while because the property was listed, so they would rent in Shrewsbury or he would commute from Bournemouth in the meantime. Mike felt better about it than the previous year. 'The timing wasn't right before,' he said. 'It will be different now, I hope.'

38.

Monday, 17 May 2021

Mike, Jacki and Charlie stood outside the hotel and waved good-bye to Simon. He was off to an old people's home in a nearby village, grumbling as he got into the taxi that what he really wanted was to follow the birds and find a good cathedral yard.

'Bless him,' said Charlie, wiping a tear. That morning, before leaving, he had asked her to be his next of kin. His health was deteriorating and they had managed to persuade him to see a doctor, who had sent him for a scan and they feared the worst. They still hoped he would get back on the road and they could visit him with a picnic and a fine red in a church garden some-where.

He was the last guest to leave.

The Everyone In scheme was over. Hannah and Neil had been moved a few days earlier, needing two estate taxis for all the things they had accumulated. Hannah had left her room in a terrible state with so many cigarette ends ground into the carpet.

Their new home was a caravan overlooking the river in the small touristy town of Ironbridge at the back of a B&B that had seen better days. Hannah scrubbed it clean, hung fairy lights over the window, scattered colourful cushions and pinned up some of her art, and was excited when a deer ran by. Yet it was cramped, stifling on hot days and far from anything. 'Temporary accommodation is not the answer,' she said. 'We all need our own space and front door.' The couple had grown to love Shrewsbury and were hoping to rent a flat there.

Shaggy had ignored the taxi sent for him to move to the Travelodge and disappeared without saying goodbye, leaving his room full of dirty needles. He was back on the streets, collecting cardboard to sleep on, a doorway up from Derek Tyrer. One evening he passed Mike in the hotel lobby with a bulging pillow-case over his shoulder, then raced up the road.

'What was in the bag?' Mike asked the guards.

'Sandwiches,' they said.

Mike was confused. 'What?'

'He gets them from begging all day, then is going to swap them for drugs,' they explained.

Mike sighed. 'It's all so complex. So people buy them sand-wiches, which they convert to heroin. It's all about drugs and being part of the gang who take them. It seems to take over their minds until the only thing that matters is obtaining the next fix.'

Nine months back, he had thought they had cracked it, but he realised they were naive, that getting out of this vicious cycle required more than a hotel, nice food and support. In the end, a hundred homeless people had stayed at the hotel over the past fourteen months, but there had been fewer complete successes than they had hoped for.

Laura Fisher, head of housing for Shropshire Council, thought they were setting their standards too high. 'For many of these individuals, this is the longest period they have been accommo-dated in one place in their adult life,' she said. 'To me, success is not just those who moved on to private accommodation and got jobs, but also those who are now living in hostels like Stokesy in Number 70, which would have been unthinkable a year ago.'

Lenny, the housing coordinator, agreed. 'It's the little things that stick in the mind. The quiz. The birthday cakes. Seeing them go to the pub like normal people when lockdown ended. The real biggie was making them feel someone cares about them, many of them have never had that.'

And some of their former residents were sorting themselves out. Peter had popped back to tell them he had got a flat, a new job as a chef in a restaurant in town and was paying his bills. 'My life has changed dramatically,' he smiled. 'I may even have a lass in my life.' It was still a struggle getting to see his children. 'If I've heard one excuse from my ex, I've heard twenty,' he complained. But by holding down his job and flat, he was hoping this would change.

Hope had settled into her sheltered accommodation and got her cats back, and was cooking her own gluten-free meals using the appliances she had ordered.

Paul had a new place, was still meeting up with his old head-master for walks and brought them each a bottle of wine to thank them. 'Good stuff, not my Lambrini!' he laughed.

Martin the boxer was still working and looking after his flat while waiting for his assault case to be heard. The hearings had been delayed because of Covid.

Deb, the Welsh woman who had been tied up and abused for twenty-seven years by her husband, had got her own place in shel-tered accommodation for over fifties in her beloved Wales. 'It's small but it's nice, near Morrisons, and on a bus route,' she said.

Chris Bennett and Stokesy were still at Number 70. Bennett had a torn ear after having been punched by a friend of Shaggy and was miserable. One day he had been in Stokesy's room, he said, and someone had thrown a Japanese flying axe through the window. 'If it had been two inches to the right, it would have gone in my head.' He wanted to do a digger driver licence – 'then you can travel the world' – but to do it needed to be off drugs and he was struggling. 'I feel like I am caught in a vicious circle,' he said. 'I can't get my own place and a job without getting off the drugs, but without those, it's hard to get off the drugs. I should never have left the Prince Rupert when I did. At least there you felt you had a future, not just down and out.' Flicking through his photo album of his holiday with his family in Turkey, he asked, 'How can I have gone from that to this?'

Dave Pritchard turned out to be at his mum's, sleeping in a tent in the garden and finally receiving some help.

Tyler had tried to join the army, telling the recruitment centre that he had been 'told by Olaf from *Frozen*' that they should take him. As soon as the shops reopened, he had been off to the Harry Potter shop to buy a new glass-top cane and to the opticians for a pair of sunglasses, which he never took off.

Bev was babysitting almost every day for her grandchildren while her daughter-in-law was working as a carer. 'Eight of them under the age of ten!' she said. 'I'm shattered but I love those babbies.' In between she often popped by for a cuppa. 'People will never believe I lived here,' she said. 'One day I will tell my grand-children the story.'

'Of all the great stories in the pandemic, what the Prince Rupert did has to be my favourite,' said Dame Louise Casey, who had started the scheme to bring homeless off the streets. 'To discover such kindness in this place in the shires, this nugget of everything that is Britishness, it's symbolic of all that I want for my country.

'But people got stuck too long in hotels.'

A cross-party commission* headed by the former head of the civil service, Lord Bob Kerslake, would later declare Everyone In a success, finding that of 37,000 people taken off the streets, 26,000 had been provided long-term housing and many lives had been saved. Research conducted by University College London found that during the first wave of the pandemic alone at least 266 lives had been saved and 1,164 hospital admissions avoided.

---

* 'When We Work Together – Learning the Lessons', interim report from the Kerslake Commission on Homelessness and Rough Sleeping, July 2021.

'This could have been a big tragedy, but it wasn't,' said Lord Kerslake.

Matthew Downie, then policy director of the charity Crisis (and subsequently its chief executive), called it 'one of the most extraordinary things to have ever happened to the homeless in this country'.

It showed that with political will and some cash, rough sleeping could be ended. The question was what happened next. 'It was a real opportunity,' said Darren Baxter, the housing specialist from the Joseph Rowntree Foundation. 'But the real challenge is for the government to use this to do things differently and address the fundamental problem of supply of affordable housing and inadequacy of benefits.'

The Kerslake Commission called on the government to learn lessons from the initiative and develop a 'clear cross-government plan to end rough sleeping and prevent homelessness'. It estimated that the government needed to continue spending an extra £82 million a year to meet its manifesto pledge of ending rough sleeping by 2024. Although it was a 32 per cent increase in current spending, Kerslake described it as 'frankly a drop in the ocean' – pointing out that an analysis of public spending had shown that it was '14 times more expensive to deal with someone who has been on the streets for a year than if they are caught early [£20,128 compared to £1,426].

'We are at a pivotal moment,' he added. 'If we fail to learn the lessons from Everyone In, all the signs are that the situation will get worse and homelessness and rough sleeping will increase. That would be an enormous lost opportunity.'

When the Prince Rupert had reopened in April for outside dining in the courtyard, they were inundated – they did 210 covers on the first day. First to grab a spot was Hannah, who ordered a coffee and a large Chardonnay and didn't like it when Jacki gave her a bill.

Some of their old staff started coming back. The chef, Paul on reception and Trevor the porter. Gabriella had moved on to work in a new restaurant outside town. She was about to turn twenty-four and no longer needed to have her mother nearby. Both she and her mum hoped to use their experience working with the homeless in the future. 'It's been an amazing year,' she said.

Mike's dream of hiring some of the homeless guests had not really come to fruition. Hannah might have made a good hostess but she was too unreliable. Needing housekeeping staff, he had tried to hire Jess as a cleaner. 'This is your opportunity to show what you can do,' Charlie told her, but Jess looked at her as if horrified by the idea.

There was one exception. Throughout April, Titch had been popping by. Mike paid him to clear the courtyard and the car park. On the May bank holiday, Mike started him on trial as a kitchen porter. New fridges had arrived and he needed someone to clear out the old ones and unwrap the new ones. Jacki collected Titch from the Holiday Inn on her way to work. He had dressed in his black gangster suit and was so excited they had to stop him drinking too many energy drinks, as he would not stop talking. On the second day he had clearly used mamba, arriving red-eyed and swaying, but Jacki gave him a good breakfast of an egg and bacon butty. He fought it and worked like a Trojan, mopping and cleaning.

'I do need to employ a kitchen porter,' said Mike, 'and no matter who you employ in that job, it's low pay, so they are usually volatile and often people you can't trust. I do trust Richard. I know if I leave my wallet or phone in the kitchen, he won't take it. If anything, he will be feeding us with information, little snitch. Sometimes you need that, telling you that the chef is taking three steaks home with him at night.

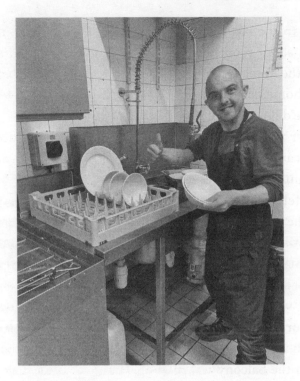

'I know it will be a bumpy ride but want to give him a chance,' Mike added. 'We'll never close the door on Titch.'

Shortly after Simon's departure they placed the crystal sherry decanter back on the front counter and opened a new logbook. That Monday, 17 May, was the grand reopening after what was hopefully the last lockdown. Colourful bunting had been hung round the town centre, proclaiming 'Shrewsbury's Open'. Mike knew most hoteliers would be ecstatic, yet he felt the complete opposite.

Over the weekend, he, Jacki and Charlie had all been so stressed they were getting on one another's nerves. Jacki would be going back to her office above the kitchen to do the accounts. Charlie would be upfront greeting guests with her big smile, back in a suit and heels.

Right to the last minute, Charlie had hoped he would change his mind about reopening. 'If Mike turned round and said we're keeping the hotel as a hostel, I'd be doing cartwheels!' she said.

Back home, she looked at the photos of her beloved Mez. 'I reckon he'd be proud of us,' she told Gabriella.

'I never realised how rewarding it can be helping people,' said Jacki. 'I can't go back to just sitting in front of spreadsheets. I never wanted to be an accountant in the first place.'

Mike felt really down. The night before he had wandered around the hotel remembering the ups and downs of that year, the troubles, the tiredness, the situations and the goodness. Afterwards he had sat in the lounge with a glass of whisky, feeling terribly sad. 'That's it, it's over,' he wrote in a text to Charlie. 'We did our best. Our very best. Something unique. We risked all we had, our health, our families, to help others. Now it's just a memory and one which we must never forget. The incredible food, our jogs, our nights on the balcony wrapped up, being together. Just the three of us. The experience brought us together. Now we have to adjust but we must always, always remember what we did. I'm going to miss it so much just as you will too.'

Normal guests would soon start trickling through the door, though bookings were slow, for it was unseasonably cold and wet for May. People were also worried about travelling with a new Indian variant (later known as Delta) of the disease 'spreading like wildfire', according to Matt Hancock, then the health secretary.

The first four guests were due to arrive after lunch. 'Time to paint on the smiles, as Deb would say,' said Charlie, as she, Mike and Jacki assembled in the lobby in front of the painting of Prince Rupert. Soon Trevor would be bringing in the cases, they would pour a glass of sherry and start swiping credit card details. The security guards had gone. Titch was out the back and there was a bottle of sanitiser at the entrance, but otherwise it was as if none of it had ever happened.

'You know it was like a fairy tale,' smiled Charlie ruefully. 'I adored them all.'

Jacki rolled her eyes and laughed. 'Okay, for the first time I will say it,' she said. 'They were lovely.'

Epilogue

Tuesday, 23 November 2021

The roads had been closed off to traffic and crowds were gathering in the market square for the annual turning on of the Christmas lights, which was back to being a public event unlike the previous year. The town's black-and-white timbered frontages were strung with decorations and many of its quaint little shops were open late, their windows twinkling with fairy lights and staff proffering mince pies. A choir of local children on a specially constructed stage were singing carols, though the recent rise in Covid cases meant the usual lantern parade had been suspended again.

There were more homeless back on the streets – Christmas Lights night was always a lucrative time for begging and eighteen months of pandemic had left more people than ever with nowhere to live. More than 180,000 families had lost their homes since Covid, according to the charity Shelter, and Shrewsbury was no exception. Derek Tyrer and Shaggy were out on Pride Hill and Dave Pritchard had re-emerged back in town, as well as others who had passed through the Prince Rupert more briefly. More women had appeared.

The following morning the Ark was busy with people coming for breakfasts of cereal or scrambled eggs on toast and complaining about the coffee. Tracy was cursing and holding court loudly. A recent arrival called John said his story alone would need a whole book. Others were taking a shower or brushing their teeth in the bathroom in the garden. With a storm forecast to bring icy winds and snow, Wendy and Rose were handing out arctic sleeping bags and green waterproofs.

'Numbers are up again,' said Wendy. That month would see 521 visitors, of whom 30 were new and 85 were regulars. 'It's like a revolving door but the best we can do is be there for them,' she said. The previous month they had managed to get four into accommodation, yet it wasn't enough. 'More homes are needed,' she added.

In a small room upstairs, local GP Dr Nicky was doing Covid vaccinations – boosters for some, second jabs for others. Just a couple of days later, a new Omicron variant would be discovered in South Africa, even more infectious than previous ones, prompting more restrictions on travel, as well as once again making mask-wearing compulsory in shops and on public transport.

Among the former Prince Rupert residents gathered at the Ark was Julie, but she was busy upstairs helping sort things out for its forthcoming move to much-needed larger premises down the road in a converted former pub, for she was there as a 'friend of the Ark' rather than a client.

Now back in Shrewsbury, she was off drugs, working weekends in a pizza parlour and thinking of having driving lessons. It had been a long journey. While staying in Wem, where she had moved from the Prince Rupert, fellow guest Samantha had ended up in the room next door. 'Samantha was nothing but trouble,' said Julie. 'One day she was bleeding from the neck, so I called an ambulance, which came and carted her off, but then I wasn't allowed back, so I was homeless again.'

Julie was moved to Birmingham where she spent twelve weeks, but just as she was settling, she was transferred to a hotel in Wolverhampton. She arrived at night, only to find the council hadn't released the money for the room, yet managed to get

Wendy on the phone who sorted it out. From there she was moved to Halesowen. 'I lasted one night,' she said. 'I was depressed as I hadn't got the letter from my girls I usually get in June, and when it didn't come, I was worried if they were all right and phoning the Ark every day, losing my temper. Then I had a run-in with my mum because she said the girls were better off without me. I told her to leave my kids out of it! My whole head went. I said, "What would you do if I took an overdose?" She said, "Nothing." So I swallowed a load of tablets then left her house and went to sleep outside. I didn't kill myself, I just had a terrible stomach ache, so I came to the Ark crying and they took me to A&E. By then it was fourteen hours later, but I'd thrown up so many times, it was out of my system.

'After that I was sleeping rough back in Shrewsbury but not in the town centre because of the drugs and people being attacked – I couldn't take it. I got the hardiest possible sleeping bag from the Ark and made a place outside behind a bush near Mount Pleasant doctors and the nursery. It wasn't far from my mum and dad's and one night when there was a really bad storm, I was dripping wet and cold so went and asked if I could stay – they said one night but no more (her father appeared not to have died after all).

'I stuck it out on the streets two months but I hated it. Eventually last month I went to have my ingrown toenails done at the Ark and they said I could move into a bed and breakfast, 70 Tudor, so I did. It's noisy and there are lots of drugs, but I am trying to stick it out so I can get a place of my own.'

Putting people who had just come off drugs in the same accommodation as people still shooting up did not seem a wise idea, particularly when it was such a hard journey.

What had turned things around for her was when Andy implicated her in his drug dealing charge. He pleaded guilty, she not guilty. 'I got the letter from the crown court with all the trial dates and in March I walked into court and was handcuffed,' she said.

'The judge gave me a stern warning, then to my surprise said to me this is your lucky day, you're free to go, but I don't ever want to see you here again.

'I walked out so relieved. I did a pipe to celebrate, but then thought, This is my fucking chance. My solicitor said for God's sake keep yourself clean.

'It wasn't easy. I spoke to Mind and SRP and the Ark. There is help if you want it, but you have to want it and then there's a waiting list – six to eight weeks for a prescription. By then you've had a relapse and say forget it.

'I used to think I needed the white but now I know I don't. Since I gave up, I've got more energy – I am sleeping better, eating better and when my alarm goes off, I get up.

'These days I walk through town and think, Really? I see homeless selling the *DOPE* [an alternative magazine produced by a small anarchist publisher that they can pick up for free], which saves asking for money: if I do it, I buy tobacco and food, but as soon as they have £10 they buy drugs. If someone said go and get yourself a bag, I couldn't, I couldn't even do white. Yesterday someone lit up in front of me and I said, "Well, that's £10 wasted."

'Now I look back and think the amount we spent on drugs was ridiculous. Andy was working but all our money went on drugs. We could have gone on holidays …

'Now people think I'm boring. I don't even do weed, just smoke normal cigarettes, but I'm quite happy to go to bed and watch telly.'

She was hoping for a Christmas DVD of her daughters. In the meantime she was planning to visit Andy in jail. 'I know it's probably not a good idea,' she said. 'But he has made a family of swans from paper which he wants to give me.

'I want to get my own place and get back into work and turn my life around. I want to be able to get up in the morning and think, I'm working today 8.30 to 5, then go to work, go back home and get back to normality. I'd like to work in retail, a café, or cleaning. People say drop in a CV but I haven't even got a CV.'

When Julie did her first shift at the pizza place, she had tried to give £10 from her earnings to Wendy for the Ark, but she wouldn't take it. 'One day I want to be able to donate to the Ark,' she said. 'I don't think people should give money to homeless on the street. But when they say have you got spare change, there's no need to give them a dirty look or abuse, just say no, sorry. A lot of people walk past and ignore, as if we are nothing. But at the end of the day, these are human beings.

'I used to sit on Pride Hill in my sleeping bag and one day last Christmas a little kid came over with a box of chocolates and a £20 note. He said, "I'm sorry you've got nowhere to go for Christmas." It brought a tear to my eye and I will never forget that boy's kindness.'

Julie was not the only former guest of the Prince Rupert whose life seemed to be improving. Jess and Keele, the hotel's lockdown romance, had split up but she was working as a waitress in a bar again, learning to mix cocktails, and had moved into a little one-bedroom house. Brendan had got a job as a pot washer at the upmarket vineyard resort where Gabriella was now restaurant manager. Chris Bennett had moved back north to Stockport to be nearer his daughters but had yet to see them. He was staying with a friend and hoping to do security training, but complained he could not afford the travel. 'It was Covid that made them care about us but now it's business as usual,' he said. Simon had left the old people's home after they cut his hair and was back on the road, looking for a nice cathedral somewhere.

Peter had stopped working as a chef. 'I think it was too soon for sixteen-hour-a-day shifts with all those egos and pressure,' he shrugged. But he was still living in his flat in Shrewsbury and had started doing supermarket shifts, loading deliveries for online orders, and was very busy in the run-up to Christmas. 'It's a stop-gap but it pays the bills and very physical, so good for me,' he said. He had been signed off from the addiction and mental health services and had lots of ideas for poems and songs. 'I feel like I'm starting to be more like myself again,' he said. 'I am happier, friendlier, not getting annoyed at anyone and have a lady who says she loves me.' His girlfriend, a nurse, came to stay every weekend and they had gone on holiday to a wilderness camp – 'No phones, no wifi and a hole for a toilet!'

Best of all he was seeing his kids regularly and was looking forward to having them over at Christmas with all the presents he'd bought – fluffy pyjamas, chocolate, trainers and a tablet for them to stay in contact. 'I'm just so chuffed I've been able to buy things, not like last year,' he said.

'No matter how long you have travelled on the wrong road, you can always turn around,' he posted on Facebook. 'Though some-times you need a helping hand.'

While they were out shopping, he and his girlfriend would often see some of his fellow guests, like Titch and Shaggy, on the streets. 'They ask for spare change but you know what it's going to go to – not food or hot drinks …'

Life was also getting better for Hannah and Neil, who had left the caravan and managed to get their own house near Shrewsbury Hospital. There were fairy lights in the window and inside it was cosy. Neil had painted the walls white, with grey around the windows, hung turquoise curtains and laid carpet, and they had sourced sofas and lamps from Freegle, as well as a reproduction of Renoir's *Luncheon of the Boating Party* to hang over the table. 'I hate it,' said Neil. 'One of the men looks like him,' insisted Hannah. She had got some of her things out of council storage and the shelves were full of her books – well-thumbed hardbacks of Marco Polo's travels and Cleopatra, as well as works on witchcraft like *To Ride a Silver Broomstick*. Her first grandchild had been born – 'a little boy with a crinkled forehead like Stan Laurel' – and she showed off photos on her phone. 'All I want now is two cats – a Persian or Bengal,' she said. She had some art supplies and was making exquisite Christmas cards.

Neil had got his tools out of storage and was doing carpentry jobs to supplement his Universal Credit. He was staying clean, meeting up with his parents, keeping busy and trying to keep away from temptation. One day, cycling along in the town, he heard someone shout his name. 'It was Shaggy and that crowd,' he said. 'I kept biking.

'It's funny,' he added. 'I was setting up an online shop today and the basket came to £40 and I thought that was a lot but I used to think nothing of spending £100 on drugs.'

At the Prince Rupert, what was supposed to be their best happy ending had gone horribly wrong. Titch had spent his first paycheque on a waistcoat, which he had proudly come in wearing, but he had then disappeared. A group of local street pastors found him flat out on mamba, on the pavement, having banged his head.

'Not again,' groaned Mike. 'We just can't risk employing him.'

Jacki couldn't believe it. 'You just want to clip him round the earhole,' she sighed.

Charlie had tried everything to keep Titch in accommodation. Mike wouldn't let him stay in the hotel while he was on drugs, pointing out the insurance implications. She managed to get him in 70 Tudor, but he kept letting others stay in the room, which was against the rules, so he was eventually kicked out. Back on the streets and always wanting to be part of the gang, he had fallen in with a bad group and one night joined them in breaking into Superdrug, smashing the window and grabbing £13,500 worth of aftershave and perfume while the alarm went off.

'For drugs, of course,' tutted Julie. 'When people do that it makes the rest of us homeless look bad.'

All were arrested and held on remand. Titch started calling Jacki from prison. 'Hi Mum!' he said. 'I'm all right. I'm gonna get myself straight.' He told her he was going to the gym, trying to get clean and had asked to be put in a different part of jail from the addicts.

Jacki shook her head. 'I've heard it all before,' she said. 'It's just a vicious circle. Even if he gets clean, where will he go when he gets out? It will start all over again.'

There wasn't much time to think, as it was the hotel's busiest time of the year. Apart from visitors for the Christmas lights, there were annual dinners, such as that of the Drapers' Company, the ancient guild behind the town's original wealth. Some of the

tourists in town for Christmas shopping wandered into Shrewsbury's charming museum, partly housed in the Victorian Music Hall where Charles Dickens had spoken. There, on the first floor, they found themselves staring at a very special exhibit in an illuminated glass box. It was a three-thousand-year-old golden sun pendant, found by a metal detector enthusiast in a Shropshire field in 2018 and described by the British Museum as 'one of the most important Bronze Age finds of the last century'.

On display for the first time, before taking up permanent residence in the British Museum, which had paid a £250,000 treasure fee to its finder, the pendant was mesmerising. Shaped like a hammock, hollow inside, it shone under the lights as if new, intricately carved with geometric motifs on one side and on the other a solar sunrise that left visitors convinced it had some spiritual significance.

The six months since fully reopening had been a challenging time for the Prince Rupert. Like restaurants and hotels across the country, they had struggled to find staff. One new starter in housekeeping had lasted just twenty minutes. Chefs came and went. Charlie and Jacki found themselves working seventeen-hour shifts, Jacki even returning from being rushed to hospital one night to do the breakfast shift.

It wasn't just staff that was the problem. A shortage of truck drivers and a slow-down of imports caused by post-Brexit paperwork had left them struggling to get supplies. Unable to source the miniature shampoo and shower gel bottles for the rooms, Charlie and Jacki had ended up laboriously refilling them from a large bottle, spilling it everywhere. When the laundry truck failed to turn up, Jacki found herself ironing sheets and pillowcases.

At the same time, guests seemed to have become more demanding. They missed their old crowd and Mike physically recoiled when people asked, 'Have you gone back to being a normal hotel or do you still have them?'

The Prince Rupert still took in a few homeless. There was a couple whose house had been condemned and a yoga instructor, a single mum and her little boy, whose landlord had sold their flat, leaving them no place to go.

Rita had come back in July to try again at living together, but Mike was so busy that he never brought her from the flat in Bournemouth. He still hoped they could make a life together, perhaps in the new year. Meanwhile, worried that he could not maintain standards in the hotel, Mike had taken the difficult decision to close for Christmas for the first time. It turned out to be a wise move. Omicron would soon bring a wave of cancellations, as daily infections soared to record levels of more than two hundred thousand and hospitals again started filling up. The UK would soon become the first country in Europe to pass 150,000 deaths. 'Do you remember how at the start, we thought this was just a few weeks?' he asked Charlie ruefully. It was all taking a lot longer, maybe it would never be over. People were tired, as once again festive parties and gatherings were cancelled, New Year's fireworks and celebrations round the world were called off and Christmas with family or friends became dependent on that single red line on the lateral flow tests.

Charlie would spend it with her family, being served on for once, as Callum and his new wife did the cooking. As always they would raise a glass to Mez. Jacki would be with her mum – the friends she normally saw had been so moved by the stories she had told them from the Prince Rupert that they had decided to volunteer at a soup kitchen in Birmingham.

In the rare quiet moments in the hotel, they reminisced about their year of being a homeless hotel. 'I wish we could do it all over again, but I'd do it differently,' said Mike. 'I wish I'd fought more for those who were asked to leave, like Dave Pritchard. I should have said, he's our guest, forget about paying for him.'

One evening, walking round St Alkmund's, Mike saw a group of men gathered with cans and bottles and who knows what else. His pace quickened, expecting some abuse. 'You're a legend, Mr Matthews!' one of them yelled.

Not everyone appreciated what they had done. 'You fucked the homeless!' Tracy would bellow whenever she saw Mike, Charlie or Jacki. 'Prince Rupert fucked the homeless!'

They still got visits from some of their old guests, letting them know their news. Julie, Brendan and Bev often dropped in. Peter had sent round his CV.

One night, shortly after the lights were switched on, the first few flakes of snow started falling wetly. Down on the river, the swans swam silently between the bridges under a pale moon. Inside the Prince Rupert, the fire was crackling in the lobby and a party was underway in the restaurant. Mike walked into the lounge to find Dave Pritchard asleep by the Christmas tree.

He woke him, gave him a drink, then went and fetched Charlie, saying, 'Come and see this.' 'Oh my God,' she said, smiling widely. As he was going home, Mike looked back through the lounge window, wondering if Dave would go before any of the guests wandered in and saw him. Somehow, however, that night, once again, there was room at the inn.

Acknowledgements

What do you do when you come out of the station and there is a homeless person on the steps in the cold or drizzle? Do you, like so many of us, walk on past? Perhaps veer away a little to pretend you didn't see? Do you fiddle aimlessly for change with an apologetic shrug? Do you read the cardboard sign that says 'Need' and wonder what – a roof, a mug of tea, a hug? Do you get on the train with the £10 note still burning a hole in your pocket? Or do you stop and listen to their story and reach out a hand?

This book started with a Zoom, like so many things in that year of pandemic. I had been invited to a virtual afternoon tea in place of the annual Women of the Year Lunch, sent a box with scones, jam and clotted cream, as well as a mini prosecco, and assigned to a virtual table with Dame Louise Casey, the homelessness tsar, among various luminaries of whom I was in awe.

Connection issues meant I joined late and my table-mates were already introducing themselves, talking about how they had spent lockdown. 'My name is Charlie,' one of them was saying, speaking fast, clearly nervous, in a not-quite-Brummie not-quite-West Country accent that I couldn't pin down. 'I am manager of Prince Rupert Hotel in Shrewsbury – we've taken in more than sixty homeless people and left our own families to look after them.'

I was intrigued. I had spent almost my entire career reporting overseas as a foreign correspondent, but Covid had put an abrupt stop to travel and I suddenly found myself reporting on my own country. I did what I had always done: went and talked to people and collected stories that focused on the human cost of the pandemic. Not just the victims of the disease and those on the front lines fighting it or keeping us going, from nurses to bus drivers, but also the millions of us who were confined to our homes, working from the bedroom or kitchen table while juggling home-schooling.

I quickly realised that lockdown was very different for different sectors of the community. From my garden I could see the top of a tower block and wondered what it must be like to be cooped up inside. I soon found out on an estate in Tower Hamlets in London's East End, where I met desperate families including a disabled single mum with four children aged eight to twenty crammed into a tiny two-bed flat, struggling to home-school with just one laptop and table in the same room as the TV where the youngest was watching cartoons.

Many of those I met were dependent on food banks. All but a few of my thirty-four years of reporting has been in the developing world and I'd always felt fortunate to be born in an affluent country, but now I realised that shocking things I had reported on abroad, like child malnutrition or slave labour, were happening on my own doorstep. The UK is the fifth-largest economy in the world yet almost a third of its children were living in poverty.

The problems were not just food and education: there was fuel poverty – having to choose between warmth and hunger – and something I had never heard of called hygiene poverty, that of not being able to afford basic products to keep yourself clean.

That's not all. We like to believe we live in a society of equal opportunity. In fact the UK has the lowest social mobility in the developed world. Most countries have inequalities but recent reports have shown the UK has the widest geographical differences, with almost half the country lagging behind. Where you are born in this country can also make a huge difference to your education – poorer children at school in Blackpool, for example, are more than two years behind their peers by the time they take their GCSEs, according to a 2020 report by the Education Policy Institute.

With so many struggling to home-school, Covid was making that gap worse. The pandemic was exposing inequalities that were already there and exacerbating them. For almost everyone I spoke to, the lack of affordable or adequate housing seemed to be at the root of their problems. And no one was more vulnerable than the homeless, most of all those sleeping on the streets.

Yet there was some good news. Among the stories I reported on during the first lockdown in 2020 was 'Everyone In', Dame Louise Casey's programme to get all rough sleepers off the streets by the weekend. I spoke to homeless people from London who were astonished to find themselves suddenly in a Premier Inn with warm beds, hot water and three meals a day, even if these were sometimes Pot Noodles. It showed that rough sleeping could be resolved if the will was there.

So when I heard Charlie talking that afternoon about what the Prince Rupert had done, my ears pricked up. I Googled the hotel while we were talking and to my surprise saw that it was a four-star with beautiful Tudor frontage, the kind of place my mum would call 'posh'. The ones I had reported from in London had been budget hotels and B&Bs.

After the virtual tea I kept thinking about Charlie. One evening I called her and asked her some more and she told me about her son dying and how looking after the homeless had helped her. She invited me to visit.

A few weeks later I walked into an eerily deserted King's Cross station where police at the entrance asked if my journey was necessary – as journalists we counted as 'essential workers' – then took a train to Birmingham. There, I boarded a Transport for Wales train, just two empty carriages, which chugged slowly to Shrewsbury.

The town's rail station was situated by Shrewsbury castle and it was a short walk down Pride Hill and along a small cobbled street to the hotel. I had never been to Shrewsbury, and, like Mike on his first flying visit from the Caribbean, was bowled over by all the Tudor houses with their intricate black-and-white timbered frontages, including the Prince Rupert.

There I met Charlie, Jacki and Mike, and some of their guests including Jess, Charlene, Simon and Titch. Afterwards I couldn't stop thinking about it. Lockdown had thrown up lots of kindness – the 750,000 people who had volunteered to help the NHS, neighbourhood WhatsApp groups offering to get shopping for those confined indoors – but these hotel staff had left their own families and risked their lives to look after people they knew nothing about.

When homeless Simon called me afterwards and asked if I could help arrange a spa visit for Charlie and Jacki to thank them for what they had done, I was even more moved.

The Prince Rupert story epitomised to me both the incredible compassion that emerged during the pandemic and the deep problems in our society. What intrigued me most was that it was the hotel staff who seemed to have been transformed as much as the people to whom they had given shelter.

I wrote an article for the *Sunday Times* Christmas edition, then I asked Mike, Charlie and Jacki if I could go back and stay, become part of their bubble. They welcomed me, for which I am truly thankful. Some of the homeless were wary at first; a few did not want to talk; others have become good friends, even offering help when my father recently died.

This book is based on all those interviews. Some names have been changed for privacy but none of the quotes.

I'd like to thank all the homeless people who shared their stories, which were often painful involving child abuse, domestic violence, addiction, losing jobs or relationships breaking down.

Many have their demons of course and sometimes the stories didn't quite add up, but most clearly had been given little chance in life and no one to catch them when they fell.

Among those who generously gave of their time to share their experience were Tim Compton, Laura Fisher and Lenny Worthing from the housing department at Shropshire Council, as well as Wendy Faulkner from the Ark and her team.

I'd also like to thank Dame Louise Casey who came up with Everyone In and is a complete authority on the subject, as are Helen Barnard, then head of the Joseph Rowntree Foundation, and her colleague Darren Baxter.

I'm also very grateful to Maggie Love, Martin Wood (the world's tallest town crier) and Reverend Richard Hayes who shared stories and history of their beautiful town.

On a personal note, I would also like to thank the good friends who stuck by me in a difficult year, as well as those I knew less well who came forward to support me.

Emma Freud, you know what you did, and I cannot thank you enough.

This book would not be here if it weren't for my fabulous editor Arabella Pike and her amazing assistant Jo Thompson, the deft hands of copy editor Iain Hunt and the organisational skills of Katy Archer. I am also grateful to my agent David (Godwin) – our ninth journey together!

As always the biggest thanks of all to my wonderful husband and son as well as my mum and late father, who died as I was finishing editing. More than ever working on this book made me appreciate my own loving childhood and that when I go off to difficult places that I always had a welcoming home to come back to.

Most of all I hope this book shines a light on people who far too often we just walk by. As Titch said, it should not have taken a pandemic to help them. If after reading this book, you feel moved to extend a helping hand, please buy a coffee, give to a homeless charity, volunteer for a soup kitchen, lobby your MP for more investment in services and social housing – but above all stop, smile and say hello. At the end of the day, we are all humans and who knows – it could happen to you …

London, March 2022